Pop Culture and Curriculum, Assemble!

Exploring the Limits of Curricular Humanism Through Pop Culture

Daniel Friedrich, Jordan Corson, and Deirdre Hollman (eds.)

ISBN 978-1-64504-183-2 (Paperback)

ISBN 978-1-64504-184-9 (Hardback)

ISBN 978-1-64504-185-6 (E-Book)

Library of Congress Control Number: 2021942523

Printed on acid-free paper

Cover Image: "And Soon Judgement" (Work in Progress) by Stacey Robinson

@StaceyARobinson (Instagram)

This book is part of the Critical Pedagogies Series

Table of Contents

Introduction

Pop Culture and Curriculum, Assemble!

Dani Friedrich, Jordan Corson, and Deirdre Hollman

Pop Culture is suffused with stories and characters that reflect and defy the limits of Western, modern humanity. From supers and ultras to artificial and mechanized, to alien, mythical, and beyond reach, humans persistently include that which is, at least at some level, outside ourselves in the stories we tell. The proliferation of diverse forms of storytelling; the flow of traditions and mythologies throughout geographical boundaries; the qualitative jump in digital cinematic technologies in the last decades; and the global dominance of multimedia corporate empires push us to consider what is more than/other than/ nothing but human in ways that require deep intellectual and affective pedagogical engagements.

Clearly, the production and circulation of these critical imaginaries—which are in some regards novel, yet always connected to specific histories—are not evenly distributed, with flows of capital norming and attempting to set limits on the potentialities of these re-imaginings of the human and its others. Yet, the multiplicity of ways in which these narratives are currently consumed/produced subverts the boundaries of (corporate/policed/brokered) popular culture, defying categorizations such as sub- or counter- or foreign, with direct impact on the cultural lexicon.

This edited volume is part of a larger project that also includes a special issue of the *Journal of Curriculum and Pedagogy*. Through this project, with our collaborators, we seek to engage in the specific connections between the pop culture productions of the more than/ other than/nothing but human, and the field of curriculum studies, interrogating the production of particular subjectivities and knowledges, posing questions about the educability of those on the outside of humanity, and how our imaginings of structures, institutions, and configurations beyond what seems possible may inform the work and thinking we are currently engaged in. Dominant educational trends suggest pop culture is a tool, dead artifacts used for student engagement. Comics, for example, enter education work as a way to invest struggling readers and to make subject content knowledge more engaging. We recognize a need to move beyond utilitarian views of pop culture and of education writ large toward views that contribute to a more complex understanding of the ways in which re-presentations of the more than/other than/nothing but human in pop culture participate in the shaping of subjectivities, world views, agencies beyond the human, and pedagogic ecologies.

This edited book and the special issue of JCP share a set of assumptions that sustain the work. The first one, which might be the most evident in our field, is that pop culture teaches, and as such, pop culture is curriculum. While there is something obvious about this statement, its implications are nothing but. Whereas the concept of hidden curriculum emerged to account for that which is taught implicitly in an explicitly educational context, we would argue that the vast majority of the pop culture curricula could be understood as hidden, requiring pedagogical work to make it visible. The fact that a popular video game, a cartoon about hormone monsters, or comic book representations of superhuman teachers were not necessarily conceived as educational—combined with our assumption that they are, in fact, educating—means that it is up to us to make that which is being taught part of the analysis. At the same time, we contend that pop culture curriculum is emergent and co-constructed. The hidden curriculum is not merely uncovered, but made and interpreted through curricular engagements like those of the authors in this volume.

A second assumption is that if curriculum is to be understood as a "complicated conversation" (Pinar, 2011), the assemblages of pop culture, curriculum, and learning can serve not only to participate in that conversation, but also to push against its boundaries and rules. The foundational questions of the field—*Whose knowledge counts? What counts as knowledge? How is knowledge produced, reproduced, circulated, centered, and/or marginalized?*—continues to inform much of our thinking. Yet, the affective flows that move us when engaging with pop culture in our daily lives bring up other kinds of questions that rub against the curricular set, generating productive friction that may lead us to new insights. When wondering about how our love for this or that character or storyline—say, *Watchmen's* Lady Trieu—flows into our imaginings of ourselves, or how our fascination with video game avatars produces effects when teaching online during a global pandemic, we realize that the kinds of knowledge pop culture produces requires different tools, outlooks, and framings for our meaning-making processes.

A third assumption, linked to the previous one, is that the work of our collective imaginations always produces a surplus that cannot be encompassed by analysis. This is the horizon of possibility of the work, which simultaneously guides our project and lets us know that the project can never be completed. The essays that take part in this edited volume all share this insight. By wondering about the curricular disruptions facilitated by Africanfuturisms, or the possibilities of educating all-knowing gods, authors are not seeking understanding in the sense of control over particular phenomena. The assemblages each piece provides, as well as the assemblage that is this very book, demand of us that we expand and move our lenses, all the while acknowledging that the work of the imagination is by definition always broader, more nebulous, more diffuse. The attempt to reign it in to study it runs counter to the purpose of our endeavors. In that sense, this project seeks to enter an ongoing conversation, push against its boundaries, and leave it to others to continue it, disrupting and interrupting it along the way.

The chapters that compose the first section of the book engage with pop culture texts and artifacts that present us with more than/other than human possibilities in conversation with curriculum studies. Oluwaseun Animashaun's work, "The Hormone Monsters Are Raging: Reimagining Childhoods in Netflix's *Big Mouth*," is a playful analysis of the blurred boundaries between childhoods and adulthoods via a consideration of hormone monsters and shame wizards. These other than human characters validate children as "capable social actors and critical thinkers who can and should be trusted with all the tools accessible to determine who they are in their present and future." The chapter by Jordan Corson and Daniel Friedrich, "Of Gods and

Educable Subjects: Posthuman education in *Watchmen* and *The Good Place*," explores the question of what the education of all-knowing beings entails. By focusing on characters for whom there is no more content to learn, the traditional goals of schooling and education are upended, and new possibilities for thinking beyond the learning paradigm are opened. Finally, "Cloud Strife's Ghost: Hauntology, Curriculum and *Final Fantasy VII*," by Nicholas Stock interrogates the haunting qualities of a specific video game, as an entry point to engage with the notion of a haunting and haunted curriculum. Stock pushes us to consider knowledge produced in the interstitial space between absence and presence, between memory, nostalgia, and the present.

The second section of the book is comprised of essays that are more directly attuned to the pedagogical possibilities of pop culture as curriculum. Francisco Medina's work, "Unsettling the Educated Subject: De/humanization and the (Im)possibility of Being Uneducated," examines the educational projects of salvation narratives in the Mexican soap opera *María, La del Barrio* and the film *My Fair Lady*. Medina seeks out characters defined in these narratives by their "lack of education" as a way to push against the humanist project that ties humanity to particular characteristics associated with Western traditions. Michael B. Dando examines the pedagogical models represented by three comic book creations. In ""The Best at What They Do": Re-Considering Perceptions of Public Education through Superhero Narratives," Dando maps the ideas of teaching illustrated by Professor X, Stick, and The Elephant's Trunk onto the limits of current pedagogical paradigms and the possibilities of going beyond the individual teacher as savior. Bianca Licata and Catherine Cheng Stahl's chapter reflects on the authors' experiences teaching during the COVID-19 pandemic as the physical space of the classroom gave way to a world of avatars and digital pedagogies. In *"Thinning space: New skins for new worlds of teaching and learning,"* Licata and Cheng Stahl shed their embodied skins to explore affective pedagogies at a time in which gaming and schooling, teaching and playing, become almost undistinguishable. Wrapping up this section, Hannah Ruth Stohry, Noella Binda Niati, and Jennifer Lynn Doyle's "Academic Misfits: De/Constructing Academic Un/Belonging through *Guardians of the Galaxy*," seeks to decolonize academic spaces by intertwining personal narratives with ideas of un/belonging in connection to Marvel's band of misfits. By co-constructing a collective onto-epistemology of becoming in their own curricular bodies, Stohry, Niati, and Doyle seek out a collectivist practice of being academic misfits.

Finally, the third section of the book connects posthumanist thinking and curriculum to specific times and places, both real and imagined. In "A Curriculum of Conflation: Using Space and Place to tell *Big Little Lies*," Boni Wozolek and Gabriel Huddleston invite us to consider the agency of place in our curricular thought. Through a collection of letters sent to each other, Wozolek and Huddleston produce a fascinating exchange on schooling, race, violence and teaching the centers the affective power of space and place. Sandra J. Schmidt's chapter, "Curricular Disruptions: Signifying Nigeria through African-futurisms," explores the production of Nigeria through africanfuturist writings by Nigerian and Nigerian-American authors as a way to challenge the ways in which Nigeria and Africa are presented in US social studies curricula and American media. The YA books Schmidt examines often disrupt deficit views of Blackness by providing alternative pedagogies grounded on specific ontologies of storytelling. In their work, "More Human Than Human? Transformational Habitus, Capital, Field and the Implanting of Memories in School Curricula," Phil Wood and Aimee Quickfall engage with the future imagined by *Blade Runner* by wondering whether the implementation of a national curriculum can be likened to the implantation of memories of a past and a set of experiences that were never there to begin with. Drawing from Pierre Bourdieu's sociological framework, Wood and Quickfall produce a critical reading of a specific school reform that treats working class children as replicants to be programmed. Van Ahn Tran's "The Refugeetude of Lady Trieu: Pedagogies of Displacement in HBO's *Watchmen*" concludes this section by mobilizing a feminist refugee epistemology to consider the curricular possibilities and limitations of displaced knowledge production. Tran proposes that the intersection of identity, lineage, memory, and power, as represented by the character of Lady Trieu, provides opportunities to consider pedagogies that not only recognize, but disrupt the production of certain subjectivities as "irregularities."

The book ends with a conversation between Jordan Corson and Jack Halberstam, one the foremost scholars in cultural studies, queer theories, and popular culture, providing a fascinating dialogue with the field of education. Connecting to his latest works, Halberstam explores the place of wildness in pop culture, as well as the curricular potential of our imaginations of the posthuman.

Section I

Curriculum and the more than/other than/ nothing but human

Chapter 1

The Hormone Monsters Are Raging

Reimagining Childhoods in Netflix's "Big Mouth"

Oluwaseun Animashaun, Department of Curriculum and Teaching, Teachers College, Columbia University

Naomi Fry reviews the coming-of-age television show, *Big Mouth* (2017–present), saying, "nothing embodies the 'Big Mouth' formula better than this… gross, hilarious, weird, precise" (Fry, 2020). To consume this show is to absorb the colorful (in both sight and tone) shapes of childhoods alongside the lively ghost of Duke Ellington, rapping ladybugs, sentient dogs, French-accented Lady Liberty advising about menstruation, a talking cell phone named Risqué, Jon Hamm-voiced scallops, Hormone Monsters, a Shame Wizard, Anxiety Mosquitos, and a Depression Kitty. Indeed, the list of anthropomorphized objects and uncanny entities is endless. The show, in its thoughtfulness and eccentricities, is reminiscent of children's play, and yet provides adults' entry points to engage in similar play too. *Big Mouth* revels in the strangeness and imaginaries of childhoods to narrate a coming-of-age tale with puberty as an impetus to interrogate and rearrange priorities and relationships.

Big Mouth is a television series created and written by Nick Kroll and his childhood friend, Andrew Goldberg, that follows fictionalized versions of their seventh-grade selves as they are growing up in Westchester County, New York. As the seasons progress, the audience follows more than this initial pair; our cast of protagonists grows to incorporate their circle of friends—Jessi, Missy, and Jay. However, these characters are not the only ones who garner the attention of viewers. The show also features a pantheon of Hormone Monsters— Maurice (Maury), Connie, Rick, and Mona—bestial creatures who embody the somatic and emotional desires of the children they serve. Alongside these characters, the audience gains insight into the murky, wild west nature of puberty and childhoods. *Big Mouth* mingles middle school tribulations with nostalgic memories of crushes and infatuations, disgusting and absurd humor, and tactful lessons on holistic well-being. The show renders a landscape for both adults and children to interrogate their identities, politics, and desires through the Hormone Monsters, the Shame Wizard, and their relationships to the children they serve (or torture).

Big Mouth upends adult imaginings and constructions of childhoods as well as reconsiders what is possible in the realm of education. Throughout this chapter, I demonstrate how the show presents this terrain of possibilities through its multiple approaches to the lived realities and potentialities of childhoods. First, the show's content and structure confound temporal underpinnings of childhood, and thus undermines the boundaries that have traditionally set children apart from the dialogues in the adult realm. Second, the show illustrates the world through a socio-materialist lens (Lenz-Taguchi, 2010), which reads the world as human and non-human materialities (in this case, monstrous intensities and objects) acting with and upon each other. Through the encounters of children-Hormone Monsters-Shame Wizard, the turmoil regarding childhood, gender, and sexuality at play in current American society are visible. *Big Mouth* insists that children are capable social actors and critical thinkers who can and should be trusted with all the tools accessible to determine who they are in their present and future. With that in mind, this chapter ends with a production, enacting the lessons (and some surprises) from *Big Mouth*. The show outlines a more comprehensive range of curricular possibilities when age and time are not boundaries restricting children's movement and thinking.

Time is a Construct

The structure of *Big Mouth* does not conform to traditional animated television shows because it executes two strategies. First, it sustains the longevity of character story arcs with callbacks and interruptions of the fourth wall. Second, it upsets the artificial boundaries of childhood and adulthood through popular culture references. Through these tactics, the writing team shares that childhoods are similar to Frankenstein's monster—a puzzling monstrosity of acquired and matched peoples, places, and objects. It also helps begin to rethink how schooling, could be a space of intergenerational learning and communing if it leaves behind these artificial boundaries of time.

The animated cast of *Big Mouth* operates outside of the standard floating timeline (when the world around the characters changes, but the characters remain the same), generally applied to long-running media texts. The children are not trapped in this perpetual personality standstill, and thus the audience grows and learns with these characters. In other words, the children are growing and therefore have histories and decisions with long-lasting consequences. Furthermore, the show does not utilize the typical arc of comparative television shows. Other shows use a tight, non-continuous 20-minute episodes that permit viewers to jump into the show with sparse background information. Such a framework features a narrow and condensed format that resolves the central conflict within the timeframe mentioned above. As such, the "narration is inevitably selective... We are presented, rather artificially, with a sequence of actions and interactions that are cut-off from … a flow which could be divided up in different ways" (Burnett & Merchant, 2018, p. 4). On the other hand, *Big Mouth* disturbs that artificiality of narrative through its callbacks and breaking of the fourth wall. For instance, Maury and Connie—two of the Hormone Monsters that serve the children of the show—speak directly to the audience during their wards' watershed moments to enlighten us on how a decision in a previous episode has led to the present situations. Kroll and Goldberg have developed a system that disrupt the show's linearity and allows episodes to spin out each moment into a series of infinite smaller interactions with multiple possibilities and meanings "that are always immanent" (Burnett & Merchant, 2018, p. 8). These infinities build on each other throughout the seasons, weaving together a robust rhizomatic vision of actions and decisions playing into, against, and with each other. The structural temporal disruptions to *Big Mouth* widen the landscape for the non-human entities to play authentically with the children and the show's audience. Additionally, it constructs a space in which learning can function as a nonlinear experience, unbound to the tradition of a beginning, middle and end. Unspooling time through narrative disruptions provides intergenerational experience because it provides all viewers numerous entry points for conversations no matter their age.

Furthermore, animated television shows—such as *The Grim Adventures of Billy & Mandy, Ed, Edd n Eddy, Codename: Kids Next Door*—are traditionally created and produced by adults and are often predicated on adult beliefs and understandings of children. More often than not, the shows relive a particular type of childhood situated in purely nostalgia and unable to handle the contemporary issues of the time. In other words, the shows become stiff and static depictions of what has been and not what can be. While Kroll and Goldberg of *Big Mouth* offer their memories of themselves and their childhoods as fodder for the show, they also map onto their reimagined selves the current language, identities, and tensions of the present. Thus, the creators do not absolve themselves and their characters from grappling with contemporary issues. Although the creators choose to collapse their past and present selves into the formations of these characters they begin to resist "approaching children and their childhoods as a magnet for transference of our own adult anxieties and narcissistic wounds" that Dyer (2019) identifies as a challenge to those who work to center children and childhoods (p. 33). The warping and layering of time, in this manner, legitimizes children—both in the show and audience—are seen and valued as social actors who have anxieties and wounds as present realities, not simply consequences of hindsight.

As children playing with, accepting, and resisting the worlds of adults, they are playing with the ideas and notions that are often curtailed to the world of adults. The pop culture references highlight this so deeply and so often. What is usually accepted is that children operate in this stage of "presocial difference," but in reality, the world of adults and their references is not beyond children of the present (James, 2004). The show thrives on the integration of popular culture that the children use to navigate their realities. Andrew's long-standing crush on Diane Lane in *Unfaithful* (2001), Missy's Nathan Fillion-inspired erotica, Jay's sentient dog named Featuring Ludacris signify popular culture's role in generating and reifying the social boundaries (Kidd, 2018). At first, the references seem anachronistic. It seems a difficult challenge to imagine a child display a deep attachment to Nathan Fillion's work on *Firefly* and *Serenity* or can comment on Diane Lane's career. While popular culture may indicate where the children's social lives intersect or diverge from others, it also performs the collapse of the adult spacetime and children spacetime. Some references are dated and thus connote a past childhood, yet the children use contemporary vernacular to set them in the present such as the #metoo references. However, this collapsing of these eclectic artifacts from differing time periods proves popular culture is continuously circulating and as such, children can have access to an expansive media ecology with which to play and construct their selves and identities. In this way, childhoods become monstrous creations as they are a hodgepodge of things present, history, and possible.

Age is Just a Number

In public discourse, childhoods are framed with an insistence of time and age as markers of development due to early works in psychology and sociology (James, 2004; James & Prout, 2014). Childhoods are regarded as a biological and social step toward one's progression into adulthood, where "full status as human" is granted because now, rational and complex thoughts reign (James & Prout, 2014, p. 9). In other words, the designation of "child" fixes the person as simple, presently incomplete, and bound to immaturity. This paradigm precludes the possibility of children as complex social actors and consequently limits how adults interact with children and imagine childhoods.

Animated television shows reify this particular vision of children and childhoods. Children are generally presented with very little growth—usually represented through the lack of aging. For instance, Dora the Explorer has remained seven-years-old in the twenty years she has been on the air. Bart and Lisa of *The Simpsons* have stayed ten and eight years-old, respectively, in the over 600 episodes that have aired. The children of *South Park* have been in elementary school since 1997. The list of characters who have been remanded to the status of perpetual children can continue indefinitely. While this television trope may be motivated by production issues, it does showcase an assumption regarding aging and learning. These characters are not aging and growing, and thus are not learning. They are consistently mired in the same conversations, conflicts and quagmires in every new episode and season. Furthermore, the activities of children in the animated landscape are often relegated to side antics or a fleeting moment of rationality. There is "little account ... given of [activities'] significance to children's social life or to the variation which they reveal in the social context of childhood" (James & Prout, 2014, p. 9). In the plot arcs, very rarely are children's activities provided serious treatment and consideration by their adults. However, *Big Mouth* offers an alternative and critical understanding of childhoods through its various plays with time and age.

As the show's theme song announces at the head of each episode, these children "are going through changes" (Kroll & Goldberg, 2017). Centering the lives of children as they experience puberty entails that the characters and their contexts are always mutating, and therefore, the children are still learning something about themselves. Jessi welcomes her menarche in the show's second episode; over the course of two seasons, the audience follows Jessi as she struggles with the ramifications of this watershed moment that irrevocably alters Jessi's relationship with her body and her own understandings of herself. Connie, her newly arrived Hormone Monster, appears with a list of dos and don'ts—"You want to shoplift lipstick, you want to listen to Lana Del Rey on repeat while you cut up all your T-shirts. You want to scream at your mother and then laugh at her tears…From now on, you call her Shannon" (Francis, 2017). Jess obliges and performs these activities despite them being a significant departure from her earlier self who "was interested in social justice, the kind of female warrior and empowered woman" and dreamt of being "the next Elizabeth Warren" (Moser, 2018a).

The beauty of witnessing the changes in Jessi's behavior is her reflection and learning in those moments. Months later, she tells Connie, "I used to smile a lot before you showed up" (ibid). At first, this could read as Jessi denouncing the changes that her biological development has wrought on her body and identity, but more significantly, this is a moment in which Jessi is demonstrating an awareness of herself and her context. It is a realization that her activities—her thefts, the slut-shaming she participated in, her resistance to her mom—the playing with her identity—is not producing the happiness she once understood herself to have. This critical reflection is often absent from animated children because it requires a complexity of thought that adults often presume children do not have.

Critical childhood scholars trouble the impact of age on contemporary understandings of childhood. The writers of *Big Mouth* follow their lead by promulgating the notion that children are not excused from complicated feelings and actions. Jessi's childhood is beset with a maelstrom of "ugly feelings" (Ngai, 2007). Her age does not excuse her from the difficult feelings and conversations with herself. The writers of *Big Mouth* do not pin children's learning solely on their biological development of the children. Missy, as a young Biracial girl, struggles with both her gender and racial identification, and so her childhood on the show is her processing her identities in the world. Through her tense and abusive conflict with her nemesis, Mirror Missy, Missy battles her insecurities, faults, and ignorance. This relationship comes to a head with Missy's creation of Mosaic Missy—the incorporation of her many selves such as Space Missy, Nanshe Missy, etc.—that honors her realization that *they are all her*. She says "Oh, there I am. I'm all these Missys. All of 'em" (Stone, 2020). This demonstrates that children are playing with and making critical decisions to take up or resist identities and ideas about themselves. This is a criticality that is often not afforded to children as it rejects the simplicity that early psychology and sociology works have assigned to children. More importantly, Missy's creation of Mosaic Missy offers an important tenet of critical childhood scholarship: the designation of the category "child" and therefore childhood is socially constructed and dependent on historical, cultural, and material contexts (Dumas & Nelson, 2016; James & Prout, 2014).

Finally, as an added wrinkle to experimenting with notions of childhoods, Coach Steve (one of the many characters voiced by Nick Knoll), despite his mature age, shares similar experiences with the children. Most importantly, he too also sees and converses with the Hormone Monsters and Shame Wizard that are invisible to all other adults of the series. Despite his age, he is undergoing similar turmoil to that of his students. Children and childhoods are tenuous and unstable boundaries that shift depending on race, gender, sexuality, class and other such conditions.

This show performs a strange balancing act as it operates as a multitude of things: a fever dream of nostalgia and memory; a reckoning and crashing pad of both adult hindsight and contemporary issues of desire and behavior; reckoning of contemporary issues of care—all wrapped in an animated package of racy humor and expletives. It maps out all the dangers, the landmines of puberty. In all this, Kroll, Goldberg, and the writing team demonstrate the tenets of critical childhood by depicting children outside of the universalizing and naturalizing approaches and instead considering children as designers of their realities in their own right. The creators acknowledge that age does not preclude children from having different conversations about themselves and identities. Consequently, the Hormone Monsters and Shame Wizard, whom we encounter in the next sections, exist and provide a fertile posthumanist landscape for difficult conversations as well as beautiful and ugly feelings.

Monsters Live Here, Too

Since the writers of *Big Mouth* supply an alternative relationship of time and age with regards to the childhoods on television, the show's landscape is wide open for different entities and conversations to be present. This, in turn, offers educators the opportunity to rethink and reimagine their curriculum as co-constructed with children and non-human materialities and entities that also reside in the classroom spaces. To develop this argument, I examine the Hormone Monsters who represent the uncontrollable affects that interrupt the scripts of schools and society. I then explore children—Hormone Monsters— Shame Wizard encounters as resistance to adult-controlled narratives and adult censorship.

In shared public domains, children are inundated with various scripts regarding childhood. Bernstein describes a script as a "set of invitations that necessarily remain open to resistance, interpretation, and improvisation" (Bernstein, 2011, p. 12). As explored earlier, children are expected to be demure, unsexed, innocent presocial beings. Schools are one such site in which children are consuming these implicit lessons about their identities, their lives, and their roles in their various communities. As children predominantly spend their waking hours in schools, there are myriad opportunities for children to resist and change scripts regarding their performance of childhood, gender, and sexuality. The Hormone Monsters are the effects that interrupt and resist particular scripts regarding the performance of childhoods.

To Whom They Appear

As mentioned previously, the Hormone Monsters are central characters of *Big Mouth*, that serve as bestial manifestations of children's pubescent urges and desires. Maurice (Maury), Connie, Rick and Mona perform as caretakers for the different children of the show. As

Maury puts it, the mission of the Hormone Monsters is to make the children and themselves "feel good" (Kroll & Goldberg, 2017). However, the pursuit of pleasure is achieved under the nose of adults. In spite of their magnanimous appearances to their wards, the Hormone Monsters run amok as invisible specters to the show's adults with the exception of Coach Steve. The specificity of their hauntings implies how children play and desires are forced underground and out-of-sight because they do not fit preconceived assumptions of children as naïve, innocent, and unaware of public discourses regarding cultural conditions. Despite their invisibility to the adult world, the Hormone Monsters support the children as they combat restrictive narratives of their beings. One way the writers of the show contend with the scripts of particular childhoods is how they manipulate how and whom the Hormone Monsters approach.

Nick, a boy deeply insecure concerning his lack of biological growth compared to his peers, has a series of Hormone Monsters show up for him. They run the gamut—an immature and novice Hormone Monster, a mumbling elderly Hormone Monster, a hypermasculine Hormone Monster. However, the longest-running Hormone Monster is Connie, a female Hormone Monstress, whose impact permits Nick comfort and joy in his own body as well as physical and emotional development. Butler (1997) writes that part of the script of boyhood (or manhood) is "repudiating femininity as a precondition for the heterosexualization of sexual desire and its fundamental ambivalence" (p. 137). This boundary-crossing of a different gender Hormone Monster transgresses the socio-cultural notion of boys will be boys. Nick only begins to enjoy and discover the pleasure of his body when his Hormone Monster's gender is not aligned with his sex or gender. In fact, his first time masturbating to completion is under the caring tutelage of Connie. His performance of his boyhood does not falter for him because of his different gendered Hormone Monster, and in this way, the script that boyhood must be visible through a particular set of tropes. Nick's trajectory demonstrates that there are still questions about the performance of gender in childhood and adolescence.

On the other hand, Missy and Jay, the lone children of color, do not initially receive Hormone Monsters of their own. At first, this seems an odd sidelining of these characters as they are not afforded the Hormone Monsters as consistent mediators of their childhoods.

While their White counterparts frame their hormones as monstrous annoyances, Missy and Jay accept their hormones as a lived experience. This lack of monsters seems to align with the adultification of Black and Brown children present in mainstream discourse (Dumas & Nelson, 2016; Muhammad & Haddix, 2016; Price-Dennis et al., 2017; Toliver, 2019). The claims under the umbrella of this discourse are never far away: their bodies are "too big" or "too developed," their behaviors are always approaching danger and criminality. However, I venture that the absence of Hormone Monsters for these children serves as an interruption to the presumptions of childhood. Jay's practice and play to understand his own sexuality earns him the moniker of "a goddamn prodigy... he's his own Hormone Monster" (Moser, 2018a). He crafts his own journey to his own bisexuality with his own experimentation with Susan the pillow and Brad the couch cushion. Jay comes to stand in his own sexual power, blatantly advertising that he is "open for all." Jay's ability, as a boy of color, to determine on his own what fits or sits right with him troubles boyhoods. It is not that Missy does not have desire and performs sexuality, but instead has found ways that are right for her. She has her Nathan Fillion-inspired erotica and her androgynous uniform of overalls and yellow t-shirt. While she, like her peers, are reckoning with the biological changes of their lives, she also has to consider these intersectional dialogues of race and gender. Both Missy and Jay's exercise of their sexuality and desire seems to rely on adultification, but ultimately contend that children—especially children of color—learn their way in the world that does not offer handholding for them. The writers of *Big Mouth* engage in tenets of critical childhoods and recognize that there are complexities in who is able to be considered a "child." Nick, Missy, and Jay's relationships with (or absence of) a Hormone Monster goads adults who serve and work alongside children to reconsider what has been imagined to be the parameters of childhood. Are naivete and innocence sustainable baselines for childhood? What critical questions are children interrogating when adults are not looking? How does learning from childhoods that are raced, gendered, classed differently able to complicate and broaden contemporary understandings of children.

Coming In and Showing Out

Within the context of the show, The Hormone Monsters disrupt the scripts that undergirds the hidden curriculum of schools. In the debut scene of the pilot, the leading children—Nick, Jessi, and Andrew— are in a co-ed health class in which the teacher is discussing the female reproductive system. The mention of a vagina conjures Maurice, who persuades Andrew to attend to his growing erection. In a fight to keep himself engaged in the lesson, Andrew rebukes Maurice, "I should tell you; this is school and we need boundaries" (Moser, 2017). This opening moment engages with interruption of multiple scripts through multiple entry points. First, the teacher's voice drones and fades into the background, while the children's discussion enters the forefront. This shift changes the attitude regarding children's classroom conversation from off-topic, distracting, and inappropriate noise to significant dialogue. Second, Maurice's emergence demonstrates that however straightforward and cut and dry a subject is presented, it is impossible to control all the responses that the subject might elicit and inspire. Maurice, and therefore Andrew, are entirely enthralled by the word, "Fallopian." By presenting the sex organs through scientific terms, one may imagine that an educator escapes instigating illicit thoughts; however, this moment attests to the fact that affects flow in and out of classrooms without any consideration for the classrooms or curricular scripts. Lastly, Andrew's rebuke "speaks to the bleak differences between what adults want for children and what children desire for themselves... school [perceived] as an adult-controlled space where children do as they're told until they can play" (Yoon & Templeton, 2019). Andrew does recognize that this action does not fit within script for him as a student. A school is a place of learning and a site that is outside the realm of bodily desires; school recognizes him as a student but does not honor the realities of being a human with sexual inclinations. However, Andrew eventually decides to masturbate in the school bathroom because he chooses to privilege his happiness and emotional well-being.

In a later episode, the writers of Big Mouth demonstrate how children further complicate and resist scripts of their childhoods in school. Connie, the female Hormone Monstress, supports Jessi and Nick as they contend with misogynistic narratives in the form of their school's newly instituted dress code. While this episode contends with the wide-ranging set of implications and consequences for dress codes, what rings out clearly is the children's performances in interrupting numerous narratives. In this way, the dress code operates as a "scriptive thing that broadly structures a performance while allowing for agency and unleashing original, live variations, that may not be individually predictable" (Bernstein, 2011, p. 12). Upon the launch of the dress code, Nick finds himself confused as to why he was at odds with Jessi. Connie, as his Hormone Monstress, processes with him so that they both come to the understanding that he "just stood there and said nothing. Like Billy Bush" (Suarez, 2019). While Nick was not actively vocalizing misogynistic notions, his silence was noted as a dismissal of his girlfriends and complicity in the harm induced by the dress code. Nick becomes aware that he has upset his friend with his inaction *and* begins to reckon with the larger power dynamics within which is situated. At this moment, Connie helps Nick in critical reflection; this opening to consider how one's actions and context produce particular power dynamics is often denied to children as it registered as too complicated and complex for the realm of childhood.

On the other hand, Jessi displays that she is wise to the narrative the dress code invites and glorifies— that boys are animals and thus girls must defend themselves from their uncontrollable behavior. Connie rages with Jessi as she calls out her male friends for subscribing to this narrative. Consequently, she decides to machinate a Slut Walk to protest the dress code. She chooses to wear a see-through crop top and jean shorts which inspires a monologue rife with anxiety and uncertainty regarding outfit choice—"I don't know what I'm doing and that I'm objectifying myself, and maybe this is just a terrible idea." Jessi and Connie both decide to put their bodies on the line to prove their resistance to the aforementioned narrative. However, the significance of Jessi's stunt lies in her intentional rejection of passively receiving particular scripts and cultural practices. As Bernstein (2011) explains, children are "experts in the scripts of children culture… and expertly field the narratives and material culture… as [they] collectively exercise agency" (Bernstein, 2011, pp. 27–28).

Nick later discovers that he just "cannot win" as he is denigrated by his male friends for trying to be an "ally with the girls." Connie is as flustered as Nick as they attempt to determine with whom to align, which demonstrates that the children are always in conversation with themselves as well as larger social narratives. Jessi releases her endless frustrations of being a girl such as "the whole world tell[ing] you how big your boobs should be." Ultimately both children and their shared Hormone Monstress determine that this "just might be this long conversation we all have to keep having." Connie says it best when she proclaims at this resolution, "Damn, y'all are in middle school and you havin' this big ass conversation" (ibid). Through the analysis of this episode's pivotal conversations, the Hormone Monsters serve as instigations that demonstrate the complexity of childhoods through these critical conversations and reflections. These animate (d) "affect [s] was already doing pedagogical work outside of the teacher's conscious intentions or control" (Niccolini, 2016, p. 241). Hormone Monsters—while albeit seemingly wreaking disaster on their children's lives, they are pushing against the boundaries of what has been cordoned off as inappropriate for children to think about, name, and consider. Time and time again, the children of *Big Mouth* are made aware of their lives within larger contexts and networks of power and with the support of these uncontrollable affects, they are bolstered in their ability to engage with those dynamics critically.

Be a Fence

However, the Hormone Monsters are not the only nonhuman entities to materialize and produce particular effects for the cast of children. The Shame Wizard—a floating specter with heterochromatic eyes, grayed and haggard hair receding from the hairline—enters as an antithetical force to the children and their Hormone Monsters as he seeks to regulate their behavior. Unlike the multiplicity of Hormone Monsters, the Shame Wizard is an individual entity with a grand reach that reflects Ahmed's (2014) illustration of affect as not localized in the individual, but instead circulated through sociocultural practices to "produce the very surfaces and boundaries that allow the individual and the social to be delineated as if they are objects" (Ahmed, 2014, p. 10). In other words, affects come through the narratives and behaviors that are shared between and among people and non-human entities. With this in mind, it is evident the Shame Wizard operates as a censoring mechanism to re-affirm proper social etiquette as well as strengthen presumed boundaries of childhood.

In his first encounter with the Shame Wizard, Andrew is escorted to Shame Court and is tried due to his penchant for "jerking off." Shame Court is a place in which The Shame Wizard presides as judge, prosecutor, and jury. The Shame Wizard, as prosecutor, aims to condemn Andrew not for "doing bad things" but for being a "bad thing" (Moser, 2018b). To support his argument, the Shame Wizard parades in the objects of Andrew's masturbation as witnesses to his so-called depravity. One witness, a sock, bemoans that Andrew "separated him from his partner" and did not use him for his intended purpose— "an object for feet" (Moser, 2018b). This testimony uplifts an implicit narrative about the shame with regard to propriety and childhood. The problem is not merely that Andrew masturbated, but that he took a sock and remixed his relationship to it to suit his own needs and desires. This reimagining of the sock's potential uses goes against the notion of children as passive consumers and enactors of received knowledge. The Shame Wizard, by placing this witness to the stand, attempts to curb Andrew's ability to be original and creative in his thinking. Another witness, a webcam girl, claims that of all her clients, Andrew is the "most perverted" because he watched her smoke from her vagina. Andrew explains in a sidebar with his attorney and Hormone Monster, Maury, that he was simply "curious about the mechanics." Andrew is being judged and penalized for his curiosity, when like many children, he had no other place or space to ask such questions. So often, children are condemned for their learning processes; however, their context does not provide alternative spaces to play out and critically examine their curiosities. The Shame Wizard denounces Andrew for "the many wretched things that [he'd] done in [his] pathetic life" (ibid), but truly the wizard is attempting to curb Andrew's curiosity and experimentation in the name of social order and maintaining a pristine vision of childhood.

However, Andrew is not the only one harmed by the stinging touch of the Shame Wizard. In his full-scale entrance, the Shame Wizard circulates throughout a school-wide sleepover, haunting all the school's children with their deepest insecurities. He proclaims that "whether they know it or not, people need shame. It protects them from the sickening filth that festers within their humiliating inadequacies, self-destructive proclivities ... their fundamental otherness" (ibid). The project of the Shame Wizard is to protect children from "their filth... their fundamental otherness," which inevitably silences their Hormone Monsters. Throughout the myriad scenes in which the Shame Wizard appears to the children, the Hormone Monsters are either silent or altogether absent. The interruptions that the Hormone Monsters incite are lost in Shame Wizard encounters as the children attempt to grapple with the narratives of who they should be and who they are finding themselves to be. As the children confess to each other that they have all received visitations from the Shame Wizard, they air out the sources of their shame. One such confession requires attention. Gina is a new supporting character who becomes Nick's love interest; she becomes Nick's first experience with intimate touching. Despite that the act happened behind closed doors, the news quickly circulates among Nick and Gina's peers. From this experience, Gina shares that the Shame Wizard "told me I was a slut. In fact, all of you told me that I was a slut" (ibid). Gina's confession brings forth two significant ideas. First, there are limitations to children's curiosity and experimentation as they learn about themselves. Gina was slut-shamed for sharing a private moment with someone she liked. Second, it substantiates that children are not unaware of the narratives and ideologies that circulate around them. The Shame Wizard was not alone in her slut-shaming, so children are hearing and taking up these larger complicated discourses and playing with them as they determine who they are.

While the children and monsters run amok, the adults only see the aftermath of their attempt to exorcise themselves from the shame. The adults—the educators and principals'—next steps are to seek out punishment for what they read as. The children collectively exorcise and banish the Shame Wizard. They turn their un-chaperoned school sleepover into a festivity of their wildest fantasies. As Yoon (in press) writes, "In spite of regulatory measures and attempts to control play, children have historically found ways to play, taking it underground in literal or figurative spaces, away from the adult gaze" (p. 3). The next morning, the school's principal and educators return to see the gymnasium as a wild and revolting site. Immediately, the educators seek out the perpetrators and attempt to dole punishments for what they read as abuse of school facilities and inappropriate behavior. They use the language of shame—labelling the acts as "debauchery"—to compel students to come forward. As Jenkins (1998) notes, "adults have framed moments of children authoring their play as "localized moments of resistance in moralistic categories of 'naughtiness' or in developmental psychological terms as 'testing limits'" (p. 31). In this scene, the educators take up this interpretation and completely miss the relationships repaired and trust built between the children because there was no longer the feeling of being "terrible and alone" for doing the same activities that the others were. Their confessions pushed them to understand that their play—whether masturbating, humping, or making out—were not shameful shared experiences. Furthermore, their interruptions to the scripts of childhood, gender, and sexuality become normalized experiences in spite of the Shame Wizard's attempts to make them feel other and abnormal. The children's resistance to the Shame Wizard provided the children the ability to push back against a world that discredits their curiosities and interests and "impose adult values" on their activities (Jenkins, 1998, p. 31). This show validates childhood and puberty logics, read as nonsensical by those who once lived within it.

If, as I suggest, the Hormone Monsters are symbolic of the unruly and uncontrollable desires of children and serve as interruptions to the scripts of childhoods, then I must also account for the practices of the adult world that attempt to inhibit the practices of children, which manifest in the mode of the Shame Wizard. The Shame Wizard circulates the sociocultural narratives regarding propriety that adults use to maintain the illusion of children as innocent, pure, irrational humans that require guidance to become "complete humans" and productive members of society. Interestingly enough, the Shame Wizard's policing and censoring mechanisms showed up within the show and in the reviews of the show. In discussing the reviews, I aim to explicitly highlight adults' anxieties that restrain the curricular possibilities of expanding our notions of childhoods.

One reviewer from *The New Yorker* wrote this show worked as "a great prod to getting serious about the parental controls on my television" (Patterson, 2017). The reviewer continued that the show "tests taboos" and showcased "the crude rituals and abject humiliations of pubescence [that] will toy with forbidden thoughts" (Patterson, 2017). This review is one of many that, in one way or another, alluded to the "gross" and/or inappropriate nature of this show such as Fry (2020) and Patterson (2017). The writing team of *Big Mouth* themselves calls these reviews into the show through the children's conversation of another show within the show. Nick shares "I know… I mean, the main characters are kids, but the show is so filthy." Andrew agrees with "It's too much." (Salaff, 2020). Such comments are underpinned by the notion of children always in need of protection or being fragile (Vandenbroeck, 2007). In that vein, adult censorship becomes rooted in these anxieties regarding their children's particular content intake, as demonstrated in these works (Guidotti-Hernández, 2007; Jenkins, 2007). Adults are deeply concerned with moving away from what Blaise formulates as monstrous childhoods—"those that are not 'normal', innocent, sanitised, and decontextualized [and] lurk throughout these uncanny more-than-human encounters" (Blaise, 2016, p. 618). As such, the shaming language of "gross," "filthy," "taboos" appear across the reviews as if to steer children away from the show's content.

In Conclusion, Rage with the Monsters

Big Mouth audaciously imitates and develops the underground logics of childhoods that run parallel to the worlds of adults (Jenkins, 1998; Thorne, 1993). Both a wild and horrific horror show and a vortex into dynamic imagined worlds of children, the show does not take for granted children's logics and behaviors even when they are read as insensible or illogical to adults. These monstrous childhoods on display in *Big Mouth* are a provocation that "activates extraordinary thinking about childhoods, enabling different kinds of lives to flourish beyond the normative conceptions of developmental psychology" (Blaise, 2016, p. 618). Even in its clumsiest moment, the show legitimizes the landscapes of childhoods—the monsters and wizards, all the imagined and anthropomorphized animals, statues, and other miscellaneous objects that are a part of the world. Thus, all children are able to play out the wildest desires and work through those myriad effects of their intra-actions with the surrounding non-human entities and intensities as well as adults.

Big Mouth opens up the possibilities of intergenerational learning because the show recognizes that children are social actors that are constructing their experiences alongside and against the dialogues that are simultaneously happening in the adult world. Throughout this show, the children, in bawdy and veracious fashion, consistently play out these seemingly large and looming issues into the everyday decisions they make with or against their monsters. The children play with and practice this new round of language and critical concepts such as gender as a spectrum, toxic masculinity, consent, shame, and well-being. This show opens a gateway to re-conceptualize our notions about what children are capable of knowing, addressing and internalizing. Buckingham (2011) acknowledges there are conflicting notions of how society imagines children and what their experiences of childhood should be. This show ultimately rejects the projection of innocence on childhoods and permits the horrors and wonders of changing bodies, contexts, and new conversations to run rampant across the screens. The child–Hormone Monster–Shame Wizard encounters help to re-consider what is intentionally permitted in the classroom—what play and exchanges are possible in the classrooms to ensure that children have access that adults have attempted to cordon out of their site. If educators and adults who work with children stopped censoring ideas that have been deemed "too complicated," then there is a chance to co-construct realities that afford all children myriad opportunities to experience all types of life.

In order to examine the curricular possibilities that *Big Mouth* for-wards, I conjure my own monsters to speculate and freedom dream a new script alongside them using my childhood memories as fodder.

Olu: So please first welcome to the stage, Vicki, my Hormone Monstress, who has remained by my side through thick and thin.

Vicki: This monster isn't under your bed, BABY! Not in your closet, boo. HA HA! It's your pleasure to make my acquaintance.

Olu: Also joining us is Ada, my Academy Genie.

Ada: What sis won't tell you is that I've been ghostwriting this whole chapter. I want my citation.

Olu: Last, but not least, Ms. Sis, my Educator Boo.

Ms. Sis: Happy to scare up some joy while sharing the stage with this hormone goon and pretentious know-it-all. Goodness!

Olu: So folx, we have made it this far and inquiring minds want to know. What does it mean to have you all living and breathing in the classroom? How can educators make room for beings like yourself?

Vicki: With or without an invite, we will show up and turn out. There was this one time—I'm not trying to put you on blast, but still—you were in 6th grade watching that movie, *Glory*, you know, the one in which that one solitary tear slides down Denzel's chiseled cheekbones. And even though, you were upset about everything in the film, I showed up and we just had to revel in Denzel's FINE self. Now I don't think that we expected Ms. K to say anything about how fine he was, but for sure, she could have at least acknowledged the other things that set you off. She just expected us to take the film at face value (get it?). She didn't even pretend to notice when some of our crew rolled our eyes or squirmed in anxiety. Like that was it.

Ada: Somehow, you have managed to say something interesting. I can build on here and say that Ms. K should have taken up a "reckless pedagogy" which Niccolini (2016) describes as a "messy mode of teaching … that allows for more movement of bodies and interaction among objects than her supervising teacher's pedagogical practice" (p. 237). Remember she did see your reactions. And she told us to "fix our faces." She may have seen the discomfort and anger in the moment but did know what to do with it. Even if she did not know, she should have been able to openly say, "I notice that there are some reactions in the room to this scene. What's happening? Why?"

Ms. Sis: But she had a job to do and it was to make sure that you understood the dynamics of Union soldiers during the Civil War. That was the aim and she got you there. Don't forget that we have supervisors and other powers that be to whom we answer. If we allow for mess, how can we ensure that learning is happening?

Ada: What Ms. K could have made room for is potentially a critique of *how* these stories about the Civil War are constructed.

Vicki: Yah, because Olu was irked by how much screen time *Sex and the City*'s husband was getting.

Ada: Exactly. It could have been a time to wonder and critique the White savior narrative that is continuously repeated throughout texts about the Civil War—and even antebellum and postbellum America.

Ms. Sis: This is, surprisingly, interesting point being made by both of y'all. That perhaps by giving up space and trusting children to come into their own understandings, there are openings for conversations that we usually don't expect from them. That, in fact, my teaching is not the only learning that can be done. This has me wondering where else my curriculum can open for children to take space.

Ada: Ms. Sis. Now you're thinking. And I think that's a question you have to ask the children. They are always ready to teach us about themselves. Remember that time Olu's students were writing about their cultural background and one of her students wrote about internet culture as theirs. In that open-ended narrative work, that student was able to express her life through the language of TikTok and Instagram. When she shared it with the class, she and her classmates were able to interrupt notions of children's lack of digital literacies.

Ms. Sis: You are making me think about how school structures are not built to trust students with their own learning. Instead, we should be co-constructing curricular opportunities with them.

Vicki: Yes! Ms. Sis! Come through, but we also have to consider the rest of us that in the room with these children. We sitting here too and the humans be feeling us all around them. So how can we also be seen in these spaces too?

Ada: And not just as interruptions but as welcome co-partners in these inquiry moments.

Olu: You all just ran the conversation without me. As a human in this space, I think our job is to name you all. If we do not speak of you, we cannot call you into the conversations.

Ms. Sis: It's not just about speaking on us, monsters. It is also about not shaming our existence. How often are educators goaded to keep pushing past our existence in the name of grades, in the name of paperwork? I think we need to deeply think about how we have censored lives that are not portrayed within this presumed narrow bandwidth of childhoods.

Ada: Yes! We need to allow all types of play in classroom! Not just the ones that were acceptable when the adults were kids. None of these perfunctory and moralistic tales of "When I was a kid" that ends with "you kids just don't…"

Vicki: Yes, because Aunty stays forgetting that I was haunting her behind too. Swear, these adults think that amnesia is on the other side of puberty. All this convenient forgetting… that turns into their own anxieties, guilt, and shame.

Ms. Sis: What if these conversations were less of "Back in my day" but more questions like "What is catching your attention today? What has you thinking and moving differently?" In that way, we have children, us, and adults making meaning together with all these histories and possibilities mingling together.

Ada: That's a start! Let's see if we can find Lil' O. Olu's inner child has to be around her somewhere. Maybe she can co-plan some of these possibilities with us.

Vicki: OOOO, Lil' O is a trip. Let's do it.

Olu: Anything else I would add seems perfunctory at this moment. So we will all just bid adieu.

References

Ahmed, S. (2014). *The cultural politics of emotion* (Second edition). Edinburgh University Press.

Bernstein, R. (2011). *Racial innocence: Performing American childhood from slavery to civil rights.* NYU Press.

Blaise, M. (2016). Fabricated childhoods: Uncanny encounters with the more-than-human. *Discourse: Studies in the Cultural Politics of Education, 37*(5), 617–626. https://doi.org/10.1080/01596306.2015.1075697

Burnett, C., & Merchant, G. (2018). Literacy-as-event: Accounting for relationality in literacy research. *Discourse: Studies in the Cultural Politics of Education, 41*(1), 45–56. https://doi.org/10.1080/01596306.2018.1460318

Butler, J. (1997). *The psychic life of power: Theories in subjection.* Stanford University Press.

Dumas, M., & Nelson, J. D. (2016). (Re) Imagining Black boyhood: Toward a critical framework for educational research. *Harvard Educational Review, 86*(1), 27–47.

Dyer, H. (2019). *The Queer Aesthetics of Childhood: Asymmetries of Innocence and the Cultural Politics of Child Development.* Rutgers University Press. https://doi.org/10.2307/j.ctvscxrd5

Francis, B. (2017). Everybody Bleeds (Season 1, Episode 2). In *Big Mouth.* Netflix.

Fry, N. (2020, December 21). *"Big Mouth" Is Still Changing—For the Better.* The New Yorker. https://www.newyorker.com/magazine/2020/12/28/big-mouth-is-still-changing-for-the-better

Guidotti-Hernández, N. M. (2007). Dora The Explorer, Constructing "LATINIDADES" and The Politics of Global Citizenship. *Latino Studies, 5*(2), 209–232. https://doi.org/10.1057/palgrave.lst.8600254

James, A. (2004). Understanding childhood from an interdisciplinary perspective: Problems and potentials. In P. B. Pufall & R. P. Unsworth (Eds.), *Rethinking childhood* (pp. 25–37). Rutgers University Press.

James, A., & Prout, A. (2014). A new paradigm for the sociology of childhood? Provenance, promise and problems. In A. James & A. Prout (Eds.), *Constructing and reconstructing childhood: Contemporary issues in the sociological study of childhood* (pp. 6–28). Taylor & Francis Group.

Jenkins, H. (1998). Introduction: Childhood innocence and other modern myths. In *The children's culture reader* (pp. 1–37). NYU Press.

Jenkins, H. (2007). Going bonkers. In *The wow climax* (pp. 159–184). NYU Press.

Kidd, D. (2018). *Pop Culture Freaks: Identity, Mass Media, and Society*. https://www.taylorfrancis.com/books/9780429493287

Kroll, N., & Goldberg, A. (2017, present). Big Mouth. In *Big Mouth*. Netflix.

Lenz-Taguchi, H. (2010). *Going beyond the theory/practice divide in early childhood education: Introducing an intra-active pedagogy*. Routledge.

Moser, J. (2017). Ejaculation (Season 1, Episode 1). In *Big Mouth*. Netflix.

Moser, J. (2018a). Smooch and Share (Season 2, Episode 9). In *Big Mouth*. Netflix.

Moser, J. (2018b). The Shame Wizard (Season 2, Episode 2). In *Big Mouth*. Netflix.

Muhammad, G., & Haddix, M. (2016). Centering Black girls' literacies: A review of literature on the multiple ways of knowing of Black girls. *English Education, 48*(4), 299–336.

Ngai, S. (2007). *Ugly feelings*. Harvard University Press.

Niccolini, A. (2016). Animate affects: Censorship, reckless pedagogies, and beautiful feelings. *Gender and Education, 28*(2), 230–249.

Patterson, T. (2017, November 17). *The Extreme Puberty of Nick Kroll's "Big Mouth."* The New Yorker. https://www.newyorker.com/culture/culture-desk/the-pre-teen-spirit-of-nick-krolls-big-mouth

Price-Dennis, D., Muhammad, G., Womack, E., McArthur, S., & Haddix, M. (2017). The Multiple Identities and Literacies of Black Girlhood: A Conversation About Creating Spaces for Black Girl Voices. *Journal of Language and Literacy Education, 13*(2), 1–18.

Salaff, A. (2020). Cafeteria Girls (Season 4, Episode 4). In *Big Mouth*. Netflix.

Stone, D. (2020). Horrority House (Season 4, Episode 9). In *Big Mouth*. Netflix.

Suarez, B. (2019). Girls Are Angry Too (Season 3, Episode 2). In *Big Mouth*. Netflix.

Thorne, B. (1993). *Gender play: Girls and boys in school*. Rutgers University Press.

Toliver, S. R. (2019). Breaking Binaries: #BlackGirlMagic and the Black Ratchet Imagination. *Journal of Language & Literacy Education, 15*(1), 1–26.

Vandenbroeck, M. (2007). Beyond anti-bias education: Changing conceptions of diversity and equity in European early childhood education. *European Early Childhood Education Research Journal, 15*(1), 21–35. https://doi.org/10.1080/13502930601046604

Yoon, H. (in press). *Popular Culture and the Aesthetics of Play: Children as Cultural Critics*.

Yoon, H., & Templeton, T. N. (2019). The Practice of Listening to Children: The Challenges of Hearing Children Out in an Adult-Regulated World. *Harvard Educational Review, 89*(1), 55–84.

Chapter 2

Of gods and educable subjects

Posthuman Education in Watchmen and The Good Place

Jordan Corson, Stockton University and Daniel Friedrich, Teachers College, Columbia University

Introduction

It is 2012 and you hear the word posthumanism for the first time. Two years later, you are at a conference, learning the contours of post-humanist theories from posthumanist scholars. Sometime after that, you have started writing about posthumanism and considering the ways it challenges dominant understandings of education. Five years from now, you will learn new theories that move beyond posthumanism, shifting your perspective once more. If these moments exist as separate entities along a linear track of time, they fit into the progressive, developmental structure that traces the foundations of modern schooling. Over time, through ongoing learning, gradual knowledge acquisition builds toward expertise. Here, knowledge is power. Education is change. Curriculum is a matter of progress moving along a single track.

What if, however, all of these times existed at once? Or rather, what if someone/something could exist simultaneously across time and space in such a way? This being would experience time, and thus education, in a fundamentally different way. Moreover, what if this omnipresent existence carried corresponding omniscience, where they are both ever-present and all-knowing? Education would here start at an impossible endpoint of knowledge. If one starts with all the knowledge in the world, what would education look like then? Would it even be possible?

This paper explores two such figures, Dr. Manhattan from the

HBO series *Watchmen*, and Janet from the NBC series *The Good Place*, to use these singular characters who always already have all the knowledge in the world to push against the humanist boundaries of our discipline. We offer sketches of these characters in descriptions brimming with spoilers. We describe how their godliness offers something a bit different in common writings about posthumanism and education. Focusing on the idea of them as *finished* products means that, at least from a humanist perspective, these two are essentially uneducable, which opens up the possibility to wonder where that ineducability leaves us when going beyond the human. Continuing with a train of spoilers, we articulate how education emerges for them only once they become human (or at least human-like). We then make another turn, moving with Janet and Dr. Manhattan's humanist education to explore the possibilities of education for gods who know everything. The chapter concludes with some questions about the limits of posthumanist education. Ultimately, through this chapter we seek to understand and argue for a posthuman education that stands outside of knowledge and rests on different ontological relationships.

Two Beings

Watchmen and *The Good Place* are both character-driven, *bildung*-type shows. Looking at their protagonists, the shows follow an educational journey. In *The Good Place*, Eleanor Shellstrop suddenly wakes up in the afterlife and, throughout four seasons, becomes friends with others like her who seek to understand what it means to be a good person. Over the course of the show, thanks to the care of her friends, an education in moral philosophy, and listening to the little voice in her head that tells her to be better, she develops from being an "Arizona trash bag" (sic) into a really *forking* good person.

As she arrives in the afterlife, Eleanor meets Janet. Janet knows everything, literally. She is a vessel of knowledge equipped with all the information in the universe, and capable of fulfilling any material desire expressed by The Good Place's inhabitants. Say someone wants a cactus. Janet just blinks her eyes and the cactus materializes in her hands. As certain events transpire, however, the characters are forced to "kill"—and thus reboot—Janet multiple times. With each reboot, Janet evolves, shifts into a being that is less subservient, developing both will and emotion. She falls in love with Jason Mendoza, an impulsive amateur DJ/dance crew leader from Jacksonville, Florida, who thinks the answer to any problem is to throw a Molotov cocktail at it. Janet's classification is particularly hard to lock down. She routinely corrects Jason, reminding him that she is "not a robot" and "not a girl." Yet, after dozens of reboots, Janet is certainly something other than an omniscient helper. She is never anything else but a Janet.

In both the graphic novel[1] and the television show *Watchmen*, Dr. Manhattan is framed initially as the all-powerful superhero, using his power to change the world. Characters frequently refer to and treat Dr. Manhattan as a god-like character. Where a superbeing/metahuman like Superman mostly fights for "justice, truth and the American way" with less attention to politics, culture, or really any interrogation of what that saying means, Dr. Manhattan is presented more like a deconstruction of the archetype, a character born of the material, moral, and political consequences of superhuman qualities. His consciousness occurs simultaneously across multiple points in time, meaning he almost always knows what will happen (with the rare exception of tachyon particles to obscure his perception of time), yet he cannot alter the course of history. As he says in the comic, everyone is a puppet, Dr. Manhattan is just "a puppet who can see the strings" (Moore & Gibbons, 1986, chapter 9, p. 5). This manner of experiencing time renders Dr. Manhattan less present within what others perceive to be the present since he is also always simultaneously somewhere in the past and future. He can physically control matter and is impervious to harm, and is the only being with superhuman characteristics in his universe. These seemingly limitless abilities leave him disinterested, disengaged, without challenges.

Almost everyone in the show thinks that after the events of the graphic novel Dr. Manhattan has left Earth to live on Mars and remains only a distant, ghostly presence. In reality, though, he spends time on a moon of Jupiter until he returns to Earth where his disconnection from human affairs is interrupted when he meets Angela, a woman he knows will fall for him as he falls for her. For him, all is foretold, up to a point he is not able to see anymore. For Angela, the relationship with this god-like figure is both enthralling and deeply unsettling, as we will explore further down.

Janet and Dr. Manhattan are not literal gods, but they carry god-like traits. They are, in fact, singularities beyond all attempts at categorization. They also share three particular traits that closely inform the possibility of understanding a posthuman education. First, they are all-knowing. They know every fact, every event, each particle of information. Their omniscience also relates to the manner in which they experience time and space. Both characters see time not as a linear thread but as something with intricate contours. They experience all times they occupy simultaneously ("To me, remembering moments with you is the same as living in them", Janet tells Jason as they say their goodbyes). Second, Dr. Manhattan and Janet both have the capacity to create. We don't mean to create ideas or works of art. As described in detail below, they both literally create (after)life. Third, at least initially, neither character is agentive. For all their power, despite their super/metahuman abilities, neither of these characters can change anything. Again, they may be able to see the strings, but they are still puppets. They operate in worlds where they cannot simply snap their fingers and solve every problem.

Though creating shares much with humanist understandings of education, omniscience and non-agency stand in direct opposition. The notion that humans become agentive creators who impact the world is a fundamental trait of humanist education. Thus, if education is a possibility for these two, it is ultimately something beyond knowledge, something other than learning, and a thing standing outside the realm of progress over time.

A New Posthumanist Figure

Pederson (2010) suggests that education within modern Western societies is so deeply entangled with humanism that they have essentially become synonymous. Emerging from the Enlightenment, education is about "becoming human," by "cultivating certain cognitive, social, and moral abilities" (p. 237). Here, education is a matter of perfecting the self through learning, becoming a productive, useful part of society. Through diverse conceptualizations, posthumanist thought challenges the primacy of humanism—some of these ways of thinking question who and what counts as human (Wynter, 2003). When human (specifically the educated or educable human) in this sense is evoked as a universal figure, it conjures a particular notion of Man, one that disregards a seemingly irrational Other. Indigenous and decolonial beings stand outside the categorical and liberal tradition of humanism. That is, in the crudest sketching, humanism places those Others marked on the margins of or outside this framework as uneducated and in need of humanism's educative light. Posthumanist thought, in contrast, presents the human as a political, contingent figure. In doing so, posthumanism offers the possibility of being and encountering different kinds of humans and different ways of knowing without a normative reference point.

Snaza and Weaver (2015) argue that posthumanism reconceptualizes the relations among humans, animals, and machines. Here, in addition to decentering colonial ways of thinking about humans, posthumanist ideas move against the supremacy and centrality of humans as a species. This shift moves humans away from being the predetermined unit of analysis when it comes to thinking and doing. In research, posthumanist approaches open up questions of thinking forests (Kohn, 2013) and agentive things (e.g., Latour, 2005). Human imagination is neither the center nor the singular driving force behind the thought. That is not to suggest that humans and their educational endeavors should be banished from the world (though some may make a compelling case) but that humans exist in relation with non-human animals and all kinds of things. Finally, there is even a notion of humans not as singular figures but as hybrids, meshing with animals and machines, breaking down the rigid borders of categorization (e.g., Haraway, 1985). All of these configurations pose a rethinking of who and what research should focus on when examining questions of thinking, learning, or making.

Most of these ideas challenge a clear hierarchy of thought. Humans are not some educational apex or unique thinking-making beings; animals and objects too can take up educational questions of planning (Snaza & Weaver, 2015). Snaza and Weaver recognize that posthumanism contains many permutations, only some of which scholars have begun to consider. Gods or god-like figures offer not only one such permutation, but they may also challenge the entry point of posthumanist work. Carstens (2018) explores the possibility of humanism's exploitation of an unthinking non-human Other, with human pursuits (including those of education) in the Anthropocene requiring domination and control of animals and other kinds of subjectivity. This suggestion is very much the opposite of Dr. Manhattan and Janet. They are unexploitable, all-powerful, pure knowledge. If they could be considered unthinking, it is simply because they have already reached the end of the intellectual line. They have all of the thought, all of the knowing. Humans, as the measure of all things, are a mundane topic beneath their knowledge and concerns (at least at first). In the way that posthumanist scholars consider humans as historical and cultural products, Dr. Manhattan and Janet literally operate outside of history.

Thus, exploring the education of gods starts at a seeming educational endpoint, with figures beyond the human. Pederson (2010) draws on Sloterdijk to provoke similar ideas in a critique of humanism, suggesting a "posteducation" in which humans use education to improve toward an endpoint where education is no longer necessary. Yet, this framework still relies on progress, development. It is through constant, rigorous humanist education that humans could theoretically exceed education. A posthumanist education for gods as singularities begins at this terminal moment. Welcoming gods into the conversation does not abandon posthumanist commitments to disrupting universalizing, colonial human-centered hierarchies, but it does open new questions about the role and possibilities of education beyond humanist approaches. More than adding new figures into the constellation of posthumanist thought, Dr. Manhattan and Janet offer a new form of ontological relations. It is not only a new type of being but a new manner of being in relation to the world, one that generates different kinds of questions about a posthumanist education.

Humanist Dreams

In one of Dr. Manhattan's first scenes in the show, he abandons the ordinary concerns of humans and Earth, heads to Europa, and builds a paradise. On that moon of Jupiter, he makes an atmosphere, constructs gardens, calls forth liquid to spring from the rocky surface and forms a pristine lake. He literally creates human life. Similarly, Janet conjures the neighborhood, the paradisiacal main setting in *The Good Place*. She makes majestic landscapes, serene ponds, and frozen yogurt shops. Every millimeter of the neighborhood supposedly responds to the characters' desires. Later in the show, Janet recreates the neighborhood and makes hundreds of people from herself to populate the neighborhood. In their respective settings, these characters create a seemingly perfect place. Encountering all that they offer and all that they contain, these places appear, at least initially, to be small societies of complete freedom. They can, furthermore, be read as an extension of these characters' educational lives.

For those who see education as a way to make a better world filled with humans making themselves better people, Janet and Dr. Manhattan have generated kinds of educational utopias, like the realization and achievement of the wildest dreams of educators like Horace Mann or Francisco Ferrer. Education as preparation for life, career, or the world in general serves little purpose as these worlds exist in and of themselves, with no need to prepare or move toward anything. Unlike Lewis' (2020) suggestion that study can be an act of pure means, these worlds are pure ends. There are no mechanisms moving toward something else, no more questions (for Janet and Dr. Manhattan can answer them all). Problems have disappeared. The planning and progress of humanist education have reached their endpoint. Agentive living, hardly a matter of concern for these characters who already know the future, recedes from view. Though Dr. Manhattan creates a kind of Adam and Eve in Eden on Europa, their function in the show is little more than puppets in Adrian Veidt's[2] theatrical games. That is not to say that they are enslaved but rather it is a world created by Dr. Manhattan and thus largely devoid of will and choice. On the surface, change itself has vanished. A horizon towards which lifetimes of learning strive has been reached. The world that Dr. Manhattan builds, and the neighborhood Janet makes, are stuck in time, a stasis of perfection.

But utopia is not as it seems. The good place, under its veneer of heaven, is a sinister, torturous, bad place. Every idyllic thing is slightly askew, intentionally creating sustained, low-grade suffering that could be endured across millennia. After all, what is frozen yogurt if not a vile reminder that one does not have ice cream? In fact, even the actual good place, once the characters arrive by the end of the show, is far from perfect. It may be a place of wondrous, endless utopia, but this stagnation in "perfection" turns to a dull bliss. As Adrian Veidt says about Dr. Manhattan's paradise, it is not only that "heaven is not enough," it is a prison. Rather than ushering in the perfect world of which so many educators have dreamed, achieving the many goals of humanist education is a trap. It is also not the product of cooperative efforts to use education to change the world and construct something otherwise and better but rather a world made outside of the world by characters standing outside of the world. Furthermore, these characters even stand outside of their own creation. Perhaps, then, education as a way to pursue utopia need not be a central focus of education. Before we turn from these ideas, though, let us linger in humanism just a bit more.

Un/Educable Gods

What about the creators themselves? Does their own perfection mean an impossibility to be educated? Returning to the notion of "posteducation," a humanist perspective suggests that figures like Janet and Dr. Manhattan are essentially uneducable. They have nothing to learn. They see no agency in the world. Imagine with frustration being a teacher and having Janet in your global history class. Think of the futility of trying to teach Dr. Manhattan biology. Likewise, an image of Dr. Manhattan or Janet as teachers inspiring students and changing their life trajectory is impossible. Janet and Dr. Manhattan do, in a way, serve as instructors: they provide information and in some cases, guidance. Yet, they do not teach as they cannot connect either with learners or with the very notion of learning. The dialogic education that so many strive for (e.g., Freire, 1970) is impossible. In *Watchmen*, for instance, Dr. Manhattan always finishes his girlfriend Angela's sentences. Rather than a sweet affect of a couple who intimately know each other's rhythms, this action irks her to no end. No matter what Veidt, Angela, or any of the other characters know or say, they cannot teach Dr. Manhattan anything, at least as it relates to knowledge acquisition.

As a Janet, Janet is made to contain all the knowledge in the universe and dispense it. She provides answers to all that is knowable but does not question. In her initial state, there are no episodes where Janet considers being anything other than a Janet. She never reflects on why things are what they are or how they might be otherwise. For Janet, the afterlife simply is and knowledge is there for sharing. It may thus seem that Janet and Dr. Manhattan fall into the educational position of perpetual teacher. Yet, teaching and learning are deeply entangled. Instructing or informing is not education. Education demands responsiveness, exchange, and mutual work. One cannot only teach and still engage in education if they never study, struggle, and learn. Moreover, this entanglement suggests that in the act of teaching, the teacher themself is changed. Students impact teachers just as teachers impact students. These god-like characters never change, never alter the course of who they are or how they are. Again, even though they create life, they do not see their own positions as ones that can enact any kind of change.

Looking to the foundations of modern education systems, educability is bound up in one's position. As singularities, neither of these figures take up the categories necessary to engage in education, such as "children", "learners", or "unfinished." Categories define the kinds of education one encounters. Teachers offer a certain kind of pedagogy for certain types of children. Language learners, for instance, might need a distinct curriculum or even a specific space to guide them. Keeping with a humanist mindset, education would thus only become possible for Janet and Dr. Manhattan if they were to become (more) human and, in that movement, categorizable. In both cases, a turn toward becoming human is exactly what occurs. Every time the characters in *The Good Place* hit the button that resets Janet (and they do this hundreds of times), Janet becomes more complex, less like other Janets, and more like the humans in the show. Suddenly, Janet is not merely a vessel for information but a character who has to figure out her feelings and learn how to adapt to the world around her. It is this resetting that makes Janet educable. The reset causes Janet to change and become someone else, a different kind of Janet. She never learns anything new, but something changes. With each reset, she develops new personality traits and shifts into more of a thinking-feeling being. Together with Janet's resets, the worlds she created are reset as well, as the imperfections in paradise become untenable and in need of some course correction. Janet's learning is intertwined with the world learning with her.

When Dr. Manhattan meets Angela, he first has to prove to her that he is who he says he is. He does so by anticipating the future (among which is the certainty that they are meant for each other). However, their inequality becomes unsustainable, and it is clear to her that their being together hinges on Dr. Manhattan taking on a human form. With the technological help of Adrian Veidt, Dr. Manhattan's abilities to manipulate matter, and a cadaver in a morgue in Vietnam, Dr. Manhattan becomes human. He lives in the body from the morgue. Thanks to the tachyon ring Veidt provided, he is cognitively unaware that he is or ever was Dr. Manhattan, thinking only that an accident caused him to lose his memory. He is suddenly, at least in one sense, Cal Abar, Angela's husband. In this human form, Cal learns to be a father and husband. Where Dr. Manhattan simply existed, doing no learning or changing, Cal learns with the people in his life. Cal and his children discuss their beliefs. He fights with his wife and learns from the conversation. Once again, as Dr. Manhattan becomes able to learn, the world changes as well. His abandoned paradise in Europa begins a revolution (his human creations revolting against his absence), and Earth descends into the abyss with the impending risk of white supremacists staging a plot for domination.

Dr. Manhattan's embodiment of a human reflects Janet's trip to Earth. Hoping to positively intervene in the characters' lives, halfway through the show Janet sneaks from the afterlife to Earth. She still possesses all of the knowledge in the universe, but this knowledge stops updating when she arrives. Her physical strength and conjuring powers also diminish. For the first time, both Dr. Manhattan as Cal and Janet on Earth must grapple with curricular questions of whose knowledge counts, who is included, and what counts as desirable knowledge. Encompassing all knowledge, omniscience has no inclusion/exclusion. Suddenly, they must consider pedagogical questions of how to live and what to do in the world. They are no longer outside of power. Prominently, Dr. Manhattan moves from a character standing outside of time and space to a Black man in the United States. Hiding his identities and powers from himself, he is forced to navigate a world populated with racist militias and deal with racist people in ways other than killing them with a wave of his hand.

Humanist education is also about a subjectifying question of what kind of person one becomes. It is about learning and understanding bodies of knowledge and ways of being. Such positioning is irrelevant to singular beings. Janet is not-a-girl and not-a-robot. Dr. Manhattan is essentially a being of collected particles that can assemble and transform other particles. When they turn toward humanness, these characters' identities coalesce around their attachments to others, their feelings and values, and emergent understandings of the world. One possible interpretation of this quite typical move in science fiction of portraying a turn towards humanity by beings that are other than/

more than human in order for them to learn is that learning and education are essential characteristics of the human, and the closer one is to humanity, the likelier it is one can learn[3]. This is the core move of humanism: taking the (Western) human gaze as a universal template and measuring rod for all other entities' behaviors. Those populational categories falling outside this universal require the normative work of education to make them more desirable humans that contribute to producing more desirable worlds. Yet, we wonder whether the turn towards humanity by these entities is a reflection of our lack of imagination for educations otherwise, a limit on our conceptualization of beings other than humans, or a combination of both. Their educability as human-like beings certainly reflects the vast allure of humanism and the difficulty of escaping this dominant educational framework.

Yet, our focus here is not on the trap of humanist education but on the possibilities of education for these characters who know all, never change, and see no ability to change things. In what remains, we mobilize posthumanist ideas to push against this interpretation by decentering the human as the normative core of education and considering other ways of assembling pedagogies that are other than/ more than human.

Beyond Learning:
Toward Posthuman Educations

It is inherently restrictive to see education as nothing more than the accumulation of knowledge, skills, and dispositions (the "mind, body, and soul" of educational standards). Dr. Manhattan and Janet, as god-like beings, both engage in educations that reveal that progressive, humanist learning is far from the ends of education. In fact, as others have indicated (Biesta, 2013; Lewis, 2020), learning itself can be a limiting discourse for education. Many, particularly Biesta, frame education as a leap into the unknown. For omniscient beings, though, there is no unknown. Posthumanist researchers, as well as those working and thinking in and with Indigenous thought, also pose such education as attuning to things and non-human animals (Snaza et al., 2014; Tuck, McKenzie, & McCoy, 2014; Escobar, 2020). But these gods already know and feel the intimate molecules of everything. Thinking with Dr. Manhattan and Janet beyond humanist conceptions, would education be possible for them? Is there a pathway outside of a humanist education other than becoming human? In other words, what would be an education of gods?

As mentioned above, Janet and Dr. Manhattan function in a universe beyond knowledge. They are not part of some Deleuzian becoming; they already are. In fact, perhaps their educations are better conceptualized as not-being, as relinquishing their singularity in a process that begins not in themselves (in their will to know, to learn, to improve) but in them being moved. They are moved to relinquish not by a teacher or a curriculum, but by a sudden encounter, an emergent realization that the world around them is not as separate from themselves as they thought it was and that the world's movement is inextricably tied to their own movement as part of it. In this section, we offer two points related to a posthuman education bound up in the movement of and with the world. One such quality—love—reveals a shared potential for these characters' education beyond humanism. We then explore a divergence, showing Janet's posthumanist education and Dr. Manhattan's ultimately uneducable state.

Love

As stated above, both characters are jarred out of their stasis by the hint of love and the curiosity towards being otherwise than they have thus far. Yet, in both cases, their movement towards change is not necessarily a choice, in that the very concept of agency (foundational to humanist views) is difficult to apply here. Dr. Manhattan continuously wonders about the irrelevance of free will or agency when everything is predetermined. He does not approach Angela because he feels attracted to her; he approaches her because that is what happens in that particular place at that particular time. The world around him moved him to that role, and he is fully aware of this. Janet, on the other hand, is time and again rebooted, forced to reframe herself in a new context, with new rules, and different affinities. Her will to know or to change (together with her less subservient nature) does not emerge from within and may not be considered, in fact, a will. Janet's relinquishing of her singularity literally changes the world (that she created) around her, and those changes lead in turn to new reboots. Janet is one with the world, and in those new worlds, her love for Jason is the largest gear in a complex engine.

Within these shows, love is an educational act. Both figures love through ultimately understanding something. It is not learning, but it is a movement, an embrace of something they already knew. Dr. Manhattan is forced to face the fact that Angela's love for humanity implies the facing of impossible odds and giving up on Cal as a human. Angela's decision to do something fated to fail—taking on a heavily armed group of white supremacists—shows Dr. Manhattan something. It is a moment that has, for Dr. Manhattan, always existed, but it is still a moment of realization, a realization that he loves her. Ten years earlier, when they meet in the bar, he tells her that he does not know that he loves her yet, but there is a moment that he will come to love her. Back in the present, as Angela turns to confront the group, Dr. Manhattan tells her, "this is the moment." He tells her with absolute certainty that she cannot save him. She tries anyway. The attempt, knowing it will fail, triggers his realization. Similarly, as he dies, the final words Dr. Manhattan says to Angela are, "I love you." The arc (though such an arc is difficult when one does not change) is a curricular path of love, not one that comes about through years of study but one existing all the time, in every moment. The education of Dr. Manhattan is an education in his relationship to both an individual and a world that, while preordained, still contains openings for a surplus. Love shifts how he is in the world. In his final moments, this being that always seemed detached, aloof, not in the world, teleports the other characters away and keeps Angela next to him because he doesn't want to be alone when he dies.

In *The Good Place*, Janet loves Jason. He is the first person to show a genuine interest in her as a being (even if he does routinely call her a girl), an act that stirs and disrupts Janet's way of being in the world. Over time, this love becomes reciprocated, including Janet and Jason marrying and later pursuing a relationship. This kind of love is, in a way, learned. Janet's love, though, is not bound to her humanity. It is not a matter of self-discovery and coming to understand her feelings. Instead, loving Jason is something incomprehensible, almost causing her to literally explode. That is not to say that it is something about which she needs to learn more. It is beyond knowledge. Janet comes to love Jason's irrationality, his improvisational and impulsive approach to the world that resists the stasis of a singularity.

The love that moves these two singularities shifts their ontologies, in a direction that seems to be contrary to the humanist progressive learning discourse. Whereas in the latter, any good education leads to the production of change agents, that is, individuals aware of their own power, will, and politicality, the radical love experienced by Dr. Manhattan and Janet produces a rupture with the self as a contained entity, a leaving behind of all that power and a realization of Ubuntu's premise: "I am because we are." Both characters need to relinquish the fantasy of being creators and instead embrace their part in a commons that is never exclusively, or even primarily, human.

Divergence

At this point in the story, the education of both characters diverges. Whereas Janet's new ontological status becomes integral in a move towards a new beginning for her and her community, Cal is forced to go back to the singularity of Dr. Manhattan when the world needs saving. In other words, the world of *Watchmen* does not tolerate god-lessness, and Dr. Manhattan's path is interrupted once again.

Angela, in her own role as the hero of the story, feels responsible for the fate of the world, and when the moment comes, she seems to have no option but to "kill" Cal (and their love) in order to wake up Dr. Manhattan. After a short period of confusion, Dr. Manhattan is back to being his blue, godly self, knowing already that he's fated to sacrifice himself to prevent white supremacists from accessing his power. He is back at being *the one*, the single presence that will alter everything. While his power sets him outside of humanity, his role as savior is the ultimate humanist dream. Curricular histories are filled with heroic subjects, individuals who overcome their own settings and use their power for good. Do not despair! The John Deweys, Paulo Freires, and Michael Apples of our field are here to help! And who is more educated than our heroes?

Perhaps, within the ultimately humanist education of Dr. Manhattan, he has become a learned subject. In an inversion of the Ubuntu premise, "you all are because I am" becomes the statement of a hero's education. In this curriculum, an objective could be stated as: "The student will learn to appreciate his own power to change and save the world". The activity, "The student will briefly relinquish those ideals and experience losing himself in the commons." The assessment, "The student will be called upon to fulfill his duty and save us all." Dr. Manhattan, the godly student, has passed the course in humanity. And, like all progressive narratives, he needs to remain imperfect, incomplete. Reflecting on what he could have done with all that power, Angela's grandfather Will Reeves—the first masked hero of that universe, the Hooded Justice—tells her upon hearing of his sacrifice: "He was a good man... but considering what he could do, he could have done more."

Janet's education is much more difficult to pinpoint. Knowing everything across all time and space and being able to conjure up any desire probably renders the (after)world mundane. Of all the people Janet could love, she chooses quite possibly the stupidest person to ever live (according to, among others, Michael, the neighborhood's architect). Her love of Jason reflects an education bound up in improvisation. This kind of improvisation is not one of venturing into the unknown but of acting in desirous ways.

In these acts, Janet becomes someone else, someone who grows from all of the resets. Whereas Cal's ultimate reboot and return to Dr. Manhattan is Angela's final move in what seemed like a sophisticated chess game ("We always knew this moment would come", Angela tells a puzzled Cal before she kills him to bring back Dr. Manhattan), Janet's resets keep adding layers that transform the totality of Janet, without ever turning her fully "human," yet moving her away from godliness. In the final episode of *The Good Place*, all the human characters finally leave the paradise in which they can realize all their desires as they come to terms with the fact that "whenever you're ready" "it's time to go." One by one, humans cross the door into the unknown and Michael, the demonic architect of the Good Place, is given a chance to live a few decades as a human, back on earth. Yet Janet stays behind. Janet is neither human nor demon, Janet is still a Janet. But the Janet she was is not the Janet she is, as her ontological status as a servant to the desires of others has shifted. Janet *is* because of the Good Place, and she needs to be there, not as a personal sacrifice, but as a communal understanding of existence. Her ontological status is not based on her own free will, yet it is also different from her previous existence as pure knowledge. She does not save, nor does she need saving, and her love for Jason (who at this point has moved on past the final door) is in itself a love for the space she inhabits. Since Janet is inseparable from the Good Place, her learning cannot be fragmented into objectives, activities and assessments, as there is no individual being there to assess.

Conclusion:
What's the Point of a Posthuman Education Anyway?

Clearly, both Janet and Dr. Manhattan emerge out of particular kinds of human imagination, and as such, they cannot escape the limits of our language, our understandings of the world, and the capitalist machine they (as characters in TV shows) so comfortably sit in. Yet, part of the effort of this book is geared towards exploring possibilities beyond such limitations, by thinking through the assemblages of pop culture, curriculum studies, and posthumanist thought, and the surplus that overflows common understanding of these terms when taken separately. In that regard, we think that the figures of Janet and Dr. Manhattan have something valuable to offer when considering their educations beyond humanist tropes.

The main challenge in considering the relevance of seemingly all-powerful characters is that, at least, at first sight, nothing should ever be able to change them. If you can solve everything with a blink or wave of the hand, why does it matter if you are in love? Why not simply make a utopia beyond the façade? An infuriating question lingers over *Watchmen*: If Dr. Manhattan can create life and move the molecules of imperfection toward a perfect world, what is the point of anything else, even of this story itself? Learning to be better seems a bit useless in the face of knowing everything you have done and everything you will do. If, in the Foucauldian sense, knowledge and power operate as a manifold, Dr. Manhattan and Janet's knowledge suggests they are all-powerful. And if the goal of education is to get one to be the best one can be, these beings as they are initially conceived are already finalized products; singularities, and as such, outside all measuring rods that could indicate improvement or lack thereof. If Janet is a Janet, who is to say what the best Janet is?

One of the most interesting provocations of posthumanist thought lies in the questioning of the "one" in that educational goal stated above. Posthumanism seeks to move against the enclosed definitions of humanity, particularly in defining the utopic ends of education as an individual matter of salvation and selfhood. The accumulation of knowledge, skills, and dispositions can only serve as goals if education is about improving the individual, even in progressive dreams in which that individual is then to use those tools to help or liberate others. Janet and Dr. Manhattan's arcs both push against the limits of those ideas, inviting us to wonder about educations that lead to relinquishing knowing all and being able to do all, not in the name of improving the self (or even improving others!) but as a way to enter into different ontological relations with our surroundings. Of the two characters, only Janet's situation becomes somewhat sustainable, whereas Dr. Manhattan is called upon to fulfill his duty as savior.

We could end the chapter with a promise: an education that decenters the individual and promotes different ontological relations with the surrounding entities would get us out of trouble. We could go further, stretch our minds, and propose concrete steps to get there. However, that would clearly just transfer salvation onto a new buzzword. What we offer instead, then, is a wondering: what other possible worlds could come out of that reframing of education? How would this assemblage (and perhaps all the others introduced in this book) of pop culture, curriculum, and posthumanism move us to push against the boundaries of our current practices?

Notes

1. Alan Moore and Dave Gibbons' graphic novel Watchmen (1986) is likely one of the most influential pieces of (graphic) literature of the 20th century. However, for the purpose of this chapter, we will almost exclusively focus on the unauthorized sequel, the HBO mini-series with the same name (2020).
2. Without going into much detail, Veidt is a character that orchestrates a genocide that saves the world from nuclear war. Dr. Manhattan deals with him by granting him his wish of creating a society for him to rule over in Europa.
3. When thinking of learning in the animal kingdom, the same framework tends to dominate: animal behavior is only considered learned when that learning mimics human functionality (language, obedience, social and emotional dimensions, etc.).

References

Biesta, G. (2013). *The beautiful risk of education*. Boulder, CO: Paradigm Publishers.

Carstens D. (2018). The politics of animality and posthuman pedagogy. In M. Zembylas, R. Braidotti, T. Shefer, & V. Bozalek (Eds.). *Socially just pedagogies: Posthumanist, feminist and materialist perspectives in higher education*, London: Bloomsbury, 63-80.

Escobar, A. (2020). *Pluriversal politics: the real and the possible*. Duke University Press.

Freire, P. (1970). *Pedagogy of the Oppressed*. New York, NY: Bloomsbury Publishing Inc.

Haraway, D. J. (1985). Cyborg Manifesto: Science, Technology, and Social-Feminist in the Late 20th Century. *Social Review, 80*, 65-108.

Kohn, E. (2013). *How forests think: Toward an anthropology beyond the human*. Berkeley: University of California Press.

Latour, B. (2005). *Reassembling the social: An introduction to actor-network-theory*. Oxford: Oxford University Press.

Lewis, T. (2020). Education for potentiality (against instrumentality). *Policy Futures inEducation, 0*(0), 1-14.

Lindeloff, D. (Producer). (2020). *Watchmen* [Television broadcast]. Holywood, CA: HBO.

Moore, A. & Gibbons, D. (1986). *Watchmen*. New York, NY: DC Comics.

Pederson, H. (2010). Is 'the posthuman' educable? On the convergence of educational philosophy, animal studies, and posthumanist theory. *Discourse: Studies in the Cultural Politics of Education 31*, (2), 237-250

Schur, M. (Producer). (2016). *The good place* [Television series]. Holywood, CA: NBC.

Snaza, N., Appelbaum, P., Bayne, S., Morris, M., Rotas, N., Sandlin, J., Wallin, J., Carlson, D., & Weaver, J. (2014). Toward a posthumanist education. *Journal of Curriculum Theorizing, 30* (2), 39-55.

Snaza, N. & Weaver, J. A. (2015). Introduction: Education and the posthumanist turn. In N.

Snaza & J. A. Weaver (Eds.). *Posthumanism and educational research*. New York: Routledge. (1-11).

Tuck, E., McKenzie, M., & McCoy, K. (2014). Land education: Indigenous, post-colonial, and decolonizing perspectives on place and environmental education research. *Environmental Education Research, 20*(1), 1-23.

Wynter, S. (2003). Unsettling the coloniality of being/power/truth/freedom: Towards the human, after man, its overrepresentation—An argument. *CR: The new centennial review, 3*(3), 257-337.

Chapter 3

Cloud Strife's Ghost

Hauntology, Curriculum and Final Fantasy VII

Nicholas Stock, University of Birmingham, UK

...[T]echnologies inhabit, as it were, a phantom structure. (Derrida, in conversation with Payne & Lewis, 1989, p.61)

A memory is something that has to be consciously recalled, right? That's why sometimes it can be mistaken and a different thing... (Tifa in *FFVII*)

This chapter, primarily embodying the Derridean concept of hauntology and the framework exemplified in Mark Fisher's *Ghosts of My Life* (2014), seeks to explore the idea of curriculum as pop culture hauntology. Inspired in part by the notion of the curriculum as a séance (Ruitenberg, 2009), that is, the idea that the curriculum could be reimagined as a summoning of the spectres of the past for pedagogical import, I examine the now unthinkably ambitious 1997 game *Final Fantasy VII* (*FFVII*). This is a timely chapter, as *FFVII* has recently been re-released under the title *Final Fantasy VII: Remake* (the very existence of which speaks to Fisher's writing on hauntology), therefore summoning the spectres of the 1997 game to the consoles of today's youth. Broadly, I see the need for a rethinking of what already constitutes the curriculum as something that is inherently ghostly, that is, not as stable as we might perhaps believe. In both its nature as a figure of presence and through its act of killing that which it excludes, there may be more ghosts haunting the curriculum than we realise. But further, I call for a reimagining of the curriculum as deliberately or innately ghostly. If we[1] accept the structure of the curriculum as always-already haunted, then we should seek to allow it to summon ghosts, perhaps the ghosts of capital, Empire, Marx, and ourselves. Consequently, we can begin to reimagine the curriculum as something entirely different, and in turn, imagine our futures differently, too. I believe the game *FFVII* conducts this hauntological act in a manner that conventional curricula cannot, both on a personal level, and on a more holistic one too. Indeed, in line with Derrida's proposition that technology 'inhabits... a phantom structure' (in Payne & Lewis, 1989, p. 61), we could say that games, with their firmly technological presence, are more inherently hauntological than other texts like the novel or film—something that will become clearer as I examine gaming in more depth. Consequently, it is through experiencing games *like FFVII* that the séance could be achieved.

Hauntology and the Curriculum

Though what constitutes a curriculum may be highly contested, the very *concept* of the curriculum indicates a figure of presence. It functions in virtuality as a list of knowledge deemed essential for acting effectively in our reality. Indeed, 'in modern school curricula with their strict delineation of content' (Flint & Peim, 2012, p. 145), the texts, skills, histories and ideologies that it purports are deemed to be the correct ones, indicated by the way they integrate with assessment. For, what a student must engage within the curriculum is 'symptomatic of the taken-for-granted organization of school subjects and conventional contents' (p. 145), that is, broadly commonsensical educational content. The notion of curricula is exactly that which determines what a student should, or *must* learn, decreeing its stability as a fixed pool of knowledge. But some complications arise when we probe the presence of the curriculum: What if this set of knowledge, skills, and texts are, to put it strangely, not exactly *there*? What if it is only a sort of half presence, a flickering being that comes and goes out of our reality; what if it is haunted by ghosts of that which it has excluded, or rather, that which it has killed? It is by thinking about things *hauntologically* that we can ask these sorts of questions. Hauntology, Derrida's 'portmanteau of "haunting" and "ontological"' (Stock, 2020, p. 2) (still pronounced 'ontology' in its original French—an ironic linguistic quip that implies all ontology is silently haunted somehow) is a concept I argue is needed in our approach to curriculum studies and indeed education more broadly. It is also through a grasping of hauntology (and it will always remain a grasping, never a full clutching) that we can approach *FFVII* in terms of its value as contributing to a ghostly curriculum.

The semantics of haunting are integral to understanding this approach, for what is a *ghost* or a *spectre*? Ghosts, spectres, and phantoms are liminal, caught in between the past and the present, 'neither entirely present, which is why we don't believe in them, nor entirely absent' (Caputo, 2012, p. 116). Their translucency makes them hard to grasp or depict. Ghosts are everywhere, as traces of the past continue to haunt us today. Centuries of colonial murder and pillage still haunt the comfortability of modernity, and yet, we often refuse to acknowledge them, to 'speak to the spectre' (Derrida, 2006, p. 11) of those lost people and places. Hauntology thus interrogates the stability of the things that we deem absolutely present in our reality. How much of what we deem present is really there, and how much of it is *haunted* by the "presence" of the past (or indeed, as I will elucidate via Fisher, the future)? To give the Derridean example of an adage from Shakespeare's *Hamlet*: 'The time is out of joint' (I.V). As the play commences, we are '*waiting* for this apparition' (Derrida, 2006, p. 2) of the murdered King, but what comes is 'some "thing" that remains difficult to name: neither soul nor body, and both one and the other' (p. 5). And yet, the almost-presence of the King is what lingers over the remainder of the play, lurking in the waters that drown Ophelia and the sword that slaughters Polonius. The past remains as much a part of Hamlet's present as anything temporally, *actually* present.[2]

Viewed from a different perspective, Derrida explicates hauntology by tracing the ghostly language employed by Marx. The infamous opening line of *The Communist Manifesto*, 'A spectre is haunting Europe—the spectre of communism' (Marx & Engels, 1848, p. 1) yields a doubled meaning: the haunting presence of the spectre that Marx summons in his prose is the collective spirit of the burgeoning communist revolution that was to sweep Europe, a spirit made (spectrally) visible in the organisation of workers. But this line also refers to the ghost that haunts the dreams of the capitalists as they sense their system may collapse. Of course, this spectre is not exactly *there*. Both the communists and the capitalists of Marx's narrative await the arrival of this revenant, expecting it to appear in its totality; and yet, it has been reified in the world through the actions of the people. It is an *absence*, whilst at the same time a palpable *presence*. Though this chapter is not about Derrida's explication of Marx *per se*, it will be made clear how these Marxian spectres indeed continue to haunt us now, and I shall elucidate why it is important we ensure that 'hospitality [is] offered to the *guest* as *ghost*' (Derrida, 1999, p. 111), rather than sending them back to the grave.

Mark Fisher's usage elucidates that hauntology not only summons ghosts of the past into the present, but also ghosts of the future into the past. Some are ghosts of 'that which is (in actuality is) no longer' (Fisher, 2012, p. 19) like the spectre of communism or King Hamlet's vengeance, those that are compelled 'to repeat' (p. 19). In comparison, other ghosts are 'that which (in actuality) has not yet happened, but which is already effective in the virtual' (p. 19). The futures that were lost in the past continue to haunt us now; they are the 'spectres of lost futures' (Fisher, 2014, p. 27). Through the musical genre of 'vaporwave' we can summon these spectres, electronic music that samples and loops fragments of retro pop music, Muzak, advertisements, or ostensibly anything audible from previous decades. There is a spectral quality to the sound, as the 'editing [is] often jagged and unexpected', accentuated by purposeful acoustic errors to conjure a 'vaporized' (Tanner, 2016) aesthetic. Something uncanny unfolds as it washes out recognisable riffs and jingles predominantly from the eighties and nineties. In the phenomenological experience of listening to vaporwave we find its futural spectrality, as when I listen to it (or watch nostalgic media like *Stranger Things*, as says Watson, 2019), I am not just transported to the past. Vaporwave's preoccupation with neoliberal culture allows me to bathe in the *futures* dreamt up in the late twentieth century. I am taken to the mythical world that those samples exist in as if I walk through the newly opened mall of a small town, and with it, I summon the optimistic futures that belonged to those people of the past. For this future, one that was promised in the era that vaporwave samples, one where the seduction of technology promised genuine hope and change, has now seemingly dissipated into nothing: 'the *not yet* of the futures that popular modernism trained us to expect, but which never materialised' (Fisher, 2014, p. 27). This experience allows us to travel to a time when there was still hope for better things than we dream of today.

This preoccupation with a lost future is, of course, troubling. Fisher proclaims that amidst the sprawl of neoliberal stasis, the future is now cancelled, notably quoting Beradi's aphorism of 'the slow cancellation of the future' (2011, p. 18). To explain briefly, Fisher reads Beradi as claiming that pop culture once had the vision to disturb the projection of our futures. We imagined utopias and dystopias that depicted radically different futures from the ones we seemed to be hurtling towards. Amidst the age of the internet, the massification of technology, the apparent absence of war and the 'alleged disappearance of history trumpeted by Francis Fukuyama' (Fisher, 2014, p. 16), the future seemed bright, or at least it does in the mythical form summoned by vaporwave and nostalgic television. But over the last four decades, these visions started to, and continue to, fade away. Thus, generations such as my own find themselves craving these lost futures and grasp for them in a virtual retelling of the past; I try and recapture the futures that belonged to those of the past. Indeed, *FFVII* also belongs to this era, the time of the PlayStation as a dazzling new hope for the future; thus, perhaps there is something important about late twentieth-century culture in the ghostly curriculum.

What is important about my phenomenological encounter with vaporwave or *FFVII*, however, is the way in which it highlights the spectrality that occurs in personal experiences as well as holistic ones. In *Ghosts of my Life,* Fisher identifies the hauntological intersection between pop culture, the past, future, and *his* present. *He has been haunted* throughout his life by ghosts that are effective in their virtual presence—some of them ghosts of the past and others of a lost future. In part, I selected *FFVII* as the pop culture text to propose the ghostly curriculum because it is one of the ghosts of my life, a haunting presence of my youth that has *presenced* a lost future of what I perhaps thought I would become at age twelve. Though it did not make me think I would save the world, I often wonder if the ghosts that this game floated around me deeply affected my worldview and sense of consciousness more than any formal education. It is thus my contention that the *sort* of spectral presence it offers is necessary in the educational realm, for curricula need to allow personal ghosts to enter in—the same text will not do this every time for every student. Assigning students *FFVII*, vaporwave or *Stranger Things* will not necessarily incur the séance it does for me, yet what my experience does exemplify is the *sort of things* we should be looking for in pop culture for a ghostly curriculum. This said, *FFVII* does possess innately hauntological qualities that others might experience, as will be made clear in later sections.

Ghostly Curricula

And so, what does hauntology have to do with curriculum? In part, this raises the question 'Whose absences haunt the curriculum?' (Ruitenberg, 2009, p. 305). Who has the curriculum killed? Via the 'taken-for-granted organization of school subjects and conventional contents' (Flint & Peim, 2012, p. 145), which dominant narratives are being purported in the curriculum that serve to keep the ghosts of the past, of Empire or capital for example, in the ground? Inherently, the curriculum *ignores* the spectres that haunt students to ensure that they are bound to the narrative of the status quo. Zembylas' work approaches this lack through a subversive pedagogy of hauntology to address the 'disappeared victims of a war or of a dictatorship' (2013, p. 69). He purports that

> a crucial pedagogical task [is] to "listen" to spectres as they gesture toward a still unformulated future within a society that has suffered disappearances... a call to responsibility for educators and learners to remember and reinscribe inherited shared histories and possible futures in ways that they may not yet be prepared or willing to consider. (p. 86)

For Zembylas, in his construction of an education that deals with the atrocities of war and dictatorship, we must ensure that curricula allow space for the ghosts of those lost to re-enter. Education cannot gloss over these histories, but rather must welcome them in. Ruitenberg speaks of a similar pedagogical stance, conceiving of 'education as séance, a coming to (speaking) terms with ghosts' (2009, p. 296). We can interpret this sort of thinking as curriculum or pedagogical strategy that acknowledges the ghosts of the past and allows time and space for a dialogue about them, and most pivotally, considers how they are still effective in virtuality today; they have 'at least an appearance of flesh' (Derrida, 2006, p. 157), that is, some sort of material presence in the classroom, but one that we too often ignore or *do not believe in.* This sort of thinking is vital, as it reminds us that we need to encounter these ghosts to strive for a different future, a goal education often strives towards, or at least purports to.

That which is killed by the conventional notion of a curriculum can be found in objects beyond the things we deem conventionally educational: 'They are in our dreams, our language, our ideas, our habits and rituals, our books and paintings' (Ruitenberg, 2009, p. 297). Consequently, it is through mass-media, pop culture, and, here specifically, video games, that these ghosts might be encountered. Pop culture's educational significance in a hauntological sense is affirmed by Tavin, who believes that the haunting nature of some visual culture creates a new paradigm altogether for education; it 'may open up a discursive space for the critique of fossilized positions while providing the possibility for future change' (2005, p. 114). What we henceforth aim for here is a ghostly curriculum, one that welcomes in the spectres of the past and the futures we have lost. Where this chapter diverts from Ruitenberg, Tavin, and Zembylas, is that I contend it is through games or texts like that of *FFVII* this sort of ghostly curriculum can be achieved.

The Ghosts of Pop Culture

For Fisher, students are now 'exhausted and overstimulated' by the state of 'de-eroticised' (2014, p. 15) late-capitalist culture, and inherently the curriculum that both expound and correlates with it. We should be wary, therefore, of any kind of pre-existing curriculum that merely bolsters itself with pop culture. These lazy utilisations of media texts do little to welcome ghosts and rather sustain the dominant narratives that seek to keep the past in the ground. The terrain of mainstream media is generally dominated by neoliberal ideology (Fisher, 2014; Blouin, 2018) that quells the ghosts of capital and colonialism. As the empires of Disney, Netflix and Amazon continue to grow, it is, of course, no surprise that much of the media they produce is coloured by capitalist ideology. Quite so, a cultural lethargy and the 'compulsion to repeat' (Fisher, 2012, p. 19) is made vastly apparent by the stream of sequels, prequels, nostalgia pieces, and remakes that are relentlessly released. It is unsurprising, therefore, that *FFVII* has received its own remake released in 2020, a game that certainly does no disservice to the original, but perhaps lacks some of the qualities that make the original so "haunting".

To return to Fisher's framework, he proposed that the ghosts found in particular forms of pop culture, hauntological ones, refuse to let us settle into the 'mediocre satisfactions' of late capitalist culture (2014, p. 22) by challenging the dominant paradigms we find in our reality. Fisher's examples primarily revolve around music, such as the spectral sounds of Burial and Joy Division; he evaluates not only the haunting quality of the texts that everyone can experience (as I will do with *FFVII*), but also demonstrates how these texts are in particular haunting for him. These are both important elements to consider in a ghostly curriculum; as I previously mentioned, the same text will not generate the same experience for every student. However, some pop culture texts, especially those made in the latter parts of the twenty-first century, are significant in this discourse due to their *innately* ghostly quality. As Derrida claimed in an interview with Payne and Lewis, it is in technological media that we find hauntings:

> contrary to what we might believe, the experience of ghosts is not tied to a bygone historical period, like the landscape of Scottish manors, etc., but on the contrary, is accentuated, accelerated by modern technologies like film, television, the telephone. These technologies inhabit, as it were, a phantom structure. Cinema is the art of phantoms… (1989, p. 61)

I wonder if the glossy aesthetic of contemporary cinema would have yielded the same response from Derrida as it did in 1989, but nevertheless, cinema, a form of media enframed by technology, speaks the voices of those who are absent. It is a summoning of ghosts onto the screen, accentuated by the imperfections of the camera (a quality that has inversely withered as technological standards have increased, thus diminishing their phantomatic structure). However, neither Derrida nor Fisher raises the importance of hauntological video games. Video games, especially when we look back to the era of the SEGA and PlayStation 1, a time when low-quality resolution and MIDI soundtracks still dominated the field, possess similar qualities as that of cinema for Derrida.[3] *FFVII*, a ghost of *my* life, is much like the experience Fisher has when turning on Joy Division's *Unknown Pleasures*. Though we may all find something spectral about the sound of Joy Division due to the eerie aesthetic, for Fisher, Joy Division 'matter now more than ever… because they capture the depressed spirit of *our* times' (Fisher, 2014, p. 50). Though the listening experience is personal and perhaps less haunting if you have no early memory of listening to Joy Division to recollect, the ghosts may still be universal for all of us. In parallel, though it is personal to me as it recalls many weekends sitting with the curtains closed and clutching the PlayStation pad, a game such as *FFVII* could be hauntological for others too due to the very phantomatic structure it holds. For, *FFVII* 'animates the ghosts that have the most fecundity; those with the greatest potential to start us thinking in powerful new ways' (Kenway, 2007, p. 6); though the personal spectre may be absent for many, there are still ghosts of 'fecundity' to be found here. Certainly, it is most potent for me as it recalls a time from my youth, but other games might offer similar things for others thus constitute the sort of pop culture that would create a ghostly curriculum. The search for pop culture that holds these *personal* ghosts that can be made *universal* is perhaps a vital task to follow in this chapter. It is because of this slightly paradoxical search that the ghostly curriculum can never be a figure of presence; it will always remain metamorphic, vapor-like... spectral.

Can you hear the cry of the planet?

FFVII depicts the journey of a band of eco-rebels, revolting against the oppressive nature of the governmental Shinra Electra Power Company. The journey begins with Cloud Strife, ex-Shinra military 'SOLDIER' turned mercenary, joining the rebel group AVALANCHE to bomb a Mako reactor in the city of Midgar. Mako, the force of the planet that holds together the delicate balance of life, is extracted through reactors, turned into energy, and sold back to the inhabitants of Midgar. Green flames shoot out of the reactors into the sky, an omnipresent reminder of the 'corporate rape of the planet' (Smith, 2002). Inevitably, through this extractive capital, the social hierarchy of Midgar is made manifest: Cloud wanders around the cobbled streets of Midgar's upper-side in one scene and the left-behind slums in the next. Encounters with the citizens are often coloured by their sense of alienation and listlessness, occasionally infused with terror or hatred of the Shinra.

AVALANCHE's first reactor bombing is successful, but their second detonation is more troubling, and there are civilian casualties. Eventually, as a tactic to shift public opinion on AVALANCHE's actions, Shinra destroys the plate that supports the structure over the slums and crashes down on the people below. Many of these people die, but the venom of the survivors is directed towards the band of rebels who have been detonating parts of the city. AVALANCHE still continue on their path to redeem Midgar of its oppressors. They storm Shinra HQ but are soon captured and imprisoned. In the middle of the night, they are released, only to find many of the Shinra have been slaughtered whilst survivors whisper of the return of the mighty ex-SOLDIER Sephiroth. It is after these first ten hours or so of gameplay (and this section constitutes the entirety of the recently released *Remake* for a good forty hours), the game truly begins.

The encounter with the Shinra and the existential effects of their corporation commences the séance. Intriguingly, the ghosts summoned in these sections are reminiscent of the ones called forth by Derrida in *Spectres of Marx*. The Shinra Electric Power Company are just that, a power company; it is through the force of globalised monopoly capital that they have become a governmental force in the game. Indeed, most towns that you enter throughout the expansive world map have had reactors built in them, even against the will of the people. Now, these forgotten souls are beholden unto the Shinra for both their employment and their energy source. This reluctant dependence is unnerving, something encapsulated by the town of North Corel. Here, the meltdown of the reactor has plunged the townsfolk into poverty, a place now littered with roadside markets selling scraps. One market stall owner begs you—'Please buy something! Anything will do!'. These experiences are unsettling, certainly, but it is the spectre of Marx pervading such scenes that instigates their hauntological quality. When we play through North Corel, we are reminded of the cruelty of global capital and hear whispers of Marx's ghost. Though the 'dogma machine and the "Marxist" ideological apparatuses [...] are in the process of disappearing', there is 'no future without Marx' (Derrida, 2006, p. 14) for the people of North Corel, or indeed for ourselves. What Derrida insinuates here is twofold: partly, it is that there can be no future without Marx as his spectre is so *pervasive*; thus, it will continue to linger long after the demise of formalised Marxist institutions. But more troublingly, Derrida intimates that our status quo is doomed to remain in stasis, to have *no future* if we do not listen to the spectre of Marx; to paraphrase Fisher (2014), the future is cancelled. This is not to say Derrida calls for a communist revolution, but rather that it calls for the spectre of Marx to be acknowledged to allow a future to come beyond the one of neoliberal capitalism. It is the encounters with the angry people of North Corel that remind us of this haunting; that for them there is no future without Marx, that is, without the destruction of global capital.

Marx's spectre is deeply intertwined with the threat of ecocatastrophe. Through 'corporate rape' (Smith, 2002), the extraction of mako is gradually killing the planet in the game. Midgar is 'bathed in a queasy green radiance. This glow emanates from the city's reactors discharging an emerald-coloured fire, the by-product of their incineration of the planet's spirit' (Sykes, 2017, p. 460). Two ghostly figures appear here: firstly, the incineration of the planet's spirit implies that something has been killed, and thus this green luminescence is that of the planet's ghost. But for the people of Midgar, the ghosts of this planetary murder are clear; they just choose to (or *have to*) ignore them. The second ghost is the one it summons from our reality, neatly embodied in another section of the game. In a beautiful yet disquieting moment, the team are invited into an observatory where the village elder Bugenhagen presents a visualisation of the planet surrounded by the flow of life. A green stream sweeps between every living creature, from person to animal to plant, endlessly circling around the globe. Just as the party begins to marvel over the beauty of life, Bugenhagen sucks the flow away. Colour drains from the planet and it turns into a grey husk; it cracks and shatters into fragments. Clearly, at the level of game reality, we are being told that mako reactors are killing the planet. What this visualisation summons in our reality, however, is the futural destruction of our planet. As energy is drained for capital gain, the land is destroyed. Eventually, there will be nothing left—and it is this prospect, this ghost of 'that which (in actuality) has not yet happened, but which is already effective in the virtual' (Fisher, 2012, p. 19) that is so chilling. The reality of the game, its ontology, is enraptured by the spectre of this futural apocalypse. Wheels are in motion, and the characters wrestle with the possibility that it might already be too late.

Beyond these experiences with the left-behind and the death of the planet, the game is populated with ghosts that plague the narrative. Those killed by AVALANCHE's bombings and by the fall of the plate in the slums—*your* actions as the player of the game that have led to such deaths. It is during moments like finding your AVA-

LANCHE comrades crushed under a pile of debris, reckoning with the deaths they have caused, 'the ghostly moment *comes upon it*, adds to it a supplementary dimension' (Derrida, 2006, p. 157). Still, this is only a game. The deaths we reckon with may not be real ones, and perhaps this is where *FFVII* lacks the hauntological power of texts that summon spectres of those *really* killed by capital or Empire. To build the ghostly curriculum sought after here, there must be pop culture texts that reckon with deaths beyond those of fictional characters. And yet, the spectral traces of death that loom around other parts of the game-world may well instigate this séance like moment in the "real" world, as we sense the ghosts of a much greater slaughter in *FFVII*. References to a forgotten war in the distant nation of Wutai are made through conversations with Shinra employees and various townsfolk; it becomes clear in a flashback to Cloud's past that he joined SOLDIER to fight in the war, dreaming of the organised slaughter of Wutai soldiers like his childhood hero Sephiroth. Deaths of the people of Wutai are mostly ignored or forgotten by the people you encounter. A widow in Midgar who lost her husband in the war makes a passing reference to Wutai as 'some faraway place', as if its distance keeps the ghosts at bay. Thus, a war that appears to be a dispute over the expansion of Shinra territory in Wutai summons ghosts that are even more chilling when you allow them in, for it is clear that it is the fear of the Other that has led to the slaughter of these people and the desire to keep their ghosts in the ground.

The time is out of joint

FFVII is aesthetically perplexing, full of anachronisms and generic hybridity. It is a 'jumble of steampunk—with its alternative energy sources and clunky machinery—and cyberpunk—with its forbidding cityscapes' (Sykes, 2017, p. 462), both genres that collapse time and space into one another. Similarly, the locations you encounter range from the sprawling cityscape of Midgar to 'medieval European hamlets and bucolic expanses' (p. 462), again plunging you as a player into different temporalities. Though this multiplicity is thematically bound, as every location is blighted with the misery caused by the Shinra, it still feels as if you have moved into a different century in each new location. In *FFVII*, the *time is out of joint*. You must play within a 'disjointed or disadjusted now' (Derrida, 2006, p. 1) where epochs collapse in on one another. But not only is the time out of joint, so too is the planet:

> The lifestream is sucked out of the ground for energy, but this process infects surrounding animals, turning them into aggressive monsters. Lifestream energy is known as "mako", and compressed mako becomes materia, the crystallised knowledge of the earth that is wielded by characters as offensive weapons. Nature is used to fight nature. (Sykes, 2017, p. 466fn)

This twisted engagement with nature, an inverted logic of ecology, collapses the sense of stability to be found in being-in-the-world[4] of the game. A line of the game repeated throughout is 'Can you hear the cry of the planet?' reminding us that it is in pain, being killed, delivering its ghosts. We are made to experience the disjointed and disadjusted, even in the most mundane random battles and the equipment selection of the menu screen.

As the game progresses into the final act and Shinra's presence fades into the background, fissures appear in Cloud's backstory. His childhood friend Tifa is confused by some of the memories he recalls earlier in the game, and each time he enters a reactor or someone mentions his past, Cloud begins to stutter and break down, accentuated by strobe-like editing and white-noise; spectral dialogue appears on screen, dismembered from anyone's body, uttering ominous phrases like 'Watch out' and 'I know you…'. Clearly, something is haunting Cloud. Ultimately, we discover that before the events of the game, Cloud was 'an unwilling subject of Shinra's rampant scientific experimentation along with his friend Zack' (Sykes, 2017, p. 460). Zack is killed in an escape but Cloud escapes and 'merges Zack's past with his own, creating a new persona' (p. 460). It transpires, therefore, that Cloud is haunted by a past that was never his, 'but which is still effective as a virtuality (the traumatic "compulsion to repeat" …)' (Fisher, 2012, p. 19). He becomes Zack, and each attempt to challenge this aspect of his past only consolidates his false persona and compels him to repeat Zack's actions, or sends him into a babbling stupor. Cloud must reckon with these ghosts if he is to move forward in the game and *become Cloud*. Consequently, we have this chilling realisation that we have not been playing as "our self" so far in the game—even identity lacks a firm presence here. Such amnesiac super-soldier tropes have become ubiquitous in pop culture now, popularised by the likes of Jason Bourne, but its ubiquity reminds audiences of the way in which we are susceptible to our past being easily erased. As Tifa says in the game: 'A memory is something that has to be consciously re-called, right? That's why sometimes it can be mistaken and a different thing'. Thus, the way in which curriculum obscures, erases or rewrites[5] that which has taken place before is laid bare. Those forgotten, *killed* by the curriculum continue to haunt it, just as Cloud's past continues to haunt him.

This same compulsion to repeat is mirrored by Sephiroth, who believes himself to be the 'saviour of the planet, wishing to reclaim it' (Sykes, 2017, p. 461) for the extinct race of the Ancients, a group who lived in harmony with the land. However, we learn that Sephiroth is not a descendent of the Ancients but rather created by Shinra from the cells of 'Jenova... an aggressively virulent extra-terrestrial responsi-ble for [the Ancient's] demise. As inheritor to this pernicious genetic legacy, Sephiroth's mission to refurbish the planet will, rather, insti-gate Armageddon' (p. 461). We see the ancestral curse of repetition arise, a product of the spectrality of Sephiroth's being that he does not talk to or acknowledge. The game indeed concludes with Sephiroth summoning a meteor to destroy the planet, an act only tempered (but not stopped) by the lifestream. Both he and Cloud are thus plagued by the ghosts of *their* lives, who they have killed, who they wanted to be, who they believe they are. By choosing to ignore their past, the ghosts that haunt them, they are on a path to Armageddon. What we experience as Cloud, however, is a physical encounter with these ghosts: 'While Sephiroth is unable to deal with nothingness, Cloud, at a pivotal moment in the game, falls inside his own mind and directly addresses the despair at the bottom of his existence' (p. 468). Cloud is *literally* plunged into his unconscious mind, and in it he must physi-cally confront the ghosts of his life. A séance takes place, and Cloud emerges with clarity of self and desire to persevere. Sephiroth gets no such séance, and thus he remains doomed to repeat the mistakes of his past. We are reminded, therefore, through the internal hauntology of the game, that we must reckon with our own past, own up to the ghosts of our lives and of our ancestors if we are to continue moving forward; we must heed the 'call to responsibility for educators and learners to remember and reinscribe inherited shared histories' (Zembylas, 2013, p. 86) as Cloud does.

It's like this train. It can't run anywhere except where its rails take it.

We must consolidate the question of this chapter then: what does hauntological pop culture such as *FFVII* offer us in terms of the ghostly curriculum? *FFVII* is no fable—fabilistic pop culture is precisely that which we should be wary of when reimagining the curriculum, as they summon no ghosts, but rather teach singular messages didactically. In contrast,[6] *FFVII* is an experience that leaves the player with an apparition of the ghost of Cloud Strife, a lingering question of how they should be-in-the-world after they have been in another; how should they go on interacting with the "real" world outside of the game when it is so uncannily familiar to the world within the game? Of course, it is this liminality, this blurring of the line between fiction and reality in video games, that makes it so that the ghosts can move between them. Or rather, it is the fact that our reality is very much a spectrality formed of ghosts from multiple times and places, that which 'adds to it a supplementary dimension' (Derrida, 2006, p. 157). You see, these ghosts are really ours, not Cloud, Shinra or Sephiroth's; 'they are always there [in our world], specters, even if they do not exist, even if they are no longer, even if they are not yet' (p. 221). We must let them in, and so too should we let them into our curricula.

We identify with the character Cloud (Chandler, 2009, p. 8) and use his words to find our place within the world of *FFVII*. Thus, when we speak, we do so through another language not our own. A tool such as this, one synonymous with a critical engagement and dialogue surrounding tales from oppressed cultures that are haunted by the ghosts of Empire, allows us to 'engage and inspect [the spectres]' (Ruitenberg, 2009, p. 302), rather than just look at them, but it does so with the added spirit of the player's agency within the game's narrative. Despite the fixed narrative outcome of the game, the way in which the player builds and customises their characters, interacts with who they choose, and occasionally selects the dialogue they wish to use, incurs a much deeper agency than is available through any other form of pop culture.

Pop culture with some level of agency is of course particularly effective at welcoming in ghosts.[7] What is so pressing about games like *FFVII*, however, is the particular sort of séance that occurs. Broadly, it allows in the spectres of Marx that Derrida foretold amongst other vital ghostly entities. Indeed, as Derrida says:

> The incantation repeats and ritualizes itself… it proclaims: Marx is dead, communism is dead, very dead, and along with it its hopes, its discourse, its theories, and its practices. It says: long live capitalism, long live the market, here's to the survival of economic and political liberalism! (2006, p. 64)

What Derrida points to is that with the death of Marx and the institutions of communism, we have only his spectre left. As the market takes hold as our very way of viewing the world, as our primary mode of being, we must allow Marx's spectre in. Not because we crave communism, but because this spectre haunts the market too; they just need to come to terms with its presence. But *FFVII* extends beyond Derrida's prophecy and other essential spectres are summoned: it shows us the '*not yet* of the futures' (Fisher, 2014, p. 27) of the eco-catastrophe that threatens our reality. It seems that now, more than ever, we should be utilising hauntological games like *FFVII* as a form of curriculum. Though we cannot ignore the way in which *FFVII* exists as part of the gaming Empire, a highly lucrative arm of capital, this does not stop it summoning those 'ghosts that have the most fecundity; those with the greatest potential to start us thinking in powerful new ways' (Kenway, 2007, p. 6). Perhaps this element even contributes to the haunting nature of the game—in that we must realise that *everything* we watch, read and play is haunted by the likes of global capital[8].

Furthermore, the experience of being 'out of joint' that such games offer is something difficult to conjure so effectively in other forms of media, especially the kind normally purported by conventional curricula. Phenomenological studies of gaming report that 'by entering into the virtual world, [gamers] became absent from the real world' (Čulig et al., 2014). This process of 'Game Transfer Phenomena' (de Gortari & Griffiths, 2016, p. 470) 'induces altered visual […] auditory [and] body perceptions' (p. 478). The very *experience* of gaming is spatiotemporally undulating, as we start to merge with the mechanics of another reality not our own. But garnering understanding of how things are out of joint prevents us from viewing our reality as a moment purely in the now. We find that it is one coloured by a past that is still effective in virtuality. One can only look to current trends of resistance across the world—climate strikes, anti-racist movements, occupations—to see how an understanding of the events of the past that we may have chosen to ignore is the spirit of revolution. Dealing with our own personal ghosts is that which allows us to reckon with what we, or what our what our ancestors have done.

This chapter is not proposing that every student should play *FFVII* as part of their learning experience. Doing so would reinstate the curriculum as a figure of presence, something that hauntology teaches us to avoid. Rather, I contend that the spectral elements of this game, and indeed other pieces of media with powerful spectral agency could be infused into the fabric of learning. The curriculum needs ghosts, or rather *should be ghostly*, and there are few better places to find them than in hauntological pieces of pop culture, a medium so often haunted by the narratives it excludes. But here, I call for the sort of pop culture that *shows* us theses ghosts, not just *makes* them. Ghosts of our past, Empire and capital must be confronted as part of the curriculum, but curriculum in the loosest possible sense as that of pop culture. When travelling through Midgar, Cloud Strife proclaims that the life of the oppressed is 'like this train. It can't run anywhere except where its rails take it'. But this acceptance of the dominant narrative, this belief that things are how they should or must be, refuses to own up to the ghosts of the past and of the future. By summoning spectres into the curriculum through the mode of pop culture, we derail the train.

But we must remember that this is only part of the journey. When the spectres are summoned, and even exorcised, that is, confronted and reckoned with, the structure that created them still remains:

> …when one has destroyed a phantomatic body, the real body remains. When the ghostly body of the emperor disappears, it is not the body that disappears, merely its phenomenality, its phantomality. The emperor is then more real than ever and one can measure better than ever his actual power. (Derrida, 2006, p. 163)

Once we have welcomed them in, started a conversation with, and reckoned with the ghosts of our past and futures, the ghosts of our lives, we have only started the journey towards a different future. The structures that allowed those ghosts to stay in the ground for this long still remain, and they too must be addressed. Any ghostly curriculum must be consolidated with real practice, action, or change, but this chapter is not the place to dwell on that. For now, before such action can happen, we await the arrival of the ghost, just as Hamlet awaits the spectre of his father. As Vincent says in the game: 'The gate to tomorrow is not the light of heaven, but the darkness of the depths of the earth.' We are not to look forward, necessarily, but into the depths and darkness of our past. It is there we may find the ghosts that we seek to allow a future to come.

Notes

1. It should be noted that I use the collective pronoun "we" intentionally throughout this chapter, for it is all of us who are totalised, enframed by the universal lens of education (see Stock, 2019). The need to reimagine curriculum is not particular to one person or place, but to the structure of education more broadly. Further, it is all of us who are haunted by the ghosts of capital, Empire, Marx and so forth, thus it is a "we" that must be addressed.

2. This ontology raises another caveat to the "we" spoken of throughout this chapter. Indeed, many cultures possess spectrality in their way of being-in-the-world. It is largely the Western, post-enlightenment cultures that have dismissed spectrality from their ontology, thus it "they" (we) who I speak of here.

3. Games have improved dramatically in terms of an aesthetic representation of reality; this certainly increases their uncanny nature, as the encounter with the contemporary video game is like that of a waxwork or a corpse. However, this increase in realism does not necessarily increase their haunting qualities. The low resolution and MIDI sounds of nineties games are objectively artificial, and yet, somehow strangely lifelike as if they possess a 'real' spirit. Cloud's "blocks and triangles" character design in FFVII is ultimately artificial, yet we still warm to him. Although, as I only speak of this in retrospect, it may simply be the fact that these sounds and visuals when engaged with today possess the haunting quality of the past.

4. I do not use this phrase accidentally. We obscurely encounter the spectre of philosopher Martin Heidegger in FFVII, the architect of the phrase and its associated ontological structure (one that eventually paved the way for Derrida's hauntology). Heidegger's concept of Bestand and Gestellen (see The Question Concerning Technology, 2011) are neatly embodied by the Mako Reactors. This is not merely a philosophical interpretation; a senior member of Shinra is named Heidegger to ensure that the encounter with his ghost is not overlooked.

5. Decolonisation discourse explores these issues in great depth; see for example Bhambra et al. (2018).

6. Zembylas for example notes how his hauntological pedagogy does 'not aim to settle past injustices within familiar modes of historical lessons' (2013, p. 85), something I contend the fable embodies in its hackneyed mode of moralistic didacticism.

7. We should note that children, in particular, will find fecundity in pop culture hauntology as they may have few ghosts of their own. The ability of pop culture to depict the ghostly, both the real and the imaginary, is a powerful mode through which children can confront the ghosts that they may not be aware are out there.

8. Fisher's most famous thesis – 'capitalist realism' (2009) –posits that everything is haunted by capital, but Fisher also notably claimed that hauntology is intrinsically the other side of the coin to capitalist realism.

References

Beradi, B. (2011). *After the Future*. Canada: AK Press

Bhambra, G. K., Gebrial, D. & Nisanciogl, K. (Eds.). (2018). *Decolonising the University*. London: Pluto Press

Blouin, M.J. (2018). 'Neoliberalism and Popular Culture' in *Journal of Popular Culture*. Vol.51, pp. 277-279. doi:10.1111/jpcu.12667

Caputo, J. D. (2012). 'Teaching the Event: Deconstruction, Hauntology, and the Scene of Pedagogy' in *The Pedagogies of Unlearning*. Seery, A. and Dunne, E. (Eds). Punctum Books

Chandler, B. (2009). 'The spikey-haired mercenary vs. the French narrative theorist: *FFVII* and the writerly text' in *Philosophy and Final Fantasy. The Ultimate Walkthrough*. Blahuta, J. and Beaulieu, S. (Eds). NJ: John Wiley & Sons

Čulig, B., Katavić, M., Kuček, J., & Matković, A. (2014). 'The Phenomenology of Video Games: How Gamers Perceive Games and Gaming' in *Engaging with Videogames* [e-book]. Leiden, The Netherlands: Brill. doi:

Pop Culture and Curriculum, Assemble!

https://doi.org/10.1163/9781848882959_007

De Gortari, A. B. O. & Griffiths, M. D. (2016) 'Prevalence and Characteristics of Game Transfer Phenomena: A Descriptive Survey Study' in *International Journal of Human–Computer Interaction,* Vol.32 (6), pp.-480, DOI: 10.1080/10447318.2016.1164430

Derrida, J. (1999). 'A word of welcome' in *Adieu to Emmanuel Levinas.* Stanford, CA: Stanford University Press, pp. 15-123

Derrida, J. (2006). *Spectres of Marx* [1993]. Routledge

Fisher, M. (2009). *Capitalist realism. Is there no alternative?* Winchester: Zer0 Books

Fisher, M. (2012). 'What is hauntology?' in *Film Quarterly,* Vol.66 (1), pp.16–24

Fisher, M. (2014). *Ghosts of my Life.* Zer0 Books

Flint, K. & Peim, N. (2012). *Rethinking the Education Improvement Agenda.* London: Continuum

Heidegger, M. (2011). *Basic writings* (1st ed.). Translated by D. Krell. London: Routledge Classics.

Kenway, J. (2007). *The Ghosts of the School Curriculum: Past, Present and Future.* Radford Lecture, Fremantle Australia

Marx, K. and Engels, F. (1848). *The Communist Manifesto.* Available at: https://www.marxists.org/archive/marx/works/1848/communist-manifesto/

Payne, A. & Lewis, M. (1989). 'The Ghost Dance: An Interview with Jacques Derrida' in *Public,* Vol. 2, pp.60-73

Ruitenberg, C. (2009). 'Education as Séance: Specters, Spirits, and the Expansion of Memory' in *Interchange,* Vol. 40 (3), pp.295–308

Stock, N. (2019). 'And what rough beast? An ontotheological exploration of education as a being' in *Educational Philosophy and Theory.* Vol.51 (4), pp.404-412, DOI: 10.1080/00131857.2018.1472573

Stock, N. (2020). 'Darkness and light. The archetypal metaphor for education' in *Educational Philosophy and Theory,* DOI: 10.1080/00131857.2020.1750363

Sykes, R. (2017). '"Those Chosen by the Planet": Final Fantasy VII and Earth Jurisprudence' in *International Journal for the Semiotics of LawRevue Internationale de Sémiotique Juridique.* Vol.30 (3), pp.455-476

Tanner, G. (2016). *Babbling Corpse: Vaporwave and the Commodification of Ghosts.* Winchester: Zero Books

Tavin, K. (2005). 'Hauntological Shifts: Fear and Loathing of Popular (Visual) Culture' in *Studies in Art Education.* Vol. 46 (2), pp. 101-117

Watson, M. (2019). *Can the Left Learn to Meme? Adorno, Video Gaming, and Stranger Things.* Winchester: Zer0 Books

Zembylas, M. (2013). 'Pedagogies of Hauntology in History Education: Learning to Live with the Ghosts of Disappeared Victims of War and Dictatorship' in *Educational Theory.* Vol.63 (10), pp.69-86. doi:10.1111/edth.12010

Section II

Pedagogical assemblages in/through pop culture

Chapter 4

Unsettling the Educated Subject

De/humanization and the (Im)possibility of Being Uneducated

Francisco A. Medina, City University of New York

What comes to mind when you hear the word *uneducated*? Is it an insult, a descriptor, or a compliment? Does it conjure up images of the poor, the developing world, the ignorant, the racist? Perhaps it brings to mind voters from a particular political party, people living in public housing and trailer parks, or the lack of a college degree, illiteracy, and the way someone speaks. You might even think of people who education can *rescue*. How would you react if someone were to describe you as an "uneducated person"? What feelings would it evoke?

In this chapter, I seek to unsettle the *superhumanization* of the formally educated subject and its overrepresentation in pop culture and educational studies by analyzing the film *My Fair Lady* (1964) and the popular Mexican telenovela *María la del Barrio* (1995). I argue that the construction of the educated subject is contingent on the dehumanization of the uneducated subject who often represents a problem to be rectified in both media and academic literature— sometimes as the dangerous "other" whose ignorance is a threat to civilization and democracy, other times as in need of protection and salvation, and at times as a romanticized figure who holds the key to a "simpler" humanity. I ask: How are media depictions and images of educated and uneducated people connected to educational studies and practice? How can "uneducatedness" help us imagine another way of being?

Central to the discussion is the conceptualization of the educated subject as the savior of humanity and/or as the model of what it means to be fully human. I bring into question the ever-present, under-problematized assertion of the role that the *educated subject* will play in planetary futurity and the survival of humanity. Educators are often tasked with the missionary creation of educated, responsible global citizens who are not only attuned to environmental catastrophe, but who must attend to social welfare and global issues (Andrzejewski & Alessio, 1999; Pais & Costa, 2020; Misiaszek, 2017). These claims have not been without critique (ibid, 2020); however, the primacy assigned to the educated subject as the catalyst for human progress and the manner in which formal education has come to represent "responsibility" for oneself and others while lack of formal education is conflated with "backwardness" and "incivility" in media and educational discourses has not been sufficiently explored.

To be sure, poverty, hunger, violence, exploitation, and all other forms of inequalities afflicting the world are serious issues—and it is not my intention to undermine the role of formal education in solving these issues and fostering solidarity. My concern is with the ways in which education has come to signify the zone where the educated subject saves the uneducated person whose problems are seen as primarily rooted in their lack of schooling. So much so that political discourses are often entrenched with the language of educated vs. uneducated voters in news media coverage and academic discussions where being college educated is conflated with voting democrat[1]. For example, studies have found an increased association between party affiliation and educational attainment (Pew Research Center, 2018), giving way to dozens of newspaper articles, both conservative and liberal, about this correlation. Often, social discourses about education emphasize the role that schooling has in combating racism, sexism, and homophobia (Wodtke, 2018; Demante, 2016) as if formal education for all will fix the ails of society. Or so, most of the cultural narratives about education insist.

My point of departure here is that current conceptions of what it means to be educated (the educated person) are inherently humanist, paradoxically dehumanizing, and continue to reproduce settler colonialism, racism, ableism, and sexism— what Sylvia Wynter (2003) refers to as the "overrepresentation of Man." The terms *education* and, by extension, the *educated subject* have been made the model of what it means to be fully human. The media, for instance, often portrays cases of people who overcame their systematic struggles through formal education. The poor person who learned how to write and speak eloquently, the woman who learned etiquette and gained femininity, the obese person who learned how to eat properly and exercise, the people of color in a developing country who were saved by the miracle of schooling— they are depicted as becoming more "fully human" through education.

It is my contention that the field of education must unpack the relationship between schooling and the humanist conceptualization of the human premised on the dehumanization of those who "fail" to succeed in the formal education system and/or of those who lack a diploma/ degree. Educational levels (or the lack of thereof) result in income inequality, less access to resources, health disparities, and more— all of which intersect with race, gender, and geographical zones (i.e., global south)—which signals a reliance on formal education for social inclusion and exclusion. The insistence on access to education for all through compulsory policies fails to consider the ramifications to those who cannot or do not wish to pursue formal education. It is precisely this insistence on education as a necessity for the future well-being of *everyone* and/or as the *only* path forward that results in the inherent dehumanization of certain students in schools and universities, such as students deemed to be "at risk" of failing[2].

If we are to decenter humanism in education, the construction of the educated subject at the expense of the dehumanization of those who lack formal education, diplomas, and degrees in all intersections must be interrogated. This requires structural, systematic, and local changes such as re-thinking the authority confer on the "educated" subject and the kinds of being/knowing/doing/feeling (Wynter, 2003; Stetsenko, 2016) valued in educational research and practice. More importantly, it requires us to re-think the role that "uneducatedness" might play in re-imagining a different way of being human.

In what follows, I draw on decolonial and critical literature to explore the connection between education and the construction of humanhood. I then analyze *My Fair Lady* and *María la del Barrio* as cultural texts to explore and wonder how the *humanitas* continues to haunt the "educated" subject, including ways in which the characters challenge us to re-think "uneducatedness."

Education and The Humanitas

For Wynter (2003) the emergence of the Western conception of humanness occurred through the colonization, enslavement, and dehumanization of Black and Indigenous people who were constructed as "dysselected by evolution" to explain and justify the overrepresentation of Man. This overrepresentation normalizes the ethnoclass of cisgender, White, upper-class, heterosexual men in biocentric terms "as if it were the human itself" (p. 260) against which everyone else is measured. According to Wynter, the struggle of our millennium, is therefore to unsettle the overrepresentation of Man and to re-imagine what it means to be human beyond our present model of humanity.

Part of my argument here is that this overrepresentation has and continues to be articulated via the *humanitas*. The "*humanitas*" is the Roman reiteration of the Greek concepts of philanthrôpía (philanthropy) and paideia (education), the later which "can be thought of as the West's ongoing attempt to articulate what it means to be 'civilized' and human" (Khan, 2007, p. 2). The *humanitas* interconnects, and marks a preference for, morality, culture, rational thought, civilization, and the educated subject to provide ethical guidelines for social and political practices that exclude those who, by virtue of their social position, are not considered fully human (Ferrando, 2019).

Education played and continues to play an important part in the production of the *humanitas*. According to Khan (2007), "paideia moved education beyond simple military preparation and the construction of an aristocratic class consciousness into its becoming the institution by which a complex of cultural skills and literacies could be learned by the young, in the name of initiating them into that overarching literacy known as 'Western civilization'" (p. 2). In order to become initiated in Western literacy, education became a process where humans were split from their "animal nature" to foster a humanity that "cannot come into being except through an educational regimen of 'humanization'" (Snaza, 2014, p. 20). Being educated became synonymous with full humanhood and complete beingness. To be educated is to be fully human.

If it is through schooling that one gains the status of full humanhood in society, then we need to examine the interconnection between de/humanization and the kind of humanity promoted in formal education. If formal educational spaces are where people "dwell together to learn what it means to be human and to accumulate the kinds of skills and habits required to participate in human societies" (Snaza, Appelbaum, Bayne, Carlson, & Morris, 2014, p. 39), then we, as scholars, need to interrogate the ways in which the overrepresentation of Man dwells in and outside the curriculum through the normalization of particular knowledge, anti-Blackness, and colonialism (Rose, 2019).

Snaza and Tarc (2019) theorize the curriculum as a humanizing and dehumanizing force (in Wynterian terms) wherein what counts as knowledge, truth, and reality serves to sustain and maintain humanist logics of exclusion. The curriculum centers and verifies Man as the model of humanity by dictating what is desirable, superior, and socially belonging. Howlett (2018) further argues that the dominant mode of thought about truth and knowledge in education continues to endorse enlightenment-based commitments to disembodied rationality and abstract objectivity. This understanding of knowledge as rationality has been an effective tool to maintain "the division and hierarchization of human life, and the demarcation of many as sub-human, as animals or objects" (p. 112) and for the exclusion of different ways of knowing from the political sphere.

Scholars such as a Levinson and Holland (1996) have addressed the historical particularities of the productions of the educated subject and how becoming "knowledgeable" in and outside of schooling condition the aspirations, moral values, and styles of learning individuals are socialized into. In this sense, pedagogy and schooling are "cultural theses about modes of living" packaged in the language of learning, cosmopolitanism, problem-solving, and innovation to exclude those whose modes of living differs from "the average" (Popkewitz, 2007, p. 74). The purpose of formal education is then to initiate students into this particular mode of humanhood, to categorize and rank them in the great chain of educated being.

Here, is perhaps, where those of us who want to transform the education system and society at large have the most work to do for the construct of the human is "centrally tied with being able to demonstrate rationality in a particular way" (Howlett, 2018, p. 111) that results in the creation of the educated and uneducated categories this paper discusses. Students often have to "demonstrate" their rationality through testing –be it standardized, multiple-choice, an essay, or oral presentation, which might unintentionally reproduce the logics of eugenics (Winfield, 2007). Rationality as knowledge is about the verification of humanity, it is about asking people (as students) to prove their humanhood through demonstrating rationality as academic knowledge.

Communities who do not subscribe to this humanist notion of knowledge are excluded from a curriculum model after Man. Rose (2019) demonstrates how the curriculum "snatches" the minds of Black students through constructing a neocolonial mythology that cast Black culture as lacking, uncultured, and undesirable without the European version of humanity. Moreover, this happens both at the local and global levels through the teaching of White middle-class values and tastes (some of which have been culturally appropriated) as what constitutes being a full, well-rounded human being (Rose, 2019). This has been an ongoing issue despite many scholars pointing out and proposing solutions to the ways in which racism and colonialism shape the curriculum and exclude other ways of knowing (Landson-Billings, 1998; 1995; Paris, Alim, & Genishi, 2017; Gutiérrez, 2008; Gutiérrez, Morales & Martinez, 2009; Caraballo, 2019).

What is at stake here is not only the diversification of the curriculum or sustaining students' cultures, *but the genre of the human itself.* Even when educational scholars speak of subjugated knowledge, it is usually in relationship to schooling and the emphasis is on the academic domestication and institutionalization of other ways of knowing and decolonizing perspectives. That is, how can this knowledge be of service to the education system and the production of educated subjects by *formalizing* it. But what if formalizing other ways of knowing for schooling purposes is not enough to unsettle *humanism*? What can we learn from the "uneducated" subject to move beyond what Andreotti (2021) refers to as modern-colonial desires and affective attachments?

It is through formal education that social ideas and practices are normalized, where the possibilities of being human are limited by pathologizing and monitoring behavior (Fendler, 1998). Teachability and learning become synonymous with accountability, one's ability to govern the self, and define the borders of humanity (Fendler, 1998; 2013). To be educated is to discipline "the innermost aspects of the self to comply with the developmental objectives of society" which are themselves premised on the conflation of science, rationalism, and governmentality (Fendler, 2013, p. 127). Sonu and Benson (2016) further argue that discursive practices of schooling construct the child as quasi-human and/or incomplete human being. Educational policies, assumptions about knowledge, institutional practices and priorities, and pedagogical methods come together to "expropriate and incorporate the child into its totalizing system" (p. 243) that renders them vulnerable and unready (as children) for society. In this sense, formal education is entangled with our present mode of *being*, including normative conceptions of what it means to be human.

The existence of the uneducated subject makes possible a conceptualization of humanhood that relies on enlightenment, rationality, self-government, and racialized gendered dichotomies via the educated subject. Schooling produces and reproduces distinctions between the educated and the "ignorant" by mapping people into existing hierarchies within and outside schools. People are given value based on their educational attainment or lack thereof where educational attainment correlates with income, health, housing stability, material deprivation, and incarceration at the intersection of race and gender (Chokshi, 2018; Kullar & Chokshi, 2018). To be formally "uneducated" is to occupy a space of liminal being in society.

De/humanizing the Uneducated Subject

Many educational theorists from John Dewey to Paulo Freire to María Montessori have asserted education as quintessential for human progress and becoming. All of these philosophers of education promoted humanist ideals that present education not only as unique to humans but as the savior of humanity. It is through education that people come to realize Dewey's democracy, Freire's project of humanization, and Montessori's maximum potential. The underlying argument being that people cannot know what democracy is, become fully human, or achieve their full potentials unless they undergo 'liberatory' humanist education.

Since formal education has been conceptualized as closing the gap between where humans are and where they could be— the social vision of an ideal human (Cremin, 1970)—the presence of an uneducated populace presents a problem. Anxieties about the "uneducated" subject have haunted education for centuries. Those who lack schooling, are seen as representing a threat to morality and civilization: the poor, the feebleminded, and the criminal. Schooling has been guided by the logic of rational purification and the cleansing of society through instilling moral values, hygiene, and the prevention of "socially defectives" (James, 2005). To be uneducated is to be part of a dangerous population and a supposed "social disintegration" outside respectability politics: single mothers, "at-risk" youth, drug usage, and promiscuity (Popkewitz, 2007; 2008). The uneducated subject is constructed as supposedly irrational, guided by emotions instead of known facts, and as an "unproductive" member of society— all of which cast them closer to "incivility" than to humanhood. Those who occupy these liminal spaces are excluded from the current model of humanity (Man) in intersectional ways.

Education and the *humanitas* are entangled in our being/feeling/knowing/doing (Wynter, 2003; Stetsenko, 2016) and social understandings about humanity. Indeed, our species is named homo-sapiens which translates to the "knowing human" or the wise, thinking man (Ferrando, 2019; Agamben, 2004). *I think, therefore I am [human]*. Being formally educated is conflated with full humanity. Any knowledge that falls outside the canon and the common core is deemed less epistemological, less factual, less important, and ultimately less human. There is certain irony here when considering that formally "uneducated" peoples have always produced, contributed to, and continue to contribute to the collective of human knowledge about the world and reality. Not only has their contribution been made through nonconsensual experimentation and exploitation at the hands of scientists, but formally "uneducated" and illiterate people paved the way for scientific advancements. The knowledge of midwives, smiths, miners, artisans, seafarers, and merchants, among others, has historically been linked to scientific and mathematical advancement (Conner, 2005). And yet society and formal education continue to erase and/or separate these historical contributions from conventional, formalized forms of knowledge promoted in schools.

Uneducated in this context, is not meant to be a defining characteristic of these populations nor an objective assessment of the knowledge people who lack schooling possess and produce. The term "uneducated" is employed to highlight how these people are dehumanized because of a supposed lack of knowledge and rationality in contrast to the *superhumanization* of the educated subject. This dehumanization is interconnected to the overrepresentation of Man, colonialism, and anti-Blackness that produce "the lived and racialized categories of the rational and irrational, the selected and dysselected, the haves and the have-nots as asymmetrical naturalized racial-sexual human groupings that are specific to time, place, and personhood" (Wynter & McKittrick, 2015, p. 10).

Uneducatedness relies on racist and gendered tropes about women, Indigenous, and Black people as "ignorant," "uncivilized," and "irrational" that are then incorporated into classism and educational elitism. Schooling was central to settler colonialism through the constructions of European colonists as "educated" and the Native population as "lacking education" (Dyke, Meyerhoff & Evol, 2018). This construction gave rise to boarding schools that sought to acculturate and "civilized" Native students by assigning them value based on their ability to perform European epistemologies (Adams, 1995; ibid, 2018). At the same time, the construction of women as "irrational" and closer to nature (e.g., reproduction) was used to exclude them from schooling and the profession of teaching (Goodchild, 2012; Tyack, 1974; Bissell-Brown, 1990). Taken together, racist and sexist tropes of the "other" have functioned to construct the "uneducated" subject as a social risk and to produce anxieties about an imagined uneducated society (e.g., feminized).

This is where this paper departs from posthumanist thought and emphasizes the works of Wynter (2003), Jackson (2013), and King (2017) where the inclusion of Black and Indigenous people into humanity results in an epistemic break that collapses the normative category of "the human" and the order of knowledge. This differs from posthumanist proposals that seek to center the more-than-human world under the assumption that animal and environmental rights will result in equality for marginalized communities. Yet as King (2017) and Jackson (2013) reminds us, posthumanism calls for a Eurocentric transcendentalism that ignores historical movements where animals and the environment have been valued over the lives of Black and Indigenous people[3]. Since the "uneducated subject" is co-constituted through racialization, gendering, disablement, otherization, and classing, posthumanism is not enough to reimagine education in non-humanist ways. Rather, we must unsettle the overrepresentation of Man and its colonial and anti-Black legacies. As Wynter (2003; 2007) elaborates in her work, because human beings are conceptualized and understood only in hierarchical terms, the "colonized-non-white-Black-poor-incarcerated-jobless peoples who are not simply marked by social categories, but are instead identifiably condemned due to their dysselected human status" (McKittrick, 2015, p. 7).

Instead of seeking to "rescue" or "fix" uneducated people through schooling, I wonder, what can we learn from the "uneducated" subject to move beyond humanist becomings? To be clear, this paper does not employ the terms uneducated or unschooled as synonyms with "closed-minded" or "ignorant". Too often, the label of "uneducated" is assigned to racists, sexists, homophobes at the expense, and for the purposes of, concealing the isms that exist within highly educated populations. Dehumanization, anti-Blackness, and the coloniality of power are also present in formally educated spaces such as academia and graduate school (Walker, 2020; Cruz, 2012; Scheurich, 1993). A higher education degree (i.e., PhD) is, for example, equated with full humanity (although not for everyone), while people without formal education are made the scapegoats for social problems. The type of "uneducatedness" I speak of is connected to the imagination and resistance of communities and social movements outside formal education (Dyke, Meyerhoff, & Evol, 2018). That is, the ways in which the "uneducated" embrace, however limited, a different mode of living that welcomes complexities and the messiness of everyday life.

Thus far, I have demonstrated the connection between the educated subject and the overrepresentation of Man, which is made possible through the dehumanization of those deemed "uneducated" in society. In the next section, I explore media depictions of the educated and uneducated subjects in a film and telenovela to show how the dehumanization of the "ignorant" other function as a cultural trope. More importantly, I use these cultural texts to explore and wonder about the possibilities of being/feeling/knowing/doing outside of the formally educated subject. What others way of being does being "uneducated" offer us?

Media as Cultural Texts

What it means to be human and who is fully human emerge from the kind of stories we tell. Wynter (2003) invites us to think of the human as a self-defining storytelling species, what she calls "homo *narrans*" who narrate ourselves into existence. For Wynter, "humans know, feel, and experience ourselves not solely in biocentric terms… but also in pseudospeciating terms as a specific 'type,' 'kind,' or 'sort' of being human" that derives from "each origin story's/myth's answer to the questions 'what is humankind?,' 'who am I?,' 'what am I?'" (Ambroise, 2018, p. 848). That is, humans do not come to be nor experience being human as a purely biological organism but rather through the kinds of cultural, religious, and political stories we tell that become part of our neurochemistry (Ambroise, 2018; Wynter, 2003). These meta-theories about humanity have deep implications for institutional practices, particularly education, and more importantly, the kinds of futures we are able to imagine as a society (Wynter & McKittrick, 2014; Wynter, 2003; Stetsenko, 2016).

With this in mind, I now turn to the analysis of two cultural texts to situate and understand the *superhumanization* of the educated subject as contingent upon the dehumanization of the uneducated subject. My analysis centers on *My Fair Lady* (1964) and *María la del Barrio* (1995) due to their presence, influence, and status as "classics" in the US. and Latin America, respectively, as well as the parallels between them. While many films capture the *superhumanization* of the educated subject, *My Fair Lady* and *María la del Barrio* open a window into the construction of the uneducated subject. Both María and Eliza are poor, uneducated White women who experience education as dislocating even when it provides them access to a bourgeois humanhood. It is precisely in their "uneducatedness" that María and Eliza experienced another way of being/feeling/knowing/doing that, to some extent (though not completely and at times superficially), challenged educated humanhood (Man).

The uniqueness of both cultural texts provides an avenue to explore the complex relationship (as well as refusal) between "uneducated" people and education that produce and reproduce narratives about what it means to be educated and uneducated. I identify three interconnected ways in which the *superhumanization* of the educated subject vis-à-vis the dehumanization of the "uneducated" subject are narrated into existence in each text: (1) the uneducated as a social problem, (2) the educated subject as a savior, and (3) education as (dis)empowerment. I then explore ways in which María and Eliza, as formally "uneducated" subjects, do not only challenge various cultural binaries but might point to other ways of being human outside of Man.

The uneducated as social problem

My Fair Lady (1964) begins on a rainy evening in 1912 with Eliza Doolittle selling flowers in Covent Garden when Henry Higgins, a professor of linguistics, is mortified by her Cockney accent—a marker of her lower social class, lack of education, and unlady-ness. He tells Eliza, "a woman who utters such disgusting, depressing noise has no right to be anywhere, *no right to live*. Remember that *you're a human being* with a soul and the divine gift of articulate speech" (emphasis added). He later sings, "look at her, a prisoner of the gutter, condemned by every syllable she utters, *by right she should be taken out and hung*, for the cold-blooded murder of the English tongue" (emphasis added). This sets the tone of Professor Higgins' understanding of Eliza as an uneducated subject. The plot of the movie begins when Professor Higgins makes a wager with Colonel Pickering, to turn Eliza into a woman who can pass for a "duchess." Eliza begins her transformation into a lady in Professor Higgin's home through scenes ranging from Higgin's maids forcing Eliza to bathe, to Eliza practicing the alphabet and phonetics. Slowly, Eliza's transformation into a "proper" educated lady is signaled with changes in clothing, hairstyle, hygiene, and mannerism.

"Filthiness" and "improper" speech are also a recurring theme in the telenovela *María la del Barrio* (1995), which begins with María, a 15-year-old girl who lives with her godmother in an impoverished community on the outskirts of Mexico City. María works as a picker of recyclable material in a landfill surrounded by other workers, street dogs, donkeys, piles of tires, and trash. When María's godmother dies, a priest convinces Don Fernando De la Vega, a businessman and one of the wealthiest people in Mexico, to give María a job in his home. Like Eliza, María wears dirty and torn clothes and is notoriously "vulgar" in her speech. When María arrives at De la Vega's home, Victoria—Fernando's wife— asks, "Who is that filthy girl?[4]" Other characters in the series refer to María as *zaparrastrosa* (scruffy-looking) and constantly remind her that she can no longer behave in an as if she were still in the "uneducated" slums. In a similar manner to Professor Higgins, Don Fernando takes it upon himself to turned María into a refined and "dignified young lady" to the dismay of the rest of the characters. Over time, María begins to take etiquette classes and undergoes a transformations à la *My Fair Lady* that include make-overs, learning how to walk in high heels, how to speak properly, how to read and write, how to eat with utensils, and ultimately, how to act and behave as a woman from high society.

María and Eliza's assumed state of "ignorance" and "incivility" perpetuates education as the *Ascent of Man* wherein prior to entering the formal education system people are not only unknowing but represent a "less evolved" form of humanity. This perhaps esteems from the presence of cultural-epochs theory and recapitulation theory in education that continues to see child development and student development as mirroring human evolution where students move through stages from an "uncivilized" state to a "civilized" one (Fallace, 2014). In this sense, the less educated students are, the closer to nature and "less-evolved" they are seen as. María and Eliza are portrayed as and understood by other characters as being closer to nature because of their lack of education. This nature—this assumed animality—becomes a target to be domesticated and tamed to direct their "attentions away from the body and toward forms of 'rational' thought" (Snaza et al., 2014, p. 45).

Importantly, María and Eliza embody racialized and gendered assemblages that function to make them "candidates" for formal education and "civilization" in the eyes of Don Fernando and Professor Higgins. Both characters are White women who fit the beauty standards of their respective society and time period, and they ultimately conform to the respectability politics woven in each narrative. For instance, María's rescue-ability differentiates her from other formally uneducated characters in the telenovela. Her hard-work ethic is juxtaposed to Carlota, a maid in De la Vega's mansion who spends more time gossiping than cleaning. María's "goodness" is highlighted through the otherization of Calixta, a maid who is coded as an Indigenous or Mestiza woman who practices *brujería* to harm María and De la Vega family. Similarly, Eliza is a White, single woman who, despite being poor works hard by selling flowers in contrast to her "lazy" father. In this context, Eliza and María's ability to enter and "absorbed" into formally educated humanity is mediated through racialized and ableist gendering. Their Whiteness/ableness/appearance/morality set them apart from other "uneducated" subjects and enabled them to embrace and be embraced by White upper-class values.

Nonetheless, as uneducated people, María and Eliza represent potential criminality and "incivility" and therefore have to literally and figuratively wash away the markers of lower-class status to become "civilized" feminine ladies who fit in within the upper classes. Their transformation signals an entrance into the overrepresentation of Man that defines humanity in accordance to masculine colonial epistemologies, even if their entrance into "full humanhood" is only partial and temporal. They are now able to read, write, dress well, speak articulately, and get in touch with their femininity. The threat they initially represented to society (e.g., uncivility, poverty, ignorance, unfemininity) is contained and eradicated through an upper-class education that transform them into the image of Man. In the eyes of other characters, they have become "civilized" human beings.

This transformation is co-constituted by two other tropes that make their partial "entrance" into humanhood possible. One of them is the construction of the formally educated subject as already civilized and therefore burdened with the mission to save, rescue, and civilize uneducated persons. The second is the belief in the transformative (dis)empowerment of education that "gives voice to" students.

The Educated Subject as A Savior

The dehumanization of the uneducated subject necessitates the *superhumanization* of the educated person *sine qua non* rationality. It is this rationality, this "factual" and "objective" view that allows educated subjects to position themselves as "above" and therefore as obligated to guide, teach, and discipline those who lack "proper" education. Professor Higgins in *My Fair Lady* and Don Fernando in *María la del Barrio*—while differing in their approach—are determined to save Eliza and María from what they perceive to be the bottomless pit of society. It is their duty, as enlightened men who inhabit a fully human status, to rescue María and Eliza by civilizing them and ensuring they adapt to the upper class. María and Eliza's ways of being/feeling/knowing/doing (Wynter, 2003; Stetsenko, 2016) are regarded as "backward," savage-like, unruly, immoral, irrational, and relegated to an object that must be acquired and transformed.

Higgins' desire to turn Eliza into a duchess can be seen as the educated man's burden—to save the uneducated, poor, otherwise deemed "uncivilized" and "irrational" people via schooling. This burden is exemplified through his misogyny and male paternalism toward Eliza, whom he sees as an irrational woman who will "go out and do precisely what she wants" despite the guidance of a "pensive man…of philosophical joys." Higgins contrasts Eliza's emotionality and irrationality to an "ordinary man" (himself) who uses logic, philosophy, and temper to navigate the world.

What is perhaps more interesting is the way other characters react to Eliza's lack of educational progress by pitying Higgins, who is perceived as "slaving away" to save Eliza from her condemned status as a poor, uneducated flower girl. The servants in Higgin's home sing "poor Professor Higgins, all day long, on his feet, up and down until he's numb, doesn't rest, doesn't eat" to teach Eliza who appears beyond 'salvation.' In fact, when Eliza manages to successfully pass as Hungarian royalty in a ball, Professor Higgins is congratulated because "he did it" and for his "glorious victory" undermining Eliza's own agency. She is the product of his hard work and "every bit of credit belongs to" him for transforming her (therefore saving her) into an educated woman. Toward the end of the film, he even tells Eliza, "there's not an idea in your head or a word in your mouth *that I haven't put there*" (emphasis added) to convey that she essentially owes him gratitude because he has saved/educated her.

A similar thing happens in *María la del Barrio*, where the etiquette teacher and Don Fernando and his family are championed as María's saviors who have done the inconceivable by transforming a *cochina zaparrastrosa* into a "dignified young lady." This contrasts to a previous scene in earlier episodes in which María attempts to transform herself by applying makeup and dressing up in what she considers to be "fancy." This initial transformation turns into a spectacle for the other characters who see María's attempt to pass as one of them as a parody. It isn't until she is taught by a teacher how to be a "lady" that María's transformation is validated and valued.

Both the depiction of Professor Higgins and Don Fernando depend on educational and social discourses about the missionary role of educators in society and the common assumption that teachers care about students more than students, parents, and communities care about themselves. In this view, marginalized students are always 'at risk' of failing and only teachers know what is best for them (Sondel, Kretchmar, & Hadley Dunn, 2019). Furthermore, Higgins and Don Fernando see themselves as saviors who are teaching Eliza and María not only how to be proper and educated but to lead more successful, fulfilling, and ultimately more humane lives by adopting the mannerisms of the White upper-class in each country. It is their ways of being, their poverty, and their speech that are deemed a problem rather than social inequality.

Teachers as saviors, much like Higgins and Don Fernando, are sustained by the humanist enlightenment that continues to inform educational theory and practice. Teachers are complete human beings who initiate students into a regimen of humanization (Snaza, 2014) and therefore the 'experts' who, according to bell hooks (1990), attempt to define what the oppressed are "really saying." These are perhaps best observed in the current insistence (which, I might add, have nearly become hegemonic in educational research) that education ought to "empower" students, "give" them a voice, and "provide" them with agency in their daily lives. Put in another way, students are seen as both lacking agency and knowledge—and thus, it is the job of the enlightened teacher/professor to save them from their ignorance and less than human status.

Indeed, many educators enter the classroom with the mentality of "bestowing" critical consciousness on their students in a similar manner to Don Fernando and Professor Higgins. Unironically, students who "resist" or "refuse" to be saved by critical pedagogy are often seen as naïve by these teachers and researchers who make it their mission to save them. Although most critical educators are well-intentioned and seek to "liberate" the minds of students to create a more inclusive and equitable society, such framing results in a narrative where formal education and the educated subject function as a mechanism to transforms the uneducated person into the image of Man.

And perhaps, more importantly, is the conflation of "saving" students through transforming them into Man with the full humanity of teachers. For instance, the initial refusal and failure of María and Eliza's to be saved by education threatened Professor Higgins and De la Vega family's self-conception as Man, and therefore called into question their humanity. That is, because their model of humanity relies on the educated man's "burden," failing to educate (civilize) Eliza and María cast them in a position where their humanity is *unrealized* until the 'student' becomes educated in each respective story. Their model of what it means to be human remains trapped in a search for meaning and purpose by educating "the other."

María and Eliza's knowledge of the world and their ways of being and speaking are deemed illegitimate by Higgins and Don Fernando who correct their diction, pronunciation, and behavior to re-make them in Man's image. In this way, they are unknowingly complicit in defining, sustaining, and validating what it means to be human, who is deemed fully human, and who can become human through a "'cult politeness' in which one's status, power, and—importantly—humanity [are] displayed symbolically as one's *wit, knowledge, and sophisticated manners*" (Khan, 2007, p. 14, emphasis added).

Through the power of education, facilitated in terms of the educated subject, Eliza and María are "saved" from their "backward" humanity. This salvation is illustrated through transformations in their physical appearances and behaviors. In the next session, I explore how their transformations are represented as (dis)empowering and the unexpected consequences of becoming formally educated.

Education as (dis)empowerment

Eliza and María's transformation into "proper ladies" are depicted as empowering moments that open opportunities for them in upper-class society. Once formally educated, both María and Eliza are no longer portrayed as dirty, ignorant, or naïve, but as "refined" women who elicit jealousy and envy from other women and/or captivate the romantic interest of wealthy men. Prior to this transformation, María and Eliza are coded as masculine within the narrative of the stories, something that changes through their educational becoming—a becoming that encompasses a more traditional model of femininity, such as wearing gowns, high heels, make up, and being soft-spoken. Education, in this context, represents the opportunity to not only enter the upper class, but to become 'womanly' as evident by María and Eliza's transformations from "uncivilized" women to "civilized" and feminine women [see figures 1]

Figure 1. María and Eliza before and after their transformation.

María la del Barrio (1995) from Google Images.

My Fair Lady (1964) from Google Images.

I compare these moments to critical pedagogy's belief in the healing potential of schooling and educational research (Tuck & Yang, 2014). Where schooling is seen an entry point for students to become responsible citizens and heal through learning about social problems vis-à-vis their lives. The problem with this is that like in the case of Eliza and María, it is education (the educated subject) that determines and is the driving force of what students learn and subsequently what is transformed. Students' agency, their desires, and their goals are taken for granted in favor of what the educator assumes students need (e.g., what needs to be saved). Hence, the question what did Eliza and María learned by becoming educated?

The dislocation each character experiences as a result of their new status as educated, upper-class assimilated women might point us in a different direction. María's dislocation, in a traditional telenovela fashion, occurs through a heartbreak that causes her to experience postpartum depression and to give away her child to a stranger. Eliza's experience is different, she starts off by embracing Higgins' humanism and fantasying about becoming rich and being recognized by the king of England, articulating a vision of humanity that relies on the values she learned from Professor Higgins.

Yet, when she finds out about Higgins and Pickering's wager after successfully passing as Hungarian royalty, Eliza feels displaced of her new humanhood. She asks what will become of her, where will she go, which Higgins answers by telling her to marry a gentleman. Eliza, horrified by this, tells him, "I sold flowers. I didn't sell myself." She abandons Professor Higgins' home and returns to Covent Garden only to not be recognized by her community. Her transformation, both physical and intellectual, cast her as an outsider who no longer fits in. Eliza encounters her father in the streets, who appears very different from the stereotypical lazy and alcoholic working-class man he was initially depicted as. It turns out that Professor Higgins had nominated Mr. Doolittle for a moral reform society where an American man turned Mr. Doolittle into a gentleman. In the scene, Mr. Doolittle complains that he used to be happy and free, but after his transformation into a gentleman, he is trapped in what he calls a "middle-class morality" where he is living for others and not for himself.

In this moment, I argue, Mr. Doolittle and Eliza challenge us to reconsider the idea that education results in empowerment. Each of their experiences ruptures the narrative of the educated subject as the solution to social problems and, more importantly showcases how dehumanizing and alienating education (when modeled after Man) can be. What happens when "successfully" educating students alienates them from their humanity and communities? In the case of Eliza and Mr. Doolittle, we see a different narrative where not only education has alienated Eliza from her community, but it has made her being/feeling/knowing/doing unrecognizable to herself.

Education promises to provide entry into full human status (*the humanitas*) and to open up social and material possibilities, which are themselves symbols of full-humanness. Case in point, the willingness of college students to go into debt in the hopes that a diploma will open economic and social opportunities for them. Eliza and Mr. Doolittle reverse the notion that the more educated one becomes (e.g., Ph.D.) and the type of institution one attends (e.g., Ivy Leagues) can make a person more human, super-human, or extra-human. In their case, formal education displaced them of the humanity they inhabited as poor, uneducated people in exchange for a superficial humanity concerned with assimilation into a "middle-class morality", which I interpret as the overrepresentation of Man. What happens when becoming educated does not bring the feeling of being "fully human" students expect even when this is done in the name of "liberation"?

I use these examples to think and begin to wonder if formal education (no matter how liberatory) is not enough to unsettle the overrepresentation of Man. This is not to undermine the importance of critical pedagogy, culturally sustaining pedagogies, and education more broadly, but rather to feel and think our way out of humanism.

The (Im)possibility of Being Uneducated

What can subjects like Eliza and María teach us about the possibilities of being human beyond (and outside) *the humanitas*? How might being "uneducated" help us reimagine the human outside Man's overrepresentation? Although both *My Fair Lady* and *María la del Barrio* do not address all the issues pertaining to the dehumanization of the uneducated subject, in particular, racialization and queerness (though it might be argued that these are always already implicated), both figures might help us think about the role of the uneducated subject in unsettling humanism. With the caveat that the potential of uneducatedness to unsettle humanism is limited unless it explicitly addresses the intersections of racialized, gendered, and ableist de/humanization and respectability politics that define the borders of who is seen as fully human.

If education is about initiating students into particular modes of living and being (Snaza 2014; Popkewitz, 2007; Levinson and Holland, 1996; Fendler, 1998), then how can being formally uneducated or unschooled guide us away from humanism, educated subjecthood, and the overrepresentation of Man? Dyke, Meyerhoff, and Evol (2018) have argued for the need to collectively imagine education beyond "state recognition" and "White recognition" through practices that often arise in social movements to envision and realize new futures in "the unknown void of what-is-to-come" (p. 176). Elsewhere, Britzman (1995) has proposed a queer re-orientation of pedagogy that exceeds the limits of educational knowability and thinkability and that refuses normativity. This, along with feminist theory, Indigenous studies, Latinx education, Africana studies, and Disability studies, have challenged us to re-imagine what it means to be human outside the overrepresentation of Man (Wynter, 2003) and education itself. I thus propose, being formally uneducated—in all of its complexities and intersections—as another possibility to reimagine being human beyond the scopes of the *humanitas* and/or the *superhumanization* of the educated subject.

Far from romanticizing the "uneducated" subject, which would be yet another form of dehumanization, I wonder about the ways in which formally uneducated people trouble the boundaries between school and education, between formal and informal, and between knowing and not knowing. Andreotti, Pereira, and Edmundo (2017, as cited in Andreotti, 2019) assert that *being* has been reduced to *knowing*, and epistemic certainty has been mistaken for ontological security. Prior to their formal education, both Eliza and María embraced an epistemic uncertainty alien to Professor Higgins and De la Vegas. They displayed an openness to knowledge, to learning to be otherwise, of questioning and refusal, of holding on to who they were while also embracing becoming educated—that was absent in the figures of Higgins and De la Vega family. Formal education, according to them, had given them an objective assessment of the world and, therefore, a proper way of being that when juxtaposed to the openness

97

of Eliza and María, might have limited their imagination. Schooling, for example, made Professor Higgins certain of the "correct" way of speaking and behaving in society and therefore limited his understanding of what it means to be human. It made him "closed-minded" to other possibilities of being/feeling/knowing/doing.

Those of us who grew up in the working-class *barrios* of Latin America, often surrounded by unschooled and analphabet people, or people with only a primary education, are familiar with figures like María and Eliza who think "outside" educational norms. People who are characterized by an openness to the other (e.g., immigrants) predicated on a common humanhood—not on what individuals can offer to society or "deserve," but because *"no eres mejor que nadie"* is the barrio's motto. Formal education is not a status symbol nor is it seen as making you a "better" human being. In the case of María, we see this in her relationship with maids, the rich and the poor, in the way she treats everyone as her equal before she becomes educated. Similarly, Eliza holds Professor Higgins' full humanity even when he insults her and seeks to "mold" her into an exclusionary version of humanhood. She does not question his worth as a human being even when she is critical of the way he thinks.

In reflecting on the role of the uneducated subject in *My Fair Lady* and *María la del Barrio* as well as beyond these cultural texts, I wonder if "uneducatedness" provides a space for re-thinking education outside the modality of possession, materialism, and formalized knowledge. I think of Eliza and María's willingness to admit their limitations, what they do not know, and transparency about the messiness of everyday life. I wonder with others[5] about the possibility of existing outside the urgency of the now, in community and solidarity, of not valuing people for what they do or can offer us, of being deemed "useless", and how non-academic knowledge might move us closer to a humanity that exists in the space of ambivalence and contradictions. In *barrios* like María's, imagination exists beyond materiality, people cook without recipes and measurements, understand family beyond blood relations, emotions are part of being and knowing, people mix religious practices, and do not reduce being to career success, academic attainment, or "civilizing" others. In the "uneducated" figures of María and Eliza, we see unmaterialistic ways of existing, challenges to masculinity/femininity distinctions, and an alternative way of seeing the world as a pluralistic space for co-existence.

I wonder about ways to blur the boundaries and fragmentation of formal educatedness and "uneducatedness" without exaggerating the liberatory potential of being "uneducated" and downplaying that of theoretical and formalized knowledge. How might we reconcile and refuse the dichotomy between "schooling," "education," "uneducated," and "not knowing"? In what ways might we exceed "what is intelligible" and " imagine beyond categories of thought and affective entrapments to acknowledge the inevitability of pain, death and (re) birth, and to 'sit with' the indeterminacy and plurality of the world without the need for identification and/or dis-identification" (Andreotti, 2019, p. 76). How can we move beyond disciplinary bounds and defragmented thought that trains people in specific genres of being (Wynter, 2003), so that it is no longer possible to think like a "sociologist" or "mathematician" because everything is interconnected? How can "uneducatedness" help us imagine another way of being "educated" that moves beyond the formalization of other ways of knowing for pedagogical purposes?

I do not offer answers to these questions nor seek to position "uneducated" subject as a savior. My goal is to invite readers to join me in thinking and feeling the multiple genres of the human (Wynter, 2003) co-constituted through collectividual becoming (Stetsenko, 2016; 2013) and the entanglements of being formally educated and uneducated.[6] Like in the case of María and Eliza, we might find in "uneducatedness" an openness to immeasurability, a refusal to hierarchies, and a partial, imperfect, departure from humanism.

Conclusion

Education often prioritizes methodological and epistemological questions (e.g., What are the best teaching practices? Whose knowledge?) at the expense of ontological questions of *being* (Andreotti, Stein, Sutherland, Pashby, Susa, & Amsler, 2018). In particular, I have focused on the ontology of the educated subject and have argued for the need to content with humanist legacies grounded in eugenics, rationality, and elitism that often result not only in the scapegoating of the "uneducated" and "ignorant," but in dehumanization and material consequences for them. Far from being a complete analysis of these problems, this paper barely scrapes the surface, and thus invites readers to engage in self-reflection and interrogate the ways in which our current mode of being/feeling/knowing/doing educated might be rooted in the overrepresentation of Man. Moreover, I invite readers to wonder with me: how might educated subjecthood (when model after Man) prevent us from experiencing other ways of being/feeling/knowing/doing?

Notes

1. At the same time, opposite discourses deride intellectuals, science, and education as untrustworthy.
2. A problem that is inseparable from pedagogical and ableist practices.
3. I'd also add, people in the global south, people with disabilities, the homeless, and the jobless
4. In Spanish, she uses the word cochina which literally translates to "dirty pig."
5. My friends and academic primas, Jennifer Cruz Marulanda, Marjorine Castillo, and Araceli Noriega.
6. While also addressing problems in "uneducated" communities, however, not from the position and ideologies of Man.

References

Adams, D. W. (1995). *Education for Extinction: American Indians and the Boarding School Experience, 1875-1928.* University Press of Kansas, 2501 W. 15th St., Lawrence, KS 66049.

Agamben, G. (2004). *The Open: Man and Animal.* 2002. Trans. Kevin Attell. Stanford: Stanford UP.

Ambroise, J. R. (2018). On Sylvia Wynter's Darwinian Heresy of the" Third Event". *American Quarterly, 70*(4), 847-856.

Andreotti, V. (2021). Weaving threads that gesture beyond modern-colonial desires. In Zhao, W., Popkewitz, T., & Autio, T. (Eds) *Historicizing Curriculum Knowledge Translation on a Global Landscape; William Pinar's Book Series, Studies in Curriculum Theory.* Routledge: New York, NY, USA; London, UK.

Andreotti, V. (2019). The enduring Challenges of collective Onto-(and neuro-) Genesis. *LÁPIZ, 4,* 61-78.

Andreotti, V., Stein, S., Sutherland, A., Pashby, K. L., Susa, R., & Amsler, S. (2018). Mobilising different conversations about global justice in education: toward alternative futures in uncertain times. *Policy & practice: A development education review, 26,* 9-41.

Andrzejewski, J., & Alessio, J. (1999). Education for global citizenship and social responsibility. *Progressive Perspectives, 1*(2), 2-17.

Brown, V. B. (1990). The fear of feminization: Los Angeles high schools in the progressive era. *Feminist Studies, 16*(3), 493-518.

Cammarota, J. (2011). Blindsided by the avatar: White saviors and allies out of Hollywood and in education. *Review of Education, Pedagogy, and Cultural Studies, 33,* 242-259.

Caraballo, L. (2019). Being "loud": Identities-in-practice in a figured world of achievement. *American Educational Research Journal, 56*(4), 1281-1317.

Chokshi, D. A. (2018). Income, poverty, and health inequality. *Jama, 319*(13), 1312-1313.

Cremin, L. A. (1970). *American education: The colonial experience, 1607-1783* (Vol. 1). Harpercollins College Division.

Cruz, M. R. (2012). Ni con dios ni con el diablo: Tales of Survival, Resistance, and Rebellion from a Reluctant Academic. *Decolonization: Indigeneity, Education & Society, 1*(1).

Conner, C. D. (2009). *A people's history of science: Miners, midwives, and low mechanicks.* Hachette UK.

Damante, K. (2016). Can Education Reduce Prejudice against LGBT People? *The Century Foundation.* Retrieved from https://tcf.org

Dyke, E., Meyerhoff, E., & Evol, K. (2018). Radical Imagination as Pedagogy: Cultivating Collective Study from Within, on the Edge, and Beyond Education. *Transformations: The Journal of Inclusive Scholarship & Pedagogy, 28*(2), 160–180.

Fallace, T. (2015). The savage origins of child-centered pedagogy, 1871–1913. American *Educational Research Journal, 52*(1), 73-103.

Fendler, L. (2001). Educating flexible souls. *Governing the child in the new millennium,* 119-142.

Fendler, L. (2013) Hultqvist, K., & Dahlberg, G. (2013). Educating Flexible Souls: The Construction of Subjectivity through Developmentality and Interaction. In *Governing the Child in the New Millennium* (pp. 129-152). Routledge.

Ferrando, F. (2019). *Philosophical Posthumanism*. Bloomsbury Publishing.

Freire, P. (1970). *Pedagogy of the oppressed* (MB Ramos, Trans.). New York: Continuum, 2007.

Gutiérrez, K. D. (2008). Developing a sociocritical literacy in the third space. *Reading research quarterly, 43*(2), 148-164.

Gutiérrez, K. D., Morales, P. Z., & Martinez, D. C. (2009). Re-mediating Literacy: Culture, Difference, and Learning for Students From Nondominant Communities. *Review of Research in Education, 33*(1), 212–245.

Goodchild, Lester F. "G. Stanley Hall and an American social Darwinist pedagogy: His progressive educational ideas on gender and race." *History of Education Quarterly* 52, no. 1 (2012): 62-98.

hooks, b. (1990). Marginality as a site of resistance. In R. Ferguson et al. (Eds.), *Out there: Marginalization and contemporary cultures* (pp. 241–243). Cambridge, MA: MIT.

Howlett, C. (2018). Teacher Education and Posthumanism. *Issues in Teacher Education, 27*(1), 106-118.

Jackson, Z. I. (2013). Review: Animal: New directions in the theorization of race and posthumanism. *Feminist Studies, 39*(3), 669-685.

Jackson, Z. I. (2020). Becoming Human. In *Becoming Human* [E-reader version]. New York University Press.

James, M. E. (2005). *The conspiracy of the good: Civil rights and the struggle for community in two American cities, 1875-2000* (Vol. 30). Peter Lang.

Kahn, R. (2007). Toward a critique of paideia and humanitas:(Mis) education and the global ecological crisis. In *Education in the era of globalization* (pp. 209-230). Springer, Dordrecht.

King, T. L. (2017). Humans involved: Lurking in the lines of posthumanist flight. *Critical Ethnic Studies, 3*(1), 162-185.

Kliebard, H. M. (2004). *The struggle for the American curriculum*, 1893-1958. Routledge.

Khullar, D., & Chokshi, D. A. (2018). Health, income, & poverty: where we are & what could help. *Health Affair, 10*.

Ladson-Billings, G. (1995). But that's just good teaching! The case for culturally relevant pedagogy. *Theory into practice, 34*(3), 159-165.

Ladson-Billings, G. (1998). Just what is critical race theory and what's it doing in a nice field like education? *International journal of qualitative studies in education, 11*(1), 7-24.

Levinson, B. A., & Holland, D. (1996). The cultural production of the educated person: An introduction. *The cultural production of the educated person: Critical ethnographies of schooling and local practice*, 1-54.

McKittrick, K. (2015). Yours is the Intellectual Struggle: Sylvia Wynter and the Realization of the Living. In McKittrick, K. (Ed.), *Sylvia Wynter: On being human as praxis*, (1-8). Duke University Press.

Misiaszek, G. W. (2017). *Educating the global environmental citizen: Understanding ecopedagogy in local and global contexts*. Routledge.

Rose, E. (2019). Neocolonial mind snatching: Sylvia wynter and the curriculum of Man. *Curriculum Inquiry, 49*(1), 25-43.

Pais, A., & Costa, M. (2020). An ideology critique of global citizenship education. *Critical Studies in Education, 61*(1), 1-16.

Paris, D., & Alim, H. S. (Eds.). (2017). *Culturally sustaining pedagogies: Teaching and learning for justice in a changing world*. Teachers College Press.

Pew Research Center. (2018, March 2018). *Wide Gender Gap, Growing Educational Divide in Voters' Party Identification* [Survey Report]. https://www.pewresearch.org/politics/2018/03/20/wide-gender-gap-growing-educational-divide-in-voters-party-identification/

Popkewitz, T. S. (2007). Alchemies and governing: Or, questions about the questions we ask. *Educational philosophy and theory, 39*(1), 64-83.

Popkewitz, T. S. (2008). The reason of reason: Cosmopolitanism, social exclusion and lifelong learning. In A. Fejes & Nicoll (Eds.), *Foucault and Lifelong Learning: Governing the Subject (pp. 74-86). London and New York, NY: Routledge.*

Smith, L.T. (2012). *Decolonizing Methodologies*. London & NY.

Snaza, N. (2014). Toward a genealogy of educational humanism. *Posthumanism and educational research*, 17-29.

Snaza, Nathan, Peter Appelbaum, Siân Bayne, Dennis Carlson, Marla Morris, Nikki Rotas, Jennifer Sandlin, Jason Wallin, and John A. Weaver. "Toward a posthuman education." *Journal of Curriculum Theorizing* 30, no. 2 (2014): 39.

Snaza, N., & Mishra Tarc, A. (2019). "To wake up our minds": The re-enchantment of praxis in Sylvia Wynter.

Sondel, B., Kretchmar, K., & Hadley Dunn, A. (2019). "Who Do These People Want Teaching Their Children?"

White Saviorism, Colorblind Racism, and Anti-Blackness in "No Excuses" Charter Schools. *Urban Education*, 0042085919842618.

Sonu, D., & Benson, J. (2016). The quasi-human child: How normative conceptions of childhood enabled neoliberal school reform in the United States. *Curriculum Inquiry, 46*(3), 230-247.

Stetsenko, A. (2013). The challenge of individuality in cultural-historical activity theory: "Collectividual" dialectics from a transformative activist stance. *Outlines. Critical Practice Studies, 14*(2), 07-28.

Stetsenko, A. (2016). *The transformative mind: Expanding Vygotsky's approach to development and education*. Cambridge University Press.

Tyack, D. B. (1974). *The one best system: A history of American urban education* (Vol. 95). Harvard University Press.

Tuck, E., & Yang, K. W. (2012). Decolonization is not a metaphor. *Decolonization: Indigeneity, education & society, 1*(1).

Tuck, E., & Yang, K. W. (2014). R-words: Refusing research. *Humanizing research: Decolonizing qualitative inquiry with youth and communities*, 223-248.

Walker, S. (2020). Racism in Academia:(How to) Stay Black, Sane and Proud as the Doctoral Supervisory Relationship Implodes. In *The International Handbook of Black Community Mental Health*. Emerald Publishing Limited.

Winfield, A. G. (2007). *2007: Institutionalized racism and the implications of history, ideology, and memory* (Vol. 18). Peter Lang.

Wodtke, G. T. (2018). The effects of education on beliefs about racial inequality. Social Psychology Quarterly, 81(4), 273-294.

Wynter, S. (2003). Unsettling the coloniality of being/power/truth/freedom: Towards the human, after man, its overrepresentation—An argument. *CR: The new centennial review, 3*(3), 257-337.

Wynter, S. (2007). Human being as noun? Or being human as praxis? Towards the autopoetic turn/overturn: A manifesto. Retrieved from https://www.scribd.com/document/329082323/Human-Being-as-Noun-Or-Being-Human-as-Praxis-Towards-the-Autopoetic-Turn-Overturn-A-Manifesto

Wynter, S., & McKittrick, K. (2015). Unparalleled catastrophe for our species? Or, to give humanness a different future: Conversations. In McKittrick, K. (Ed.), *Sylvia Wynter: On being human as praxis*, (9-89). Duke University Press.

Chapter 5

The Best at What They Do

Re-Considering Perceptions of Public Education through Superhero Narratives

Michael B. Dando, St. Cloud State University

Introduction

Superheroes have been enduring cultural icons who have embodied particular cultural mythologies for generations. Aspirational notions of truth and justice, good and evil, or right and wrong have been bound up in these cultural signifiers in ways that have proved both enduring and meaningful in how cultures understand themselves. These popular cultural artifacts represent the best of who we envision ourselves to be and reflect dearly held cultural values. Superheroes often reflect a society's anxieties and desires for itself, especially for their young people. These stories are often laden with heroes and heroines learning what it means to be a member of a culture or civilization through a mentor, teacher, or instructor of some kind. Comic pages have produced and reflected specific understandings of the nature of pedagogy, teaching, and learning that remain embedded in cultural consciousness.

An examination of the nature of these pedagogic relationships can afford teachers and educators insights into public understanding of what kinds of teaching and learning are considered most desirable and can provide a springboard for imagining new frameworks for approaching pedagogic practices. This analysis engages various popular conceptions of so-called good teaching as it is reflected in the pages of prominent comic book titles to invite opportunities for teachers and community members to engage in critical reflection regarding the nature and function(s) of the pedagogic relationships they engage with daily as well as to invite new strategies for creating counternarratives regarding classroom practices and praxis. The examined characters and relationships highlight the hegemonic or dominant notions of youth, functions of education, and pedagogy and the implications rethinking these understandings hold for a wider, democratic society.

To that end, I argue that comic books allow us to re-conceive understandings of teaching and learning in the public square, and to reimagine so-called common sense positionings and knowledges that shape the reproduction of social power, hegemonic structures, and possibilities and legibilities for democratic engagement in the classroom. Having a deeper understanding of how these representations are created and transmitted, and their differential effects on the public imaginary can afford educators and community members alike avenues for meaningful disruption of entrenched, dominant ideologies regarding public education and the role of teachers. To do that I, look at two foundational teachers in comics: *X-Men's* Professor Charles Xavier and *Daredevil's* Stick. I also look at a more recent example from *Shuri,* The Elephant's Trunk.

Public perceptions of Teachers

In keeping with research on teacher identity (Chen & Mensah, 2018; Hong, Greene, and Lowry, 2017; McIntire & Hobson, 2016) multiple scholars (Cole & Knowles, 1994; Hargreaves & Fullan, 1992; Weber, 1993) have noted the interconnected and interdependent nature of the stories we tell ourselves about ourselves and about each other. Often this appears in the popularly created and consumed artifacts a given culture produces. These stories are "embedded biographies" (Weber & Mitchell, 1995, p. 9) that embody social, cultural, political, fictional, public, and private understandings of self. We also carry with us representations and images that coalesce to form a collective understanding of teachers that are built upon the same. The reproduction of these norms is often a function of societal understandings which are mediated by contemporary discourses, political rhetorics, and texts. "What a teacher's job is" is often bound up in the resulting sociocultural and political disputes regarding the functions of education and for whom it is available in a particular society or culture. These common-sense understandings are often reified or contested in the relationships between popular cultural artifacts such as literature, art, or film and the public. The resultant narratives are continually contested sociopolitical terrain. As hooks (2009) reminds us, "changing how we see images is clearly one way to change the world" (p. 7). Consequently, how a given culture generates and reproduces particular narratives is linked to those same messages.

Research demonstrates that there is an abundance of narrative representation of teachers and schools in popular culture particularly in films (Bulman, 2002; Cann, 2015; Dalton, 1995, 2006; Thomsen, 1993; Trier, 2001, 2005). We might think of *Harry Potter's* Hogwarts, *Spider-Man's* Midtown High, or *Stand and Deliver* as examples. However, in a multimedia culture, films are far from the only place where the public might encounter such grand narratives of teaching and learning. Another is on the pages of a seemingly ubiquitous genre and medium: superhero comics. Recently, superhero comic books and films have become extraordinarily popular making superheroes a part of the contemporary cultural vernacular. Even if they have never read a comic book, box office receipts indicate that many people have likely encountered or interacted with them on some level. Superman, Spider-Man, and Wonder Woman, for example, are part of the shared, larger cultural consciousness. There is a socialized experience and therefore understanding of how these characters should operate and what they represent, even though every member might not be familiar with the expansive details of a given character or universe. This is based in large part on the socialized understanding of heroism as well as personal definitions created by the social, political, and cultural commitments made by an individual or group.

The same holds for constructed understandings of schools, schooling, teachers and learners. Coupled with their own experiences in schooling, people believe they have an idea of what happens at a school and what a teacher is supposed to do, and who they are supposed to be in that setting because of the mediated cultural narratives they create, share, and take in. Teachers themselves participate in this process of narrative creation drawing from their ideologies, philosophies, and experiences to create what Ayers and Schubert (1992) call "teacher lore" (p. 9).

This chapter explores how these popular cultural texts teach about teaching. To that end, this chapter centers on the need to understand how popular culture shapes a community's "everyday lives" (Lefebvre, 1991, p. 41) and how to disrupt hegemonic and oppressive motifs that might be in operation. Struggles over meaning, identity, social practices, and institutional machineries of power are necessarily based on understanding how popular culture situates the terrain. Examining how popular cultural artifacts, such as comics, frame the work of teaching and learning, invite us to reassert democratic pedagogy back into the political classroom by recognizing that the "educational force of our whole social and cultural experience actively and profoundly teaches."

Exploring a Multiverse of Possibilities in Education

Exploring how the images and understandings of teaching and learning persist over time requires a particular framing of relationships and perceptions. I take up several questions meant to examine and analyze how the cultural status quo regarding cultural functions of teaching and learning are created and reproduced and by whom. Specifically, I ask how superhero comic texts manifest the relationship between teacher, teaching, student, and learning and how analyzing these representations of teachers and teaching in comics can invite educators to re-envision their practice toward furthering democratic forms of education. Rather than simply observing that superhero texts show the existence of student–teacher relationships, I consider what is revealed about education (and the political position of this relationship) by delving into superhero comics.

Behind the Masks:
Theoretical Framing

In responding to these questions, I draw from two theoretical perspectives. The first is Critical Pedagogy, which examines the dynamic(s) of power in a given relationship, which in this case, is teaching and learning. I also take up Bormann's Symbolic Convergence Theory (1985), which explores the nature of shared meaning-making at the individual and social levels. Taken together, these theoretical frameworks provide a complex and robust approach to the creation, transmission, and disruption of these socio-cultural practices of teaching and learning that are often taken for granted as common sense.

Critical Pedagogy

Critical pedagogy is a teaching philosophy that draws from critical theory and related traditions applied to the field of education and the study of culture. It is a teaching approach that encourages participants to question and challenge domination and oppressive ideologies. Critical pedagogy holds that work for social justice and democracy are inextricably linked to teaching and learning. In other words, it is a theory and practice of helping students achieve critical consciousness or what Freire calls *conscientization*.

This is particularly useful in our analysis of comics and public perception of teachers because popular culture is a mechanism through which power dynamics are created, taught, and reinscribed. And this is particularly true in the classroom. As Giroux (2020) notes:

> [C]ritical pedagogy illuminates how classroom learning embodies selective values, is entangled with relations of power, entails judgments about what knowledge counts, legitimates specific social relations, defines agency in particular ways, and always presupposes a particular notion of the future. (p. 4)

It is through these popular cultural artifacts that students, teachers, and the public make sense of their roles, responsibilities, and expectations for the functions of education. If these cultural norms and the embodied habitus are to be disrupted, it is essential to examine the nature of the power dynamics present. In other words, it is important to understand the dominant in order to critique it.

Bormann's Symbolic Convergence Theory

A number of critical scholars (Bourdieu, Arendt, Spivak, Said) have argued that the media occupies a significant role in shaping social realities. In some cases, popular media may simply reinforce existing beliefs or even strengthen the narratives that contour an audience's constructed reality (Hawkins, Pingree, Adler, 1987; Bormann 1982a, 1982b; Charters, 1966; Roberts & Schramm, 1971). For example, Heilman (1991), argues that the popular media propagates what he calls the "great teacher myth", that is to say, that a "great teacher" is constantly engaged against the "evil" education system. This is often achieved by taking up an unorthodox approach or engaging in practices set apart from pre-existing notions of teaching. Examples include *Dead Poets Society, Dangerous Minds,* or *Freedom Writers.* This helps create a public narrative through which expectations and understandings are mediated.

Rhetorical theorist Ernest Bormann outlines the contours of Symbolic Convergence Theory, which is particularly useful in considering how publics and communities create shared understandings of societal roles and norms. Specifically, his notion of Fantasy Theme Analysis, or FTA (1973), provides a useful framework for analyzing the public perception of teachers and how public understandings are shaped, reproduced, and critiqued. Bormann argues that by participating, that is taking in and reproducing across media, audiences become agents of rhetorical, mythologized creations or traditions that result in a new iteration of reality, a psychodramatic fantasy world that may even seem more real than the real world (Bales, 1950; Bormann, 1982; Smith, 1988).

A fantasy theme is a myth, folklore, or other commonly circulated narratives, about a particular cultural artifact or event which is assumed to contain or suggest a universal truth or cultural tenet that transcends the basic story. An example of this might be one of Aesop's fables, or indeed the message of great power and responsibility that is embedded in Spider-Man stories. Frequently characters are portrayed as heroes and villains to symbolize the message or theme of the discourse (Smith, 1988). These symbolic confrontations can be classified as "fantasy types," with "good versus evil" being the most common. Smith (1988) defines a fantasy type as a "group of fantasy themes so closely related that they constitute a general thematic class." Other types can include overcoming oppression, restoration, or truth, holding up against all challenges. The shared myth, in effect, becomes a part of the user's new symbolic reality or vision of how the world is (Bormann, 1972, 1982; Littlejohn, 1989). Individuals who share the rhetorical vision become a part of a "rhetorical community, or "form of public" that participates in the drama (Bormann, 1982). As Bormann explains:

> The fantasy theme drama when shared is a key to social reality. It is not by itself the social reality. My position is that during the process of sharing a fantasy theme drama the participants come to share the interpretation of the drama, the emotions, meanings, and attitudes of

the drama towards the personae and the action. They come to share a common view of an aspect of their common experience. To my mind, this is a good definition for social reality. (1982, p. 304)

Comic books often present readers with popular conceptions of teachers and a myriad of socio-political challenges involving education that encourage consideration of contemporary constructions of schooling, public understandings of effective teaching, epistemologies of learning, and of the pedagogical purposes that drive the teacher–learner relationship. Though comic books have proven themselves a rich and valuable field of study, especially within art criticism, literature studies, and even as an educational intervention, a more robust exploration of the medium's impact on conceptualizing the cultural role of the teacher–mentor and the student dynamic remain under-researched.

A Taxonomy of Comic Culture Conceptions of Teachers

Before exploring the various styles of teaching and learning comics can present, it is useful to examine briefly how the medium functions in its role as a cultural influencer. Representations of the teacher in mainstream comic book pages, and their link to pedagogical relationships, invite exploration into how the teacher–learner has been conceived, contested, and reinscribed in mainstream culture, and highlight how public notions of teaching and learning, as well as the sociocultural and political role(s) of the teacher, can vary. These interpretations, as Jenkins (2019) points out about collected items, "coexist alongside the things we inherit from [our] mothers and fathers" and further that "different collectors can bring different interpretive frames to the same object" so rather than being a fixed or static artifact, representations of teachers are dynamic and fungible, culturally mediated and we indeed, "map our meanings onto them" (p. 318).

While there are many pedagogic and teaching relationships present in comic book stories including Batman, Robin, and Alfred or Uncle Ben and Peter Parker/Spider-Man, this chapter examines three explicit instances of teaching and learning across formal and informal settings. These examples are from relatively high-profile titles that demonstrate particular approaches and understandings of the function, role, and purpose of teaching that perform particular ideological and political functions.

Charles Xavier and the X-Men

One of the first schools to appear in superhero comics was Xavier's Academy for Gifted Youngsters in the pages of *X-Men* in 1963. In the midst of significant social, cultural, and political upheaval in the United States, Stan Lee and Jack Kirby introduced the public to the X-Men, a team of outsiders beset by prejudice, bigotry, and violence by simple warrant of being different from so-called "normal" humans. Mutants are hated, feared, and despised collectively for no other reason than that they were born with a genetic mutation that granted them superhuman powers. Quickly, the X-Men became a metaphor for race relations in the US and continues to represent marginalized populations today.

These young people attend a secluded, secretive private school in a mansion, which was tucked away in the Westchester woods. Here students were taught to explore, control, and use their powers by a mysterious benefactor named Professor Charles Xavier, or Professor X for short. Xavier typifies the era's publicly understood conventions of a good teacher. Severe, disciplined, and regimented in his pedagogic approach, Xavier runs his school for "gifted youngsters" very much like a traditional school would be in the late 1950s or early 1960s. The teaching and learning model is didactic, hierarchical and the leadership patriarchal. The students in Xavier's Academy, much like the schoolchildren of the era were expected to be receivers of instruction and of a discipline's knowledge which is provided from an authority or expert. As such there is an authoritarian air to the relationship between Xavier and his students as he commands them. In *X-Men 1* (1963) each of the students refer to him as "sir". There are grades assigned, and Xavier's demeanor is often punctuated by exclamation points and bolded commands such as "Enough!" and "Silence". In the first panels of the first issue Xavier telepathically summons his students to him, saying to them, "You are ordered to appear at once! Class is now in session! Tardiness will be punished!" This is only one of the several times Xavier expresses a zero-tolerance policy for attendance and compliance during this issue. The tension in the early days of the series is that Professor X operates as an autocratic figure who also adopts the educational and pedagogic norms of the same society that shuns them.

Xavier indeed provides these persecuted youth a haven away from a world that hates and fears them which can be seen as a necessary protection and site for solidarity. But while his intentions and goals are perhaps laudable, because of the unequal power differential present at Xavier's mansion, it is also possible to understand Charles Xavier in this era as a monied, White savior who manufactures consent.

During this era, Xavier's students are positioned as ideal learners. They are highly skilled, compliant, and dutiful rarely, if ever, questioning his judgement, tutelage, or leadership. They do not create, collaborate, or choose, but are instead deployed to enact Xavier's wishes. For example, in their first issue, they are deployed to rescue the US military from the clutches of the Brotherhood of Evil Mutants. Oftentimes, this means students act in ways that are perhaps against their best interests in the service of what is referred to as "Xavier's Dream", the end to mutant persecution and peaceful cohabitation with humankind. We see this as the teens face down Magneto in a US military base in Issue One. While Xavier provides a safe haven away from the hostility of an intolerant human society, he also unilaterally places them directly in physical danger on a near-constant basis.

During this era, readers are presented with a top-down model of education. Charles Xavier possesses all the wisdom, knowledge, and expertise and bestows it on his students. They were to prove their command of skill through high-stakes testing provided by the Danger Room as they trained for an abstract "upcoming mission". Rather than making decisions and choices through democratic processes, debate, and inquiry, everyone knew their roles within the hierarchy and were more or less spectators concerning decision-making regarding how and indeed if co-existence with non-mutant humans is to be achieved. While Xavier does get the school's students to share in his vision, they have little to no input into its formation, sustaining, or defense. They are passive observers rather than full participants in the construction and enactment of their own worldview. Ultimately the power for how the school is run, which missions and values are taken up and why, rest solely with Xavier. Consequently, it is Xavier who shapes both perception and action. He does not coerce his students through corporal punishment, but neither does he engage them in a generative or scholarly discourse. His aim is to get them to agree to participate in this relationship willingly through persuasion.

This falls roughly in line with what Chomsky (1977) argues concerning manufactured consent, wherein 20% of the populace, or the political class, has an active role to play and has been deeply indoctrinated for example his most loyal students such as Cyclops or Jean Grey while the remaining 80% is generally being trained to follow orders. We see this phenomenon occur in the comics in the Danger Room, for example. There are team leaders, and other members take orders without any questions. To be otherwise, to dissent, or hold an alternate perspective would be dysfunctional to the institution itself. One might also argue that this achieved through physical means as well, as nearly each of the first 12 issues feature the X-Men put through a dangerous physical test designed for the training of their powers, but also require them to listen exclusively to Professor X's guidance in order to be successful.

For example, a public expectation for education many hold is that a good teacher is a "good performer", is an expert in all things, or has a charismatic personality (Ayers, 2015, p. 26) and, while perhaps a benefit is not in and of itself effective pedagogy. Through this performance of expertise or charisma, teachers may go about manufacturing consent in ways very similar to that of Charles Xavier. Whether or not they challenge the dominant institution or ideology is of little concern in this view. If, for example, a highly engaging, well-liked teacher does not take up a critical perspective or trouble the status quo, then except for manners, there is little difference from more tyrannical forms of instruction. If there is no contestation of the curriculum or syllabi, then the agenda can be set by any number of outside political, ideological, and/or corporate interests (DelFattore 1992; Buras, 2010, p. 95) and will be generally adhered to by large swaths of students, teachers, and the public. Taken together, this might look like a macro school policy of saying the pledge of allegiance at the beginning of the day to more micro issues such as including poems from a select few African American poets in a language arts class in February without questioning their functional presence or the ways these texts are (mis) represented.

Xavier's idea of coexistence between humans and mutants relies heavily on persuading "ordinary" humans that mutants are non-threatening and on convincing his mutant students that his dream of coexistence is indeed worthwhile. For a large portion of real-life readers of the era, Xavier's position as the public face of the school is literally dependent on his race, gender, and class—all of which are crucial in establishing public understandings of authority and expertise. Xavier's Dream, as it is known, relies on the authority of money, masculinity, and Whiteness. Only a few years following *Brown v. Board of Education*, schooling in the US was still deeply segregated along racial lines and leadership positions still held by a White, male majority. So, while Xavier's school may have been a hush harbor of sorts for young mutants, to be accepted by public (both in the story and real-life), its outward face necessarily reflected dominant ideologies of the era. The teacher at the school was a professor, rich, White, and male. And this was as it should be according to the era's norms.

Moreover, the first roster for the X-Men (Cyclops, Marvel Girl, Iceman, and Beast) were also entirely White. While the X-Men understandably became a metaphor for race relations in the US, the "inoffensive" nature of the ideal and acceptable student was nonetheless portrayed as White. Xavier travels the globe taking mutants away from their homes, families, and cultures. There is, of course, the argument to be made that their cultures of origin are not safe for their existence and safety as mutants, but students are taught in an environment where, what Critical Race Theory scholars might refer to as normative racism of American Whiteness takes precedence. Xavier's ethos and pedagogy might better be understood an example of corporate multiculturalism, "a strategy for disavowing racism and prejudice without conceding any of the power or privilege the dominant class enjoys" (Ladson Billings, 2004, p. 56). Further, real-world institutions, similarly to the fictional Xavier School, often have a facade of inclusion and diversity while continuing to operate in ways that do not call for institutional or structural change.

Ultimately, while there is a message of acceptance, belonging, identity and multiculturalism woven throughout these early stories, readers are also given conceptions of teaching and learning that reflect, reinforce, or reinscribe the status quo, particularly anti-democratic practices. Particularly he positions his students' roles is primarily that of compliance and performance, and his as one of control, command. He is the sole source of knowledge, power, and authority. Professor X is a fictional character but a very real reflection of the norms, mores, and expectations for a school and for a teacher who, while providing a safe harbor for those who are different, may not invite them to engage in self-actualization.

The Hard Master:
Daredevil's Stick

A generation later, in the late 1980s and early 1990s, similar concerns about teaching and learning found their way into the pages of *Daredevil* in the form of a blind sensei named Stick. A significant distinction here is that the learner in this story is both deficient in some regard and "at risk" of an undesirable fate. Additionally, the teacher's goals here are the instruction of a skill set for a pre-determined, external purpose. This goal is pursued at the physical, emotional, and psychic expense of the student.

Created by writer Frank Miller during his run in the 1980s, Stick is primarily known as the blind martial arts master who trained Matt Murdock, AKA Daredevil. While introduced previously, Stick was a relatively flat character until readers are provided a backstory for Murdock and Stick's student/teacher dynamic in *Daredevil: The Man Without Fear* (Miller, 1993).

Here, Stick embodies the public understanding of educators as a blunt force, skill-delivery mechanism largely unconcerned with a holistic approach to learning, humanity, or perhaps least of all democracy. He is described as having, "No pity. No mercy. Only cold, clear purpose". Stick is obsessively concerned with the ability of his students to perform a specific function or discrete set of skills, in this case, physical combat. When Stick first encounters Matt Murdock shortly after Matt is blinded, Stick refers to Murdock as "useless" and his first words to Murdock are "quit feeling sorry for yourself," making it clear the deficit model with which he approaches his task. Unlike Xavier, Stick has no interest in being a supportive mentor or father figure for Matt Murdock. Rather, he sees his student as a weapon in need of forging in order to fight an ever-present, yet unseen threat. The only thing that matters to Stick is that Matt is ready to fight evil when the time comes.

For many in the broader public, a sign of a rigorous or high-quality education continues to be students' capacity for productive content-focused output and teachers' facility with achieving efficient production or output. That may take the form of high scores on a particular standardized test, the ability to compose a five-paragraph essay in a given amount of time, or to solve a number of given equations independently. Like Stick, teachers are often expected, and some believe it to be their purpose, to focus solely on efficient command of their discrete content area without regard for the more ethical, communal, or interpersonal facets of learning. Teaching and learning here is a transactional enterprise focused on mastery and deployment while abandoning concern with anything that might interfere or distract such as human relationships or a wider community. This traditional, binary relationship is built on a wildly unequal distribution of power and authority. The expert in the room must be the teacher and the learners are there to pick up a specific set of practical skills. Stick sees his role as teach as being to deliver discrete skillsets to his students in a brutal form of Freire's banking model.

The purpose of this mode of instruction is, at best, to be able to go to work and be productive. In US education, neo-liberal ideologies posit that a quality education means that students graduate with the ability to add to economic competitiveness, which will be of supposed benefit to the community. Historically, this was meant to ward off a supposed external social, political, or ideological threat. In 1983, at the height of the Cold War, the US Secretary of Education published "A Nation at Risk", which famously noted that, "the educational foundations of our society are presently being eroded by a rising tide of mediocrity that threatens our very future as a Nation and a people" (US Department of Education, 1983). This was followed by *No Child Left Behind* and *Race to the Top*, both of which positioned faltering competitiveness with Chinese manufacturing as an imminent threat to the so-called American way of life.

Moreover, Stick's teaching for both Daredevil and his other pupils, including the sometimes hero, assassin, and Daredevil's love interest Elektra, focuses almost entirely on skill development. The distinction should be made here about the difference between training and memorization. This is similar to the approach that Whitehead (2008) espouses as he notes that, "civilization advances by extending the number of operations which we can perform without thinking about them" (p. 46). Likewise, Hirsch (2010) bemoans critical thinking and metacognition as disconnected from the "real nature of competency" (p. 143), suggesting that a teacher's responsibility is primarily to teach facts and figures to those he labels "slower and less disadvantaged" (p. 210), which is almost always a proxy for race. Stick dismisses Elektra because he says she is too driven by negative emotions and advises Matt to "steer clear" of her bad influence.

This style of education often comes at the cost of the humanization, autonomy, and physical and mental wellbeing of the student. In *Man Without Fear*, Stick used a long, wooden staff as a weapon as a form of corporal punishment or as coercion toward compliance as he trained young Matt Murdock. Stick puts Matt through physical and emotional ordeals to prepare him for the purported oncoming, yet unseen assault by evil, Other forces. This narrative of teaching and learning as a social or cultural defense against attack from an undesirable force is a familiar one. It rears its head anytime a group utters the phrase "our way of life" and has been a driving force behind many so-called reforms to education. In Daredevil's case, this threat was an *actual* demon. For many public schools, it was a threat to Whiteness, capitalism, or property that demanded an educational response.

Many traditional forms of schooling and many teachers operate to define, classify, control, and regulate their students. So, pupils must first be rendered compliant requiring power to be located solely within the role of the teacher. This compliance disguised as discipline is a requisite mindset for those who take up the Instructor role. True education, they claim, can only be accomplished through acts of physical, mental, and emotional violence.

We see this approach taken up in *Daredevil*. Take, for example, Stick's early training of Matt. During one sequence in *Man without Fear*, Stick forces young Matt to shoot a bow and arrow at a target until his "knees wobble and red-hot pain streaks from shoulder to elbow to wrist" until he hits his target. In another, Stick physically beats Matt slapping him in the face and hitting him in the head with a bo staff until Matt successfully blocks an attack with his cane. This sort of "tough love" approach to education many would rightly argue, constituted abuse.

Unfortunately, it is the same technique and attitude adopted by many educators and one expected by many community members who perhaps experienced similar traumas. Rates of suspension, violence, and trauma are visited upon students who are seen in need of so-called tough love at an increasingly disproportionate level (Payne, 2010; Skiba and Rauch, 2004; Anyon et al., 2016) in school policies that include among others Zero Tolerance mandates. This abusive approach is often positioned as "tough love" in educational settings which has shown to have detrimental effects for students and teachers alike (Fung & Lau, 2012; Flett, Gould, Griffes, & Lauer, 2013; Zirkel et al., 2011).

So, we can see that one publicly available conception of the teacher is that of the so-called tough love disciplinarian whose position, while perhaps well-intentioned, is to produce individuals who will unthinkingly defend the status quo with their lives. Moreover, a publicly available and legible interpretation of teachers is that of an imparter of a discrete set of skills possessed by the teacher and given to the students to prepare students for the imagined real world as a defense against an ideological foe.

There is a distinct overlap between Xavier and Stick. Both deploy their students for a wider ideological purpose. Both see their students as being the last defense against an external threat. Both teachers are experts in their fields and tasked with passing on this knowledge to a chosen or select few. Both are situated as absolute authorities not to be questioned by students. And while Xavier provides safety and security for his students, Stick offers no such solace to Matt Murdock.

This is perhaps due to the formal nature of the educational relationships in *X-Men* or to the genre-specific tropes of *Daredevil*'s martial arts narrative. It could also be due in part to the changing nature of how the larger public of the eras viewed youth. In the 1960s, the idyllic young learner was often positioned as compliant and capable, cheerful and industrious, such as in the pages of *Archie* comics or on shows such as *Leave it to Beaver*. As the Cold War dragged on, and the nation continued to be "at risk", learners who were considered either unable or unwilling to support the US in resisting the threat of Communism were a threat in need of remediation or expulsion. Thus, the façade of care became a luxury in the face of what the dominant ideology considered an existential threat.

Community Council:
The Elephant's Trunk, and Shuri

The third approach to teacher identity narratives is the Community Council. This differs significantly in that it is situated in a more holistic and student-centered conception of the pedagogic relationship and the nature of the educational process. A teacher in this conceptualization is not solely responsible for the success or failure of a student but rather it is seen as a collective responsibility of both the student and the community itself. It is best demonstrated in Africanjujuist Nnedi Okorafor and Afrofuturist Vita Ayala's *Shuri* (2019) series and the group called the Elephant's Trunk. They see Shuri not as a weapon or a means to an end, but as a vital member of the community well suited to step up into a leadership role given her understanding of and engagement with the Wakandan people in a variety of ways.

Whenever Wakanda is threatened, The Elephant's Trunk is called into service. When the Black Panther, T'Challa, goes missing, his mother, Queen Ramonda, calls it into action once more. Shuri is called to a meeting tradition called the Elephant's Trunk. This was a secret group of women that met when Wakanda was in trouble, and Shuri's mother Queen Ramonda has called it into action once more. The group consists of Ramonda, Zuwena (Director of the Extraction Academy), Mansa (High School Graduate from Q'Noma Valley), Tiwa (Mother of Four, and Professor of Physics at Wakanda University), and Bube (Single Mother of Two, Dressmaker of Many). This is not a collection of patriarchal nobility or a gathering of moneyed elites but a wise cross-section of community voices and interests. Moreover, The Elephant's Trunk does not direct events, take action, or indeed impose itself other than to ask Shuri to step into service of the Wakandan people.

Shuri has occupied several identities throughout her life, and her journey of continued self-discovery is the series' central theme. The first pages point toward the centrality of her varied (super)humanness. From the literal first page of the series, we are reminded that Shuri is simultaneously a genius inventor, one-time Black Panther, and a mystical connection to the spirit realm. But rather than embodying a clichéd Action Girl trope (Pixley, 2015), Shuri fully embodies her myriad identities and draws upon them to both become fully human and thereby become an agent for change in her community. This multiplicity of identity and its embodiment of praxis of being is made explicitly clear again in the first issue when Shuri invents a set of nano-tech wings and tests them over Wakandan skies. Shuri, being called home, retracts the wings mid-air and using her anamorphic powers, flies home in the form of a murder of crows. Shuri does not require wings for flight, but her full person yearns for creative and scientific expression in a way her metahuman powers cannot provide. Similarly, her superpowers are very much a part of her biological being and exist in seamless tandem with the technological. Together, they present a fully formed Afrofuturist representation of the possible. Her smile as she flies through the night sky embodies Black joy and creativity at its very best. In her role as chief scientist and princess, she is not asked to sacrifice one for the other but is encouraged to bring every aspect of herself to respond to the challenges facing her community.

Rather than being leveraged because of her skillset, the Elephant's Trunk supports, guides, and nurtures Shuri throughout her journey. We might see this as analogous to the approaches taken up by culturally sustaining pedagogies or reality pedagogy that acknowledge and nurture lifeways, stories, and cultures of origin as pedagogic assets rather than ignoring them at best or erasing them at worst. This conception of the teacher embodies the Wynterian conception of *homo narrans* (Wynter & McKittrick, 2015) the notion that human beings developed through both biology and the storying process, as well as the spirit of the West African Bantu phrase *ubuntu*, which roughly translates to "I am because we are". Shuri and the Elephant's Trunk situate identity as legible through relation to others within the community and their stories, rather than created individually. This stands in direct opposition to the Western and Descartian notion of "I think therefore I am".

It should be noted that the writers and creators throughout time have been predominantly African and African-American, including Reginald Hudlin, Ta-Nehisi Coates, Nnedi Okorafor, and Vita Ayala. Ultimately, through *Shuri* Okorafor, Romero, and Ayala situate the Elephant's Trunk in such a way as to support Shuri in achieving her own goals—utilizing her genius for the betterment of Wakanda—and in realizing a more holistic conception of self as both a princess, prophet, and sibling.

They recognize her multiple identities and the way(s) this shapes her construction of identity when Ramonda, speaking for the Elephant's Trunk tells her that:

> "[T]he people call you Princess Shuri. The ancestors call you Ancient Future. I call you my daughter. But for a time, you were called something else, and we need you to take up that name once again."

Their consensus is that Shuri should take up the mantle of Black Panther as she did before, but Shuri refuses. Shuri's experience being the Black Panther was traumatic (she died, but was resurrected), so instead of taking up the Black Panther mantle, she focuses her efforts on finding her brother. In *Shuri #2*, this includes bringing together some of his former loves— Ororo Munroe (aka Storm) and Ikoko—who have drastically different approaches to finding T'Challa than Shuri. But even these mentors support Shuri's judgment and offer advice rather than directives. Though Shuri carves her own path and arrives at her own solutions, she is nonetheless supported by The Elephant's Trunk, a far cry from the tutelage of Stick or Xavier. Moreover, this was not considered an act of egregious defiance, but a trust that a young learner to make the necessary decisions on her own terms for the benefit of the larger society.

Nnedi Okorafor emphasizes a non-western conception of education and knowledge production, which de-centers the primacy of the individual and brings in non-male community members from a variety of backgrounds to teach and train Shuri on her path, as her own person capable and indeed well suited to make her own decisions as a leader of the Wakandan people. Rather than be positioned as someone in need of training or who lacks wisdom, skills, etc. The Elephant's Trunk recognizes Shuri as possessing all she needs to work toward the common good of all Wakandans.

What If: Envisioning New Stories about Teaching, Learning, and Schooling

For generations of readers, comics have served to spark the civic and democratic imagination. The "what if" questions have served to shape civic and democratic public discourse on issues such as responsibility, truth, justice, the so-called American Way for generations of readers. Readers had ready access to new worlds, identities, and possibilities. The capacity to dream is crucial to a thriving democracy and has shown up in revolutions works from Frederick Douglass to Langston Hughes, Dr. King, and Amanda Gorman. To build a more equitable, robust democracy, it is important to broaden the imagination of what is possible, especially with regard to teaching and learning. Dominant narratives regarding what, when, who, and how of public education is in desperate need of contesting. And it is the teachers and learners who must do so by advocating for and creating what Solazano and Yosso (2002) call "counterstories" in a variety of spaces both in the public square and in the classroom. Comics and speculative storytelling have historically been a place where counternarratives flourish and the boundaries of imaginative possibilities are stretched.

Often students and the larger public are given specific kinds of narratives on the functions of teaching and the nature of the learner. These dominant narratives aid in shaping public discourse and individualized, often internalized narratives of teaching and learning. These dominant narratives show up everywhere from the classroom to the dining room, often in ways that reinforce a deficit perspective of the learner and denigrate the importance of public education. This might be in simple sentences such as not "being good" at a particular content area, over-reliance on standardized testing, or in publicly held perceptions such as "those who can't to, teach." These are some of the dominant narratives and stories that are in desperate need of disruption and learning to tell new stories is a way this can be done in the classroom.

There are myriad examples of the potential this kind of work can have in educational spaces, on how teachers think about their practices, and how the public views educational spaces. These (re)envisionings of teaching and learning offer ways forward for educators and understandings of education in the public square. For example, the Black Speculative Arts Movement (BSAM), "seeks to interpret, engage, design, or alter reality for the re-imagination of the past, the contested present, and as a catalyst for the future" and offers avenues for teachers —especially, but not exclusively language arts educators—to engage in the incorporation of counternarratives and representation in public forms of storytelling into their curricula. This re-storying is critical in re-structuring not only what learning means, but also how it is accomplished and the nature of the teacher–student relationship.

Multiple Eisner Award winner and Rhetorics professor John Jennings currently serves as Editor-in-Chief (EIC) for Abram's *Megascope* comics imprint (Reed, 2020), which intentionally features stories of and by BIPOC writers and artists including speculative artists and scholars David Brame, Nnedi Okorafor, Ytasha Womak, and Stacey Robinson. Megascope was named after a magical telescope in W.E.B. DuBois' 1908 short story, *The Princess Steel.* This telescope could see across alternate dimensions, times, and spaces and grant the viewer a glimpse into the way(s) things might have been and could potentially be. This effort to expand the canon and the "history that gets erased by mainstream educational practices on purpose, as well as systemic issues about what gets taught" not only broadens the notions of what is possible for the students but for the teachers and for members of the community as well. The stories told through the Megascope imprint create new narratives that re-imagine and realize changes to a system that previously did not allow space for these voices. Teachers interested in countering dominant narratives of education such as what counts as real literature, for example, can easily take up these stories and meaningfully incorporate them into their curriculum, inviting the radical imaginary of the "What If". What if there were scholars, thinkers, authors, and artists that stand in contrast to hegemonic understandings and conceptions of scholarship, excellence, and expertise? What if students could not only see themselves represented in the syllabus but, unlike so many forms of education accepted and reinscribed by the public, were seen as assets or partners rather than tools for imagining a better, more just future?

There are initiatives taking up this challenge such as the Remixing Wakanda Project (Holbert, Dando, and Correa, 2020) that engages identity and iterative design work that focuses on Critical Speculative Afrofuturist Design, specifically foregrounding culturally sustaining pedagogies (Alim and Paris, 2017) in teaching and learning practices around critical literacy development and democratic education. There are those engaging in restorying STEAM pedagogies and representations of excellence and expertise in these fields (Emdin, 2017; Dando, 2020; Champion, et al., 2020). This work centers communities and narratives of origin in ways that disrupt normative conceptions of designers and design work, understanding that creation and imagination are necessarily contextual. Work is also being done (Thomas, 2018;

Toliver, 2020; Muhammad, 2020; and Lopez, 2019) to engage new forms of storying into social studies and language arts spaces in ways that disrupt dominant narratives and invite teachers to explore possibilities in creating new avenues for emancipatory counternarratives on students own terms.

Echoing Gramscian conceptions of the connection between culture and pedagogy, Giroux (2020) reminds us that this relationship exists, "not merely in schools but in a vast array of public sites" (p. 71). A crucial step in this process is to reframe and rethink the ways the public talks about and understands the teaching profession to produce new ways of understanding and positioning teachers within the larger discourse. These counterstories, both internalized and publicly available, are significant because, as Chappel, Solomon, Rhodes, and Yates (2003) remind us, an educator's identity "is constituted by the power of all of the discursive practices in which we speak and which in turn 'speak' us" (p. 41). If educators aim to bring new discourses to bear on teaching and learning in their classrooms, they must push their incorporation of comics beyond facile reading interventions and engage in rich, critical analyses with their students. Reimagining what stories are told about equitable teaching and learning has the potential to reshape ongoing discourses beyond the classroom walls. Hegemonic messages about the political, social, and cultural purposes of teaching (like those embodied by Xavier and Stick) have been written onto the public's psyche through a variety of channels, including popular media such as comics. It is by resituating the social, cultural, and political conversations about teaching and learning through the speculative that can replace tired narratives of the past with new radical and progressive imaginary aimed toward realizing an equitable and democratic public for all.

Conclusion

Many students from historically marginalized communities have been subjected to a systematic miseducation reinscribed by a colonial and hegemonic imaginary. Often this colonial imaginary of what learning is, or of the salient characteristics of a good teacher or student is reinforced and reinscribed by popular cultural texts such as comic books.

The approaches taken up by Xavier and Stick, for example, while vastly different in their tone and tenor, nonetheless demand that students distance or separate themselves from objectives, lifeways, or belief systems that are theirs in favor of someone else's. In contrast, the Elephant's Trunk recognizes and sustains Shuri's strengths and guides her in decision making even when Shuri's goals or approaches differ from those they initially offered up.

We must recognize that oppression has never lacked for imagination. And so, it must be countered with an equally robust imagination of a democratic future. This is can be achieved through epistemic and pedagogic decolonization through radical imaginaries developed by the stakeholders of these communities. In short, a different story of "what counts" as quality teaching and meaningful learning must be told. If those dedicated to public education are to re-vision what teachers do, we must, as Huddleston (2019) encourages us, "begin our own stories" (p. 28) that disrupt neoliberal constructions of the nature of education toward a more complex and complicated understanding of the craft. Indeed, we must push against the teacher as an individualistic hero and/or (White) savior trope embodied by so many narratives and consider what a narrative or counterstory focused on community and justice might look and sound like. By carefully considering the various teacher characters here and their embodiment of particular understandings of teaching and teachers, we can begin to open new educational perspectives that offer fresh perspectives for critical reflection and simultaneous affirmation of self and culture, what Bishop (1990) calls "windows and mirrors" (p. 3), regarding what kinds of classroom spaces or what ways of teaching and learning are possible, legible, and desirable for teachers.

Likewise, analyzing these characters as artifacts through which public discourses and understandings are (re)inscribed offers educators new perspectives regarding how particular forms of pedagogy are normalized, preferred, or legible and also for whom. Making classrooms transformative means educators must, as hooks (2009) suggests, "critically intervene in a way that challenges and changes" (p. 12). Doing this requires active and collective re-imagining of the relationships between teachers, students, and the public. One way to do this is to (re)consider not only how these understandings are created and propagated but meaningful avenues to critique and reinscription. And exploring comics is an appropriate strategy for examining articulated understandings because, as Low (2017) suggests, "the medium affords students a ripe terrain for critically surveying—and ultimately subverting—the conflicted boundaries of what can be said and what can be shown" (p. 27).

It is through these mappings that cultures and societies make humanness legible. This is as true for a society's understanding of children (Corson, Dauphinais, and Friedrich, 2020) as it is for its understanding of race and ethnicity, whose sparse presence is a reason for complication and critique is so necessary so that it is not misrepresented as fixed or monolithic. As Gateward (2015) notes, Black voices have, "a story you see; and sometimes that story has one voice, and other times it has a collection of many voices" (p. 4). These delineations of humanness through a story are socially and culturally mediated but never uncontested and never fixed for long. And it is these stories that shape our understandings and ourselves. As Wynter (1995) reminds us,

Human beings are magical. Bios and Logos. Words made flesh, muscle and bone animated by hope and desire, belief materialized in deeds, deeds which crystallize our actualities [...] And the maps of spring always have to be redrawn again, in undared forms. (p. 35)

We must also be critical of the stories we are told, even as they delight and entertain, and contain messages championing justice for the oppressed, quests for justice, and for truth. Popular comic book titles like *Daredevil*, *X-Men*, or *Shuri* may indeed both reflect and create shared realities as much as they reflect them as they act to "generate a sense of community and cohesion" (Endres, 2016, p. 8). They can serve to simultaneously resist and reinforce common sense notions of teaching, learning, and society. Considering these images of youth as some of the many examples of recognizable subjectivities offers several lessons for teachers. If educators are to transform both the classroom and pedagogy into liberatory spaces, we must first provide "the basic conditions for people to narrate their own lives, hold power accountable, and embrace a capacious notion of human dignity" (Giroux, 2013). The first step is to begin to dream the impossible for ourselves, to hear stories from others, and to engage in contesting grand narratives that permeate the public about what a teacher is, what purpose education serves, and what is possible when these stories are told. As Delgado

(1989) reminds us, "oppressed groups have known instinctively that stories are an essential tool to their own survival and liberation" (p. 2436). So, for educators to meaningfully engage in transformational and liberatory forms of education, they must dream of a different future and work toward realizing it alongside their students.

References

Alim, H. S., & Paris, D. (2017). What is culturally sustaining pedagogy and why does it matter. Culturally sustaining pedagogies: Teaching and learning for justice in a changing world, 1-21.

Anyon, Y., Lechuga, C., Ortega, D., Downing, B., Greer, E., & Simmons, J. (2018). An exploration of the relationships between student racial background and the school sub-contexts of office discipline referrals: A critical race theory analysis. *Race Ethnicity and Education, 21*(3), 390-406.

Au, W. "Hiding behind high-stakes testing: Meritocracy, objectivity and inequality in US education." *International Education Journal: Comparative Perspectives* 12.2 (2014).

Ayers, W., & Alexander-Tanner, R. (2010). To teach: The journey, in comics. Teachers College Press.

Ayers, W. & Schubert, W. (1992). *Teacher lore: Learning from our own experience.* New York, NY: Longman.

Bales, R. F. (1950). Interaction process analysis; a method for the study of small groups.

Bishop, R. S. (1990). Windows and mirrors: Children's books and parallel cultures. In California State University reading conference: 14th annual conference proceedings (pp. 3-12).

Bormann, E. G. (1973). The Eagleton affair: A fantasy theme analysis. Quarterly Journal of Speech, 59(2), 143-159.

Bormann, E. G. (1985). Symbolic convergence theory: A communication formulation. Journal of communication.

Bormann, E. G. (1982). I. Fantasy and rhetorical vision: Ten years later. Quarterly Journal of Speech, 68(3), 288-305.

Bormann, E. G. (1972). Fantasy and rhetorical vision: The rhetorical criticism of social reality. Quarterly journal of speech, 58(4), 396-407.

Borman, G. D., & Dowling, N. M. (2008). Teacher attrition and retention: A meta-analytic and narrative review of the research. Review of educational research, 78(3), 367-409.

Bulman, R. C. (2002). Teachers in the 'hood: Hollywood's middle-class fantasy. The Urban Review, 34(3), 251-276.

Buras, K. L. (2010). Rightist multiculturalism: Core lessons on neoconservative school reform. Routledge.

Cann, C. N. (2015). What school movies and TFA teach us about who should teach urban youth: Dominant narratives as public pedagogy. Urban Education, 50(3), 288-315.

Champion, D. N., Tucker-Raymond, E., Millner, A., Gravel, B., Wright, C. G., Likely, R., ... & Dandridge, T. M. (2020). (Designing for) learning computational STEM and arts integration in culturally sustaining learning ecologies. Information and Learning Sciences.

Chen, J. L., & Mensah, F. M. (2018). Teaching contexts that influence elementary preservice teachers' teacher and science teacher identity development. Journal of Science Teacher Education, 29(5), 420-439.

Corson, J., Dauphinais, J., & Friedrich, D. (2020). Holy Childhoods, Batman!: Configurations of Youth and Possibilities in Teacher Education as Seen through Robin Comics. The New Educator, 16(2), 171-185.

Dando, M. (2020). Re-Mixing Making: examining the Intersections of Hip Hop Culture, Maker Spaces, and Social Justice Education. The International Journal of Critical Media Literacy, 2(1), 83-102.

Dalton, M. M. (1995). The Hollywood curriculum: Who is the 'good' teacher? Curriculum Studies, 3(1), 23-44.

Dalton, M. M. (2006). Revising the Hollywood curriculum. Journal of Curriculum and Pedagogy, 3(2), 29-34.

Delgado, R. (1989). Storytelling for oppositionists and others: A plea for narrative. Michigan Law Review, 87, 2411-2441.

DelFattore, J. (1992). What Johnny shouldn't read: Textbook censorship in America. Yale University Press.

Endres, T. G. (2016). Symbolic Convergence Theory. The International Encyclopedia of Communication Theory and Philosophy, 1-8.

Flett, M. R., Gould, D., Griffes, K. R., & Lauer, L. (2013). Tough love for underserved youth: A comparison of more and less effective coaching. The Sport Psychologist, 27(4), 325-337.

Foucault, M. (2012). Discipline and punish: The birth of the prison. Vintage.

Fung, J., & Lau, A. S. (2012). Tough love or hostile domination? Psychological control and relational induction in cultural context. Journal of Family Psychology, 26(6), 966.

Gateward, F., & Jennings, J. (Eds.). (2015). The blacker the ink: Constructions of black identity in comics and sequential art. New Brunswick, NJ: Rutgers University Press.

Giroux, H. A. (2020). *On critical pedagogy*. Bloomsbury Publishing.

Giroux, H. (2013, April 09). Angela Davis, Freedom and the Politics of Higher Education. Retrieved December 03, 2020, from https://truthout.org/articles/angela-davis-freedom-and-the-politics-of-higher-education/

Giroux, H. A., Freire, P., & McLaren, P. (1988). *Teachers as intellectuals: Toward a critical pedagogy of learning*. Greenwood Publishing Group.

Gramsci, A., & Hoare, Q. (1971). *Selections from the prison notebooks* (p. 276). London: Lawrence and Wishart.

Hawkins, R. P., & Pingree, S. (1982). Television's influence on social reality. Television and behavior: Ten years of scientific progress and implications for the eighties, 2, 224-247.

Heilman, R. B. (1991). Movies: The great-teacher myth. The American Scholar, 60(3), 417-423.

Hirsch Jr, E. D. (2010). The schools we need: And why we don't have them. Anchor.

Holbert, N., Dando, M., & Correa, I. (2020). Afrofuturism as critical constructionist design: building futures from the past and present. Learning, Media and Technology, 1-17.

Hong, J., Greene, B., & Lowery, J. (2017). Multiple dimensions of teacher identity development from pre-service to early years of teaching: A longitudinal study. Journal of Education for Teaching, 43(1), 84-98.

hooks, b. (2014). Teaching to transgress. Routledge.

hooks, b. (2009). Reel to real: race, class and sex at the movies. Routledge.

Ladson-Billings, G. (2004). New directions in multicultural education. Handbook of research on multicultural education, 2, 50-65.

Lefebvre, H. (1991). Critique of everyday life: Foundations for a sociology of the everyday (Vol. 2). Verso.

López López, L. L. (2019). Woking Curriculum: Youth, popular cultures, and moving images matter!. *Race and Pedagogy Journal: Teaching and Learning for Justice*, 4(1), 4.

Low, D. E. (2017). Students Contesting "Colormuteness" through Critical Inquiries into Comics. English Journal, 106, 19-28.

Miller, F. (2014). *Daredevil: The man without fear* (Vol. 1). Marvel Entertainment.

Muhammad, G. (2020). *Cultivating genius: An equity framework for culturally and historically responsive literacy*. Scholastic Incorporated.

Okorafor, N., Romero, L., Bellaire, J., Sabino, J., & Moss, W. (2019). *Shuri*. New York, NY: Marvel Worldwide,, a subsidiary of Marvel Entertainment, LLC.

Payne, M. (2010). Educational Lynching: Critical Race Theory and the Suspension of Black Boys. *Online Submission*.

Pixley, T. L. (2015). Trope and Associates: Olivia Pope's Scandalous Blackness. The Black Scholar, 45(1), 28-33.

Reed, C. (2020, December 2). John Jennings Talks Speculative Fiction and the Debut of Megascope. Retrieved December 23, 2020, from https://www.publishersweekly.com/pw/by-topic/industry-news/comics/article/85039-john-jennings-talks-speculative-fiction-and-the-debut-of-megascope.html

Sass, D. A., Flores, B. B., Claeys, L., & Pérez, B. (2012). Identifying personal and contextual factors that contribute to attrition rates for Texas public school teachers. Education Policy Analysis Archives/Archivos Analíticos de Políticas Educativas, 20, 1-26.

Solórzano, D. G., & Yosso, T. J. (2002). Critical race methodology: Counter-storytelling as an analytical framework for education research. Qualitative inquiry, 8(1), 23-44.

Skiba, R., & Rausch, M. K. (2004). The Relationship between Achievement, Discipline, and Race: An Analysis of Factors Predicting ISTEP Scores. Children Left Behind Policy Briefs. Supplementary Analysis 2-D. *Center for Evaluation and Education Policy, Indiana University*.

Smith, M. J. (1988). Contemporary communication research methods. Wadsworth Publishing Company.

The Hidden Impact of COVID-19 on Educators: Rising Health Concerns, Lower Risk Tolerance and Benefit Gaps (Rep.). (2020, November). Retrieved December 23, 2020, from Horace Mann Educators Corporation website: http://www.horacemann.com/~/media/documents/supplemental/The%20Hidden%20Impact%20of%20COVID-19%20on%20Educators.pdf

Thomas, E. E. (2018). Critical Engagement with Middle Grades Reads: Who Lives? Who Thrives? Who Tells Your Story?. *Voices from the Middle, 26*(2), 13-16.

Thomsen, S. R. (1993). A Worm in the Apple: Hollywood's Influence on the Public's Perception of Teachers.

Toliver, S. R. (2020). Can I Get a Witness? Speculative Fiction as Testimony and Counterstory. Journal of Literacy Research, 52(4), 507–529. https://doi.org/10.1177/1086296X20966362

Trier, J. D. (2001). The cinematic representation of the personal and professional lives of teachers. Teacher Education Quarterly, 28(3), 127-142.

Trier, J. D. (2005). 'Sordid fantasies': Reading popular 'inner-city' school films as racialized texts with pre-service teachers. Race Ethnicity and Education, 8(2), 171-189.

Weber, S. J., & Mitchell, C. (2002). That's funny you don't look like a teacher!: Interrogating images, identity, and popular culture. Routledge.

Wood, L., Kiperman, S., Esch, R. C., Leroux, A. J., & Truscott, S. D. (2017). Predicting dropout using student-and school-level factors: An ecological perspective. *School Psychology Quarterly*, *32*(1), 35.

Whitehead, A. N. (2008). *An introduction to mathematics*. London: Oxford University Press.

Wynter, S. (1995). The Pope must have been drunk, the King of Castile a madman: Culture as actuality, and the Caribbean rethinking modernity. The reordering of culture: Latin America, the Caribbean and Canada in the hood, 17-41.

Wynter, S., & McKittrick, K. (2015). Unparalleled catastrophe for our species? Or, to give humanness a different future: Conversations. In K. McKittrick (Ed.), Sylvia Wynter: On being human as praxis (pp. 9–89). Durham: Duke University Press.

Zirkel, S., Bailey, F., Bathey, S., Hawley, R., Lewis, U., Long, D., . . . Winful, A. (2011). 'Isn't that what "those kids" need?' Urban schools and the master narrative of the 'tough, urban principal'. *Race Ethnicity and Education*, *14*(2), 137-158. doi:10.1080/13613324.2010.519973

Chapter 6

Thinning Space

New Skins for New Worlds of Teaching & Learning

Bianca Licata and Catherine Cheng Stahl*, Department of Curriculum and Teaching, Teachers College, Columbia University

> Worldmaking "always starts from the worlds already on hand; the making is a remaking." (Goodman, 1978, as cited in Stornaiuolo & Whitney, 2018, p. 210)

> "When people only have access to a single story—one that simplifies and flattens the complexity of human experience and excludes many perspectives from being represented—they can become constrained in what they imagine to be possible." (Thomas & Stornaiuolo, 2016, p. 313)

The beginning months of 2020 saw a collapsing of worlds for teachers across the globe. School, as we had understood it, unraveled as the COVID-19 pandemic upended routines, disrupted commutes, and pushed us indoors to help slow the spread of the novel coronavirus. As teachers in the New York City area—then identified as the epicenter of the pandemic in the US—we found ourselves occupying our and our students' homes multifariously, grasping through screens small and large at the mercy of Internet service providers for some semblance of our former, orderly rooms. The rapid shift to this online environment left us little time to transition pedagogies, repurpose lessons, or update technologies. Far from a reset, the initial move into this hybrid space felt tentative, chaotic, slippery: we were teachers becoming students.

Yet, amidst the frantic shifts, a spirited lightness moved within us, summoning our inner child-like selves. Removed from the reach of governance over what and how we teach, we found ourselves immersed in possibilities, wading through virtual space, searching for who we were to and with our students, feeling for the familiarity of who we 'ought' to be. At some point, we stopped grasping for the thick identity of who we once were and looked around, recognizing the elements of this hybrid place as familiar. It was a virtual world belonging to gamers—a place built for play, multiplicity, and possibility. It was a place we had both explored as intra-active in games like Among Us, Animal Crossing, Goat Simulator, Doom, and others. It resembled a place where we, like our students, had adorned ourselves in 'skins'—avatars, embodied identities, performed personas, materializations customized to our choosing. Skins enable players to choose to follow, deviate from, or recreate a storyline through intra-actions with biotic and abiotic beings in an 'open map,' or a world unbounded.

Aware now of this mercurial terrain, we met one spring day on Zoom to reflect on the dynamism and playfulness of this new learning space and saw our calloused skins, now shed beside us, as corded to a system of accountability that dehumanized us and our students by rejecting our multiplicities of culture, knowledge, communication, and joy. Thus, as we hear calls for a return to 'normal,' we argue for anything but. Instead, as teachers who fell into a messy, uncertain map that opened us to becoming-multiple, we argue to summon this transitory, *emergent-cy* time-space into in-person learning so that (be) coming multiple *is* normal.

In this chapter, we share and analyze a series of vignettes to map how three learning spaces—the neoliberal firstspace, the virtual gaming secondspace, and the emergency online-learning thirdspace—textured our avatars as middle-school and college teachers, and came to inform the way we believe liberatory learning could take shape. Borrowing from Soja (1996), we call these spaces a "trialectic of learning space," and conceive of them as active in the *thickening* or *thinning* of both teacher and student 'skins,' taken from the gaming world to describe our agency, power, and identity in each space. We conclude by imagining how we and other teachers might manifest a *thinning space*—an agentive and transmutable location that welcomes multiple ways of becoming—once we return to in-person teaching and learning. We propose that, just as players dispel one skin for another, so, too, must teachers learn to shed thick 'professional' skins and actively attune to ever-shifting local learning ecologies, and student histories and futurities.

Toward Critical—yes, Critical!—
Postmodernism with Soja's Trialectics

Postmodernism has been criticized for reducing identities to unstable social constructions, thereby dismissing the violence marginalized people face every day (see, for example, Koro-Ljungberg et al., 2018; Zembylas, 2018). However, as two teacher–researcher–women of Color who have found "home and alienation" (Ayala, 2009, p. 72) in formal education, we argue that a "postmodernism of resistance" (hooks, as cited in Soja, 1996, p. 102) refuses its mono-ontological precepts, like those of White supremacy. Where White supremacy values us by our proximity to Whiteness (Solorzano, 1997) and kidnaps us into believing we are inferior (Milner, 2007), postmodernism's multiplicitous take on identity as unstable and always becoming (Barad, 2003) breaks down silos of identity constructed by White supremacy, allowing us to become more-than. Thus, we reject choosing one end of the critical-postmodern binary and, instead, choose to "work the hyphen" (Fine, 1994) as teacher–researchers–learners–players–women–scholars of Color. Within this written space, we join scholars like Anzaldúa, (Black and endarkened) feminists like Dillard, and queer postmodernists like Haraway who, as an assemblage, draw power to the edges and summon our multiplicity, and who slip between worlds and shift shapes within a *thinning space*. From this rhizome of women, we turn to Soja, and recreate his trialectic of spatiality for learning spaces.

Soja's (1996) notion of spatiality resists the conscription of singularity by offering three spaces between which people can shift, move, and become: a perceived, hegemonic, and territorializing firstspace; a conceived, artistic, yet still hegemonically inspired secondspace; and a lived, experimental thirdspace. Capaciousness in each space is determined by the degree to which normative discursive histories intervene in and define the "social relations of production" (p. 46). In the context of school, we do not take 'space' to mean the physical manifestation of these histories in their infrastructure, as O'Donahue (2006) did in writing about the masculinizing structures of school, or as Krueger (2010) did in writing about the structures of surveillance at a high school. Rather, we see space—and, with it, becoming—in a Baradian sense: as a locus of entangled, intra-active bodies (sometimes disembodied), whose produced phenomena are not only created by boundaries of space, but *create* boundaries of space and, thus, extend or limit potentiality of becoming. The physicality of space, in other words, does not anchor bodies into one discursive history or another, but is *one* agent involved in intra-actions that have the possibility of doing so. We, therefore, map Soja's three spaces (respectively) onto three transmutable spaces of learning: the firstspace of neoliberal schooling, where neoliberalism is defined as social actions motivated by capital gains tied to (White) meritocracy; the secondspace of virtual gaming, where virtual gaming is defined as role-player games, simulator games, battle royales, and any other such interactive games; and the thirdspace of emergency online learning, which took place in the first few weeks of a nation-wide school shut down. We understand capaciousness in these spaces through the gaming metaphor of skins, the thinning of which resists what Soja (1996) called "binary closures" (p. 65) and moves toward the liberation of student and teacher becomings.

Critical Autoethnography:
A Snapshot of Intra-active Becoming

As two teacher–researcher–learners–space-travellers concerned with the implications our intra-active skins have on students, we turn to critical autoethnography to reflect upon the "messiness inherent within multidimensional identities that resist simplistic, binary categories" (Boylorn & Orbe, 2014, p. 75). While we recognize that postmodernists reject the human experience and, thus, singular human narratives as a basis for reality, we contend that the following vignettes are, as their etymology suggests, portions of a vine of interminable becoming that extend and intertwine with one another and with you, our reader. Like cuttings from a vine, these stories are intended to intra-act as agents unto themselves. Thus, we believe these stories—ours as indicated by each of our names, but no longer only ours—will produce shifts in thinking, being, and becoming. From this critical postmodern perspective then, we share each of our personal experiences within three spaces of varied freedom for teachers and students to become, then together reflect on these experiences in order to consider future possibilities for becoming. Our collaboratively composed chapter represents a mere beginning to this reflection—an endeavor we continue beyond these pages into a space we extend to you through our QR code at the end of this chapter.

To Be a Machine in the Firstspace of Learning

Bianca

They had warned us about tearing little squares from the numbered, lined, and labeled scratch paper provided for the State exam. I would be required, they had said, to turn in *every* bit of scratch paper because if State test reviewers discovered a piece missing—considered a 'test irregularity'—it could be construed as evidence of cheating, as the absence of an answer written from one student to another, or even from one teacher to a student. For middle schools like ours, an urban charter serving Black and Brown students, an annual pattern of competitive student test scores was the difference between receiving funding, staying open, and even expanding, to losing students and closing for good. High test scores earned us merit, and by association, our students greater access to scholarships and colleges. There was little room for low scores and none for 'test irregularities.'

And so it made sense that we went into lockdown while our Dean, a towering suit-and-tied man, and our Chief Operating Officer (COO), a tiny, fast-moving woman, dug through trash cans, unzipped backpacks, and interrogated students after our Operations team discovered a two-inch square missing from a piece of scratch paper. They were on a mission to *solve and own*—our motto at the school for taking responsibility for messy situations, for tackling problems we saw and, in the seeing, knew we had to fix.

The student to whom this paper was assigned, 'Ben,' a skinny, thirteen-year-old boy with big eyes and a smile always on the verge of laughing, shrugged and nodded that his paper had been fine when he turned it into me. Me, who was responsible for collecting test documents, but who instead allowed students to gather everything. Me, who was responsible for walking the rows to monitor students and limit irregularities, but who instead drew cartoon puns on the board (*"You clam do it!"*) and graded papers. Me, who, by Ben's admission, was responsible for losing two inches of a test product and possibly incurring harsh punishments for the school and a damning future for my homeroom.

For the next two hours, as students tucked their heads and arms inside their blue-collared shirts, unable to access sweatshirts whose pockets were deemed a cheat-risk, I ran through the consequences in my head: *Their tests will be dumped. They'll sit through another grueling two hours to take it again. I will get fired, blacklisted from other schools.* The kids knew these possibilities too, their silent frustration filling the room, growing as their bellies groaned over a skipped lunch. But among us, watching the search with a smile, was Ben, who two hours later quietly approached the Dean.

"Um, I have something to tell you."

"Yeah, Ben?"

"I...ate the paper."

"You...what?"

"I ate it! Hah!"

Our jaws dropped. We would *never* be able to restore the two-inch square to its mother page. Our fates were sealed. Some students applauded, some laughed, but most called for Ben's punishment in place of their own.

"This isn't fair! Ugh, Ben!"

"You better not make all of *us* do it again. I'm not doing it again. He can do it!"

"Can *we* please get lunch now? Just keep Ben."

Then, chuckling, Ben pointed down to several tiny, damp balls of paper under his seat, all collectively smaller than a pinky nail.

"Jus' playin'! It's here!"

For the next fifteen minutes, the Dean and COO picked apart, unrolled, smoothed out, and pieced together with tape the chewed edges of the missing square back into place.

Catherine

"It took a lot of shedding of thick skins, Bianca! Colleagues thought I was a machine, a robot!"

These were words I tapped furiously onto my iPhone screen, as the foggy rear-view window of my mind warmed to release vapor, leaving behind a moment of clarity I had not experienced in years.

"But my school was a privileged space."

"Hmm how was it privileged?" probed Bianca before continuing, "Do you think there were unspoken codes people still followed?"

And with the mention of codes, I found myself retracing the contours of my first few years of teaching in the idyllic suburbs of New England, revisiting what I had meant by 'a privileged space.' Select memories began flashing in my mind like fireworks, colored with swirling emotions. One by one, I captured and relived them.

"And... joining us this year is Catherine Cheng, our shiny, newly-minted teacher." Hearing my name pronounced into the microphone and echoing across the newly renovated auditorium, I stood up, smiled, and waved to a sea of anonymous White faces. After that fleeting moment of hypervisibility, I was once again one among many, huddled near my co-workers, teeming with nervous excitement to embark on a new school year. The descriptor 'newly-minted,' stayed in my mind. *I think this is a compliment?*

A month into my new role, I picked up that 'newly minted teacher' was a phrase my principal liked to announce with every introduction to members of the school community. Before I had a chance to share on my own terms, my words were suppressed, replaced by the reminder that Catherine was the new one, the young one, the outsider straight from a teacher education program. The label was practically rubber-stamped onto my forehead and followed me into IEP meetings, faculty lounges, open house night, the list goes on. In an effort to prove my worth as a 'professional' as opposed to 'newly-minted,' I played by all the rules of the school, followed every administrator's social cue, and nodded 'yes' to every request presented to me.

One memory remains particularly vivid: One day, while scurrying down the hallway in my heels from 'Commons duty,' the principal caught up and walked alongside me towards the 'Science wing.'

"Given your background in art history, you would make excellent contributions to our school musical as this year's producer. It would be an ideal role for you to exercise your aesthetic skills and get a feel for other aspects of our school community."

Despite having zero experience producing any performance, I responded with an automatic enthusiastic 'Yes!' *What an honor to be asked by the principal himself.*

Soon after taking the role of producer, I learned the reality of the situation: no one wanted that job. Not only was it physically exhausting, but also emotionally draining and interpersonally taxing. Everyone wanted something from the producer, and it was my role to serve. *Yes, yes, more yes.* What kept me going was getting to see some of my students outside of class—that, and my desperation to feel accepted. Quite simply, I wanted to belong, blend in, or at least avoid becoming an outsider—a felt experience all too common in my life up to that point.

Yet, in spite of the exhaustion I felt each time I answered "yes," I pushed myself to be seen working harder than the rest, without complaint. Whereas the more experienced teachers learned to collaborate and work smart, I worked alone, often past 5pm so that when the principal took his daily stroll and peeked through the square window of every door, he could see me grading at my desk or preparing in the chemistry lab. The later he took that walk, the later I stayed. And it worked: It did not take long for the administration to lift me up as a 'model teacher' and later, a 'teacher leader.' Topped with my routine 25-page-plus student learning reports, spotless meeting attendance, and meticulous emails catering to every parent's needs, I became the teacher who made taxpayers happy. To the school leaders, I was an asset whose perfectionist work ethic and eagerness to please were rewarded with handwritten notes, public praise, and chocolate bars. To my own colleagues, however, I was hardcore—hardened to the core, unapproachable, a robot programmed to nod and produce.

"...I was a machine, a robot..."

I rested my thumbs, sitting within the spaces of the ellipses on the screen. My school was a space of privilege for well-to-do parents, a space where teachers could be pressured to ensure their children had a straight path to college through the grades, extracurriculars, honor society membership, and so forth made possible only by (over)productive 'professional' teachers. As part of playing this role, I learned to get out of the way or become the obstruction that *will* be removed.

Critical Reflections of the Firstspace Travels

Though located at different points across time and space, we both occupied the same transmutable learning space, shaped by a neoliberal discourse that equates productivity with survival—of one's career, of students' futures. The explicit and implicit rules of behavior we both describe reflect a panopticon and an "obsessive fear of unruly and dangerous elements and the equally obsessive desire to bring them under control" (Hooper, as cited in Soja, 1996, p. 114). Thus, through a language that praised productivity and castigated laxity, our identities were articulated into a singular materiality: producers of students who produced meritocratically worthy (survival-worthy) test scores, resumes, and grades. This limited way of being essentializes a binary that excludes the possibility of a nuanced humanity: either become a machine or be seen as transgressive and, therefore, terminable. We argue that this binary is psychologically and emotionally harmful to multiply-marginalized (Kumashiro, 2000) teachers and students already traumatized by historically dehumanizing discourses that circulate within social systems like school.

This neoliberal firstspace of learning frames teachers and students of Color through a deficit lens (Ladson-Billings, 2006); our success is yoked to a constant ascension to (but never attainment of) Eurocentric ideals (Asante, 1991; Brown & Brown, 2020; Grant et al., 2016; ross, 2020; Woodson, 2020). It is a gamespace we cannot leave and, yet, can never win, thereby impelling us to self-destruct into anxiety, depression, and self-doubt (Tuitt & Carter, 2008). The firstspace of learning positions the voices, bodies, and gestures of Black and Brown youth like those at Bianca's school as disruptive and chaotic (Au, 2018, Ramlow, 2004; Sokolower, 2018), tasking teachers like Bianca to hypervigilantly monitor 'strong reactions' that may interfere with their ability to take high stakes tests (Lesko & Niccolini, 2016). And, although she resisted the systems of surveillance and testing (i.e., writing puns on the board instead of walking the aisles), Bianca felt extreme anxiety at losing a two-inch square of paper, duress at being seen as the 'test irregularity' that the Dean and COO had to 'solve and own', and frustration at Ben's playful wanderings on the edge of the firstspace map. Her frantic worries, like the Dean's and the COO's, reflect the psychological pressure created by this firstspace of learning to fill a singular thick teacher skin of surveillance. Yet, as Catherine's story showed, even if we were to wear this skin, we still experience the anxiety and torment of *having* to wear *only this skin.*

Catherine had struggled with finding a focus for her firstspace narrative on rules and structures because she had occupied what she called a space of 'privilege.' But as she returned through time and space to her suburban teaching years, she wondered, *A privilege for whom? And at what cost?* Was it really an 'honor' to be esteemed (and relied upon so heavily) by the principal to serve? Despite having taught in divergent contexts, Bianca's experience of anxiety and marginalization resonated with Catherine's.

Like Bianca, Catherine was labeled as 'professional,' and positioned as a 'teacher leader' among her peers. Coined by her principal as 'newly minted,' she was constructed as *the* desirable machine through a discourse that praised her competition and 'hard work' over the 'more experienced' teachers' use of collaboration. In this environment, Catherine was led to believe she had to *over*produce and to speak the neoliberal language of '*Yes, yes, more yes*' in order to have value. As a vulnerable new teacher–woman of Color in a predominantly White and monied school, she feared failure and felt pressured, as Bianca and her students did, to prove her value. Compensating for some perceived deficit—of newness, of unfamiliarity—she overworked to a point of not recognizing herself becoming-(more) Othered. She quite literally became a producer.

Wearing thick skin for both of us facilitated simultaneous feelings of suffocation and isolation. For Catherine, her armor of thick skin alienated her from those who *truly* wanted to support her and see her succeed—not in a productive way, but in a supportive, collegial way. For Bianca, the sense of being seen outside her thick skin—naked, vulnerable—produced an imagined future of isolation. For Bianca's students, their learning paths were made to be isolated and competitive by a system of testing that predicated constant surveillance. What we needed were new skins, a new map, a new space to play.

To Become in the Secondspace of Learning

Catherine

While acclimating to emergency online teaching, figuring out how to (re)create spaces of community and healing in times of isolation and fear for my first-year college students, my mind often returned to the formative days of my own youth. Much of my 'virtual pedagogy,' as I was imagining it in real-time, involved seeking inspiration from time and space travels to other moments of transitions, hybridity, and in-betweenness. One such place was Neopets, a virtual world of gaming and community that opened in 1999. It was a world that I escaped into late at night and buried myself in during a challenging transitional time in my life when my friendships were in flux, belonging felt tentative, and community was hard to come by.

Growing up, my racial identity as Asian (American) was a source of insecurity and internalized shame in my everyday school settings. My unevenly shaped eyes (shifting between single- and double-lidded) and my Chinese name 'Yanan' (whose mispronunciation made me cringe every time) were what everyone seemed to notice first and pay the most attention to. In school, I was what others expected me to be: outsider, nerd, quiet girl. Within Neopets, however, I could begin again, blend in, or play with(in) the multiple roles available to me, and participate in the construction of a lifeworld I yearned for—one of acceptance, creativity, and belonging. Not only that, Neopets served as a kind of buffer: I could stumble through the growing up process, try out different ways of being without the permanence of identity labels, and gather in the company of like-minded peers who also took refuge as an insider in an-Other world.

In this virtual world, I created for myself the player screen name of '_sweetxoxcathy_' and first name of 'Cathy' (Figure 1). Cathy was a nickname I had never used in person and associated with extroversion. It was ideal for my online identity play, for it was not until I attended American schools that I became 'the quiet student,' made legible through regular report card inscriptions like "Catherine/Yanan is encouraged to participate more in class." In place of Catherine the student, I crafted a profile that showcased other less noticeable aspects of myself.

Figure 1 *A Partial Screenshot of Catherine's User Page in Neopets*

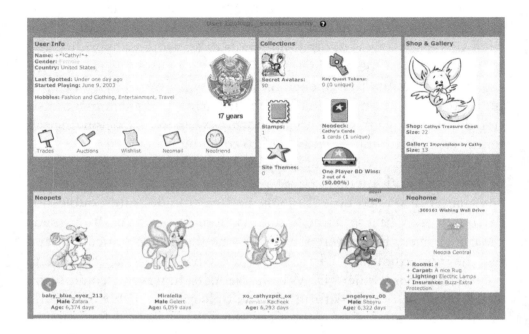

Feeling back to my early adolescent selves in this gaming world, I remember how profound each of these entities were to me: places like the Secret Laboratory and Rainbow Fountain, objects like 'faerie bottles' and 'magical paintbrushes,' and activities like 'faerie quests' and 'battledome challenges.' Each enabled or activated a more dynamic, freeform play that I could sustain with the neopoints (gaming currency) I accumulated through winning games and completing tasks. I played hard, and while the games lost their luster over time, they remained nonetheless addictive for their liberating potential. Neopoints were my entry into this other world and I was driven by a desire to earn big. With more possibilities afforded to me through my diligent play, I immersed myself in experimentation through embracing the malleability of my neopets, the uncertainty of their transformations, and the transitory period of adolescence.

"Do you know who Travis Scott is, Ms. Licata?" 'Jay' asked while looking offscreen.

"I've heard of him, but—"

"Well he's going to be on Fortnite tomorrow. Do you play Fortnite?"

'Yvonne' rolled her eyes. "She doesn't play, stupid."

"Don't say stupid, Yvonne. No, Jay, I don't play."

"Too bad. It's gonna be cool."

"No it's not," Yvonne said, turning off her camera. "No one plays Fortnite anymore."

Travis Scott performed a live concert as a giant avatar of himself on a Fortnite map while players engaged in a battle royale against each other and the encroaching enclosure of their map to be the last one standing. The event had been thrilling for students, who had been stuck inside for weeks already. But like with so many others, Fortnite had been subsumed by a new obsession, a new storyline, a new place for battle and intrigue—Among Us.

I learned about Among Us after I left my middle school position and began teaching college writing alongside Catherine. My friends still teaching there discovered that students were sharing codes to maps where they could play during online classes. Their gameplay was voracious, unstoppable, contagious. Even after the administration blocked them from emailing one another codes in an effort to stop the spread, students found ways to share information surreptitiously and build avatars to join the game.

Created by Inner Sloth in 2018, Among Us takes place on a breaking space station, maintained by players, whose avatars were chunky, armless humanoids in colorful unitards, reminiscent of the minions from *Despicable Me*. An imposter (or sometimes two) is aboard, pretending to help but actually out to destroy others. Each player's mission is to stay alive and identify the imposter, while the imposter must stay hidden. If someone discovers a body, they call a meeting, and players discuss what they saw and vote to toss one suspect into space (Figure 2). If they successfully vote the imposter off the ship, they win as a team; however, if they vote off a comrade, the imposter continues to roam, taking lives until they've killed everyone and won the game.

Figure 2 *The Meeting Panel Following Bianca's Death and That of Player "soss"*

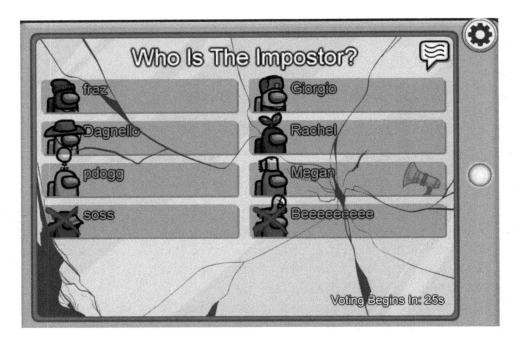

Curious, and inspired by Catherine's transformative experience in Neopets, I decided to play with friends one night during the pandemic. Immediately, I felt skin-to-skin with my avatar, to whom I added a hamster in a ball for $2.00 to eliminate ads (Figure 3). Moving excitedly from room to room, chasing and hiding, solving and plotting, I learned to move silently through this new world. I transformed into a younger version of myself, thrilled to play, determined to win. I remembered what it felt like to be small, in love with the monsters I watched my little brother and dad destroy in Quake and Doom (as I was an avid fan with unfortunate hand-eye coordination). As a mixed-raced Filipina mestiza, 'what' I was was a point of wonder, a strange and exotic object to poke at for other kids. But through these games, I saw the monster/humanoid/creature that I was as more, as beyond.

So, from my couch, I became a thirty-year-old-teacher–research-er-and-eleven-year-old-kid poking out my tongue as I (poorly) nav-igated hallways while trying to jot down notes: *fun, what is fixing?, why do I have to fix things and find the killer?* I found myself caught up in the map, becoming a humanoid, surrounded by a world, and when I/my avatar was killed, I felt anxious yet invigorated in knowing who did it and not—as the rules of honor dictate—being allowed to share.

Figure 3 *The Avatar Panel Prior to Entering the Spaceship*

Death in the world of Among Us is not an end, but a transition. Privy to the killer's identity, I floated as a ghost from room to room, beyond the walls of the slowly crashing ship, both in the game and not, (re)learning what it felt like to simultaneously exist and not, and feeling powerful in my postdeath knowledge. Like the imposter— who had the unique powers to crawl through vents, appearing and disappearing with ease—I, too, could appear and disappear, wander and explore (Figure 4). There were no borders for me. I could continue to fix the ship, watch the game, function and feel joy beyond death.

Figure 4 *The Ghost of Bianca's Avatar Floating Through the Spaceship, Crossing Barriers and Attending to Tasks*

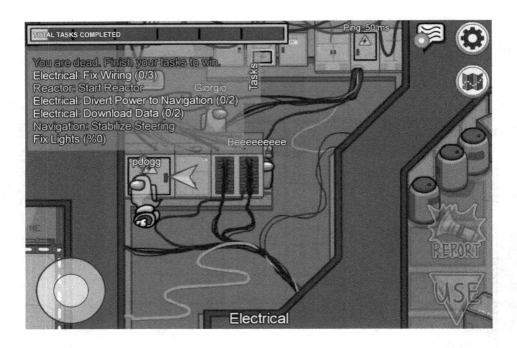

Critical Reflections of Secondspace Travels

Converging after our journeys through time and game space maps, we find ourselves having traversed the same secondspace, where we (re)learned to become-other and become-more-than. Unlike the firstspace, where we were meant to *be* machines and wear a teacher skin thick with neoliberalism, we became not only creatures but concurrent states of being, merging our futures with our pasts.

In travelling back in time to (re)experience her formative years with Neopets, Catherine remembered what it meant to play with(in) her various thin skins, and how these skins supported her transformation into becoming-another. She had restored herself through player identities, collapsing the sedimented thick skin of 'the quiet student' she had been ascribed in the firstspace, a label that had reduced her complexity as a being. In remembering these earlier times of potentiality and virtuality as an educator during COVID-19, Catherine felt her teacher skin thin and her capaciousness expand into gamer–neopet–teacher all at once, leaving her to wonder: Who else could she be beyond Catherine, the writing instructor? How could she and her students showcase other skins, hidden beneath facades of firstspace professionalism?

Similarly, having boarded the Among Us ship, Bianca imagined herself into the game space students had been occupying during the pandemic, while reoccupying her youth-game fan skin. During a time shaped by death, the thrill of gaining new powers through death in Among Us offers players not only an escape from the mundanity of firstspace expectations to produce and repeat, but also a desirable counternarrative for the finality of death—one where life after death is play. To hover on the border in Among Us—both a living player and poltergeist in a breaking machine, between human being and more-than human—is to embody what Anzaldúa (1987) calls a *mestiza* or *nahuatl* consciousness. Bianca felt herself imagining as a gamer–teacher living through a pandemic how Among Us' diminished boundaries provide students with the opportunity to expand and become, particularly students whose communities had been hit the hardest. She, too, pondered how student–teacher play *during* online classes might serve as a refuge from the constricting firstspace walls of learning.

These wonderings seemed hard to answer, though, as we recognized how our material realities in the secondspace were still comprehended through restrictive "thought things" (Soja, 1996, p. 79) from the firstspace. Each of our (re)new(ed) skins had manifested through the same competition and productivity that defined our firstspace skins. In Among Us, every humanoid had to complete a set of tasks, lest they look 'sus' (i.e., suspicious) and risk being voted out. Even to become an interloping ghost, one had to be killed. Similarly, in the world of Neopets, transformation required faerie bottles, magical paintbrushes, and other objects of metamorphosis earned with neopoints or acquired with quests, by chance, or through the charity of 'high status' players. For players with financial means, however, neopoints—and the extra freedom, power, and play that comes with them—could be purchased with actual currency. In other words, Neopets gamifies the inequitable access to resources and competitive social capital that influence public school systems across the US. Likewise, Among Us communicates that a state of transformative freedom—a stated intention of firstspace learning—is a prize and not a right. As they were experienced by Bianca and Catherine, both reproduce harmful firstspace anxieties.

Still, the secondspace of gaming is a world decidedly wider. Through "permanently partial identities and contradictory standpoints" (Haraway, 1991, p. 153), players intra-act with one another and abiotic bodies, bending firstspace narratives—to borrow from Thomas & Stornaiuolo (2016)—in ways they may perceive as too risky in the firstspace. Youth-centered research reveals these spaces as active sites of play, negotiation, experimentation, and both important and necessary sites of social learning (see, for example, Abrams & Lammers, 2017; boyd, 2014; Ito et al., 2013, 2019; Squire, 2008, 2010). In the transience of gaming, players can engage in a battle royale, take up role-player missions, or practice simulated tasks like driving a tractor (Tractor Simulator) just to feel what it is like to live differently, if only for a moment. Thus, while firstspace competition and monetized hierarchies dictate secondspace rules, players still learn to (re)assume a multiplicity through experiential play and multimodal participation in affinity spaces that might not exist in surveillable firstspaces.

Having (re)learned what it meant to become-other, we found ourselves asking how we and our students had been playing with(in) our Zoom ecosystem and how we might pursue a play that leaves behind firstspace precepts. Was this possible? How might the metaphor of skins in the COVID-19 climate of racism and xenophobia create openings in our thinking and writing about our multilayered identities—who we think we are, who we want to be, and why it can be hard to be ourselves fully? Just like in the secondspace game world of Neopets and Among Us, how could we unlock the transformative potential within students through intra-actions with human faces and non-human things, digital artifacts, conceptual ideas, stories, "and... and...and..." (Deleuze & Guattari, 1987, p. 25)?

Becoming I as We, I/We:
Thinning Skins in the Thirdspace of Online Learning

Bianca & Catherine

tests were cancelled and absent-policies relaxed

s l o w l y

    we lay down our mechanical firstspace skins

                and stepped

          back

uncovered, we slipped, slid, *fell*

    returned to what felt like a powerless, amoebic state

students played with new forms of resistance: video off, muted

        we are here and not—there is no

way to be sure

    cleaved from the panopticon

      we, too, played like secondspace argonauts within this

new map

    pushing against each firstspace wall that rose to corral

us

         rules

         routines

         grading

         feedback

crushing that which once sieved them/us into a singu-

larity beneath their/our

MULTITUDES:

anime artist, BTS fan, Hip Hop dancer, Fortnite gamer, Netflix connoisseur, Instagram influencer, foodie, dreamer, and… and… and… we found ourselves sharing multitudes alongside, pulled in unlocking a new level of teaching that was/is always

IN PROCESS:

friend, counselor, teacher, fellow pandemic survivor, gamer, dancer, dreamer

and… and… and…

left to play in these shifting skins, we let the

BECOMING

unfold:

we ate, drank coffee, listened to music, told stories behind our

names and our 'happy objects' in our surroundings, and cheered each

other on for just showing up

students Zoomed from bed, couches, cars

from behind the glow of video games and Netflix on

other screens

siblings made cameos; pets did, too

GIFs in the chat, dance moves on camera

backgrounds of a faraway paradise and Rick and

Morty

students wrote poetry, filmed videos, played with assignment

directions

(or ignored

them altogether)

missed class, overslept, fell asleep...

we stopped clamouring for our mechanistic

skins...

but in our opening to our/their multiplicity

we felt the pain

and heartbreak

once mitigated by the machine

sickness, *death*,

overworked parents, *more death*,

rising unemployment, *multiple*

deaths,

ICU beds counted daily in numbers, percentages, points

so. far. removed.

TALLY-TRAUMA (ignored and belied by the firstspace)

now underscored and amplified by protests that called

for racial justice

yet not fluent in the discourse of death

we struggled

we alone could not carry the burden (we got this now)

we turned

and released ourselves from firstspace anxiety to *fix and*

solve alone

we leaned into COMMUNITY

GoFundMe's, hard memos:

This student would have their camera off because...what

should we *do?*

That student will be missing class because they say they are

depressed, unresponsive...what should we *do?*

play, write, think, talk, listen, share, explore

tell me about the music you like

we begin each day like the last, we share rituals

Good morning, post a GIF that tells us what you

think about...

Stay after if you want to share, sit in silence, cry,

vent...

in the letting go and opening up

our skins continued thinning

with the shedding of each layer

we found ourselves bracing together against the winds

that had always been there, but which firstspace walls had

muted into a cold draft that slowly but persistently chilled us,

singularly cold

Critical Reflections of the Thirdspace Travels

Terlouw (2011) writes that following a massive economic shift in a region, people migrate and take up new industries in a new space, which in that "specific moment can create a new, but transitory, regional identity" (p. 710), or a thin identity. We think of COVID-19 as having forced a massive regional shift in our teaching, and that what occurred amidst our *emergent-cy* teaching was "transitory" in the sense that it was always in-process. The thirdspace of emergent-cy online learning was intra-active, open to the inscription of firstspace boundaries, skins, and the design of power, just like the secondspace of gaming. But this inscription was *not yet* defined in the thirdspace, as much as empowered bodies hoped it to be, especially after mandated requirements—test, strict attendance, a certain collection of points— were eliminated. In this new open map, our ever-thinning intra-active skins were portals into burgeoning ways of learning and becoming through community, play, and rest rather than competition, surveillance, and marginalizing meritocracy. The quicksilver of thirdspace becoming made it impossible for firstspace skins to stick, which was initially discomforting to us as former firstspace machines.

Just as being in the secondspace of virtual gaming is to be transformed, teaching in the emergent-cy thirdspace was to be immersed in an ecology of *constant* transformation, to experience a *thinning* of thick skins and a shifting through identities that were always becoming-more-than-teacher. The thinning moved us toward a freedom from containment that had become normal. As Soja (1996) wrote of thirdspace, the possible-freedom in this thinning space was "common to all of us yet never able to be completely seen and understood, an 'unimaginable universe'" (p. 56) and, thus, frightening. 'Ameobic' though we were, we/our students became multitudes and, in many ways, 'of the same skin' (e.g., artist, dancer, Netflix connoisseur). And while White supremacy did not disappear, our plurality and the improvisational quality of our/our students' bodies, minds, relationships, and emotions "ruptured the normative practice" (Gutiérrez et al., 1999, p. 288) of the neoliberal apparatus. Our collective care for one another in our wholeness allowed for hybrid ways of being and learning, such that objects and behaviors constructed as disruptive in the firstspace (e.g., eating or dancing during class) were normalized.

Yet, this thinning also invited the pain, horror, suffering, and depression formerly compartmentalized and buried in the firstspace to sit in our 'classrooms,' demanding to be addressed. Feelings and realities that hampered firstspace competition now drove the ways we moved through our rooms. Although as teachers we wanted to provide a 'good education' for students, we recognized that 'learning' could not happen in a vacuum, out of touch with a world that was reckoning with multiple pandemics and their aftermath. We could not 'effectively teach' until we learned to attune to students' social and emotional needs and to their entanglements with the situations around them. Even then, the greater lesson was to demonstrate humanity, to sit with knowing. Put differently, firstspace relationality had tried to manifest, but slipped away, transforming into secondspace gaming possibilities, which also slipped, renewing into something un-gamed, something that just *was*. It was becoming something that called us to go 'play in the dark' of what we did not know (Morrison, 1992).

So, through providing simple routines (e.g., *Good morning, post a GIF that tells us what you think about...*) for students who felt better knowing what came next, we nudged ourselves into the unknowing: we talked 'off topic'; we spent time in silence; we didn't force kids to talk or turn on cameras, even if we were urged by administrators to do so. In these first few weeks of emergency teaching, we sat with the unknowing, the emergent-cy of our day-to-day living, and the reality that we alone could not 'solve and own.' And so, while our/our students' multitudes included pain, joy, anger, and confusion, we became an assemblage that was expansive, more-than-human, fully alive and affectively responsive, that was no longer a simple machine.

Thus, as public discourse urges students to return to desks and teachers to resume the front of the room, we call for education to continue moving, resist settling, and keep becoming-more-than. Just as young readers in online fanfiction sites restory the identities of characters "to more accurately reflect the diversity of the world, to blur boundaries between traditional categories, or to create characters whose identities more closely mirror their own" (Thomas & Stornai-uolo, 2016, p. 321), we propose further inquiry into how students and teachers might break through sedimented ways of being, and bend their (in-person) learning environment to better align with an orientation of deterritorialization, multiplicity, and becoming.

(Re)membering as Conjuring: Welcoming a Thinning Space In-Person

New space, new rules, new becomings

Camera on/off

(un)mute

You're on mute

(laughing emoji)

Silence does not mean

> *not caring, not knowing, not paying attention*

No video does not mean

> *lack of engagement, indifference towards learning, or disrespect towards peers*

We are rewriting expectations

Troubling classroom management

Who is doing the seeing, the regulating, the monitoring?

Rethinking compliance

I participate when I want and how I want

(blue hand-raising icon)

Type in chat, play a song, make something together

I'm still here; it's just that time of the month

>*Cramps*

Let's all turn off our cameras and do something for ourselves

I need a break, so I take it

Sharing stories, sharing space, sharing bandwidth

Show and tell: here's my happy object

>*Spaces of childhood revisited and returned*

(clapping emoji)

Home and school blurred

>*Blurry background*

>*What does my background tell you about me?*

>*Who are you? What's your story? Where's home?*

How do you best feel at home?

Returning to our roots, our names

Hearing sounds from local surroundings

Private home life spills into public school life

 Unstable network

 Sibling crying, sirens wailing

 Mom, I'm in class

Rethinking interruptions, disruptions, assumptions

I'm here

I'm with you

I'm listening, deeply

 Let's honor thinking time

Play with ideas in our minds, feel them in our bodies

No physical bodies but still embodied in a way

Empathy, compassion, flexibility

Do you trust me?

(heart emoji)

Thank you for always believing in us

I am because we are

What does it mean to get to know ourselves and our students in

this thinning space?

In returning to and re-turning—in the Baradian (2014) sense of "turning it over and over again...in the making of...new diffraction patterns" (p. 168)—words, voices, and wonderings situated within Zoom chat transcripts, notebook jottings, orphaned chapter fragments from retracing memories, margin notes on PDFs, students' work, and... and... and... we found ourselves again in the middle of the thinning space, listening. Part found poem, part list poem, and part free verse (Franco, 2005), this poem merges existing words tethered to our memories with those arising impromptu *in vivo* that explore and evoke our/our students' lived experiences in the shared, blurred, and co-constructed thirdspace of emergent-cy teaching and learning. It incorporates our voices as teacher–researcher–players with that of our students—a kind of heteroglossia that softens any singular static voice. It, too, puts into conversation our multiple selves in various time-spaces, having drifted through firstspace and secondspace, and assembles them on the page, touching, feeling, skin-to-skin, summoning the thirdspace: the thinning space.

Thus, drawing from womanist, endarkened feminists, and queer feminist ontologies and epistemologies, we believe that through collective remembering, documenting, and acting upon our multitudes as part of a(n) (re)assemblage, we may conjure the thirdspace of emergent-cy teaching and learning that we experienced at the height of COVID-19 in institutions thick with long-established social structures. In so doing, we can thin these rigidly rooted structures to "the primary epistemological unit" (Barad, 2003, p. 815)—to that of phenomena, from which new ways of learning and being may materialize. Yet, because we believe all beings are a(n) (assembled) plurality, there is neither a formula for conjuring this thinning space, nor one straight path that educators might take to do so. We can, however, offer one suggested approach based on our own critical reflections and wonderings through the first, second, and thirdspace.

We first attuned to our bodies, to sensations of anguish and anxiety reflected in journals, texts, and conversations. By *seeing* and *hearing* our feelings and tracing their origins, we recognized that teachers and learners are not monoliths. Rather, we are all "bodies without organs" (Deleuze & Guattari, 1987) with a propensity to intra-act (Barad, 2007) with human, non-human, and non-living bodies alike in our becoming as teachers, students, researchers, and… and… and… Together, we came to realize that, through an assemblage of sanctioned institutions, physically surrounding us and embodied within us, we had been enculturated toward a singularity that rendered us amnesiac, that harmed (and continues to harm) us—particularly us who are multiply-marginalized, multiply-othered—emotionally, psychologically, and spiritually. In attuning to our feelings, we saw that in this hegemonic firstspace, we/our students had forgotten our plurality and, thus, been wholly silenced, made alone in our pain and singular striving for some standards we could never (healthily) meet.

Understanding a need to (re)learn to (re)member our inherent multiplicity (Anzaldúa, 1987), as a means of survival, we as teachers responded to our present situations, for, as Dillard (2012) puts it:

> Teaching asks us to be present, to care, and to be able to respond to the students and others within our purview: Being able to do so with all who gather, with care and love for the energy we bring to the endeavor, characterizes our response-ability. (p. 83)

From this place of presence, as Dillard (2012) suggests, we reached back, remembered who we are spiritually, culturally, communally, and bodily to activate our many selves, past and present, and to connect agentially with those skins so as to walk with students as they, too, gather and construct new skins. Spurred by an entanglement of conflict and crises—COVD-19 and racial unrest—we sought "to recall and rethink of again…[and] put back together" (Dillard, 2012, p. 3) the many beings we are, were, and will become in concert with the many beings around us. We felt, then, that we needed to center presence in all its forms in our practice in order to invite multiplicity.

By (re)membering multiplicities, we then critically intra-acted with *institutionalized* thick skins, in a continuous thinning of boundaries, returning to and re-turning phenomena in a constant ontogenesis, "diffracting anew…iterative[ly] (re)configuring" (Barad, 2014, p. 168). In this re-turn, we drew from the richly textured secondspace of learning: We took up various skins, pushed the edges of neoliberal maps and boundaries of surveillance by playing intra-actively with the power dynamics of teacher–student relationality. As skin-shifting gamers walking this immanent terrain, we asked ourselves, *Can I thin the way I am meant to behave with my students? Who or what can I become with/alongside/through/for them? How can we materialize new structures that invite us to explore who we are and what learning means?*

Yet, though slipped into skins ready to suss out the imposters of meritocracy and singularity, we realized that transformative teaching based in firstspace rules—that of competition, defeat, winning, binaries—would open neither us nor our students to the ongoing process of becoming. We could not single-handedly change this system, much less single-handedly solve our students' problems so that they could return to learning based in firstspace ways of knowing and to earn firstspace standards of value. Instead, we understood that true freedom would happen by constant meditation on our intentions—an iterative thinning—and by working as part of a collective.

As Love (2019) contends, dismantling firstspace barriers and eschewing whole histories of divisive and insidious White supremacist policies, calls for work "in solidarity with communities of color while drawing on the imagination, creativity, refusal (re)membering, visionary thinking, healing, rebellious spirit boldness, determination, and subversiveness of abolitionists to eradicate injustice in and outside of schools" (p. 2). Put differently, our "subjects are made in and through relationships" (Villenas, 2019, p. 156) and, thus, while our remembering may begin singularly, we must engage in (re)collective imaginings in order to clear the space of White supremacy and (re)build our agentive bodies. This collective work of "community, coalition, and solidarity [are] always in the making" (p. 158), producing warmth and power from an expansive, centrifugal, energetic body without organs in an enduring state of becoming alive.

And this conjuring extends beyond the teacher–student relationship into other tendrils within the assemblage of education, like research. For education researchers, opening a portal into a thinning space means that they must attune to and be aware of their intra-actions with those in, alongside, and around their study; to speak *with* rather than at or for educators and students (Alcoff, 1991); and to document and reflect upon the affective resonances of their own expansion. In an ethnographic study, for example, this could mean inviting participants to shape the presentation of data more directly. It might mean stepping aside to make space for them to participate not only as the observed, but the *observer* who intra-acts with people and things—not only as one about whom conclusions are reached, but as one who forms conclusions that impact them and their community. In thinning the boundaries between researcher skin and participant skin, researchers open participants up to the privileged resources of research (Villenas, 1996) to shape actions that serve their immediate needs (Beeman-Cadwallader et al., 2012; Cahill, 2007; Green, 2014). Through the (re)generative process of thinning space, researchers can engage with participants in communal discovery or, in what hooks (2018) calls, "critical love"—that is, an ethical commitment to caring for the communities in which we work in the various spaces where we inhabit, whether it be physical, virtual, or...or...or...

And...and...and...From I/We to You

The firstspace of neoliberal anti-life and necropsy (Petrovic & Kuntz, 2018) "cannot reconcile the fantasy of freedom with the lifeblood of oppression" (Vaught, 2012, p. 62) and, thus, binds bodies and becomings. When permeated by a thinning space, however, the space opens up all matter to possibilities for becoming (Barad, 2003) and becomes one rooted in love "that demands constant vigilance toward response-ability in relationships" (Villenas, 2019, p. 156). Thus, though we have shared with you here how both our time teaching at the start of a global pandemic and our concurrent traipse through a trialectic of learning spaces opened us to a worldmaking as one that begins with our inner worlds on hand (Goodman, 1978, as cited in Stornaiuolo & Whitney, 2018), we see this remaking process as ongoing. And so, we invite you to join us in our ongoing journey in, through, alongside and in reflection of a transmutable thinning space. We also encourage you to excavate the 'raw materials' for such a reconfiguration from within yourself, tap into your inner child (as we have), and activate that nascent state in recognition of the multiplicity that exists within you. Join us in the assemblage, and share your own walk virtually through the thinning space using the QR code below.

Notes

*This chapter has been equally authored

References

Abrams, S. S., & Lammers, J. C. (2017). Belonging in a videogame space: Bridging affinity spaces and communities of practice. *Teachers College Record*, 34.

Alcoff, L. (1991). The Problem of Speaking for Others. *Cultural Critique, 20*, 5–32. https://doi.org/10.2307/1354221

Anzaldúa, G. (1987). *Borderlands/La frontera: The new mestiza* (First edition). Spinsters/Aunt Lute.

Asante, M. K. (1991). The Afrocentric idea in education. *The Journal of Negro Education, 60*(2), 170–180. https://doi.org/10.2307/2295608

Au, W. (2018). Racial justice is not a choice: White supremacy, high-stakes testing, and the punishment of Black and Brown students. In D. Watson, J. Hagopian, & W. Au (Eds.), *Teaching for Black lives* (pp. 243–250). Rethinking Schools.

Ayala, J. (2009). Split scenes, converging visions: The ethical terrains where PAR and borderlands scholarship meet. *The Urban Review, 41*(1), 66–84. https://doi.org/10.1007/s11256-008-0095-9

Barad, K. (2003). Posthumanist performativity: Toward an understanding of how matter comes to matter. *Signs: Journal of Women in Culture and Society, 28*(3), 801–831.

Barad, K. (2007). *Meeting the universe halfway: Quantum physics and the entanglement of matter and meaning.* Duke University Press. https://doi.org/10.1215/9780822388128

Barad, K. (2014). Diffracting diffraction: Cutting together-apart. *Parallax, 20*(3), 168–187. https://doi.org/10.1080/13534645.2014.927623

Beeman-Cadwallader, N., Quigley, C., & Yazzie-Mintz, T. (2012). Enacting decolonized methodologies: The doing of research in educational communities. *Qualitative Inquiry, 18*(1), 3–15. https://doi.org/10.1177/1077800411426414

boyd, danah. (2014). *It's complicated: The social lives of networked teens.* Yale University Press.

Boylorn, R. M., & Orbe, M. P. (2014). *Critical autoethnography: Intersecting cultural identities in everyday life* (Issue volume13). Left Coast Press, Inc.

Brown, K. D., & Brown, A. L. (2020). Anti-Blackness and the school curriculum. In C. A. Grant, A. Woodson, & M. Dumas (Eds.), *The future is Black: Afropessimism, fugitivity, and radical hope in education* (pp. 72–78). Routledge.

Cahill, C. (2007). Participatory data analysis. In S. Kindon, R. Pain, & M. Kesby (Eds.), *Participatory action research approaches and methods: Connecting people, participation and place* (pp. 181–187). Routledge. https://doi.org/10.4324/9780203933671

Clandinin, D. J. (2016). *Engaging in narrative inquiry.* Routledge. https://doi.org/10.4324/9781315429618

Deleuze, G., & Guattari, F. (1987). *A thousand plateaus: Capitalism and schizophrenia.* University of Minnesota

Press.

Dillard, C. B. (2012). *Learning to (re)member the things we've learned to forget: Endarkened feminisms, spirituality, and the sacred nature of research and teaching* (First printing edition). Peter Lang Inc., International Academic Publishers.

Felman, S. (2013). Education and crisis, or the vicissitudes of teaching. In S. Felman & D. Laub, *Testimony: Crises of witnessing in literature, psychoanalysis and history* (pp. 21–76). Routledge. https://doi.org/10.4324/9780203700327-8

Fine, M. (1994). Working the hyphens: Reinventing self and other in qualitative research. In N. K. Denzin & Y. S. Lincoln (Eds.), *Handbook of qualitative research* (pp. 70–82). Sage Publications, Inc.

Franco, B. (2005). *Conversations with a poet: Inviting poetry into K-12 classrooms*. Richard C. Owen Publishing.

Golann, J. W. (2015). The paradox of success at a no-excuses school. *Sociology of Education, 88*(2), 103–119.

Goodman, J. F. (2013). Charter management organizations and the regulated environment: Is it worth the price? *Educational Researcher, 42*(2), 89–96. https://doi.org/10.3102/0013189X12470856

Grant, C. A., Brown, K. D., & Brown, A. L. (2016). *Black Intellectual Thought in Education: The Missing Traditions of Anna Julia Cooper, Carter G. Woodson, and Alain LeRoy Locke*. Routledge.

Green, K. (2014). Doing double dutch methodology: Playing with the practice of participant observer. In D. Paris & M. T. Winn (Eds.), *Humanizing research: Decolonizing qualitative inquiry with youth and communities* (pp. 147–160). SAGE Publications, Inc. https://doi.org/10.4135/9781544329611

Gutiérrez, K. D., Baquedano-López, P., & Tejeda, C. (1999). Rethinking diversity: Hybridity and hybrid language practices in the third space. *Mind, Culture, and Activity, 6*(4), 286–303.

Haraway, D. (1991). A cyborg manifesto: Science, technology, and socialist-feminism in the late twentieth century. In *Simians, cyborgs and women: The reinvention of nature* (pp. 149–181). Routledge.

hooks, bell. (2018). *All about love: New visions* (765th edition). William Morrow Paperbacks.

Ito, M., Horst, H. A., Baumer, S., Bittanti, M., boyd, danah, Cody, R., Stephenson, B. H., Lange, P. G., Mahendran, D., Martínez, K. Z., Pascoe, C. J., Perkel, D., Robinson, L., Sims, C., Tripp, L., Antin, J., Finn, M., Law, A., Manion, A., … Yardi, S. (2013). *Hanging out, messing around, and geeking out: Kids living and learning with new media*. The MIT Press.

Ito, M., Martin, C., Pfister, R. C., Rafalow, M. H., Salen, K., & Wortman, A. (2019). *Affinity online: How connection and shared interest fuel learning*. New York University Press.

Koro-Ljungberg, M., MacLure, M., & Ulmer, J. (2018). D...a...t...a..., Data++, Data, and some problematics. In N. K. Denzin & Y. S. Lincoln (Eds.), *The SAGE handbook of qualitative research* (5th ed., pp. 462–484). SAGE Publications, Inc.

Krueger, P. (2010). It's not just a method! The epistemic and political work of young people's lifeworlds at the school–prison nexus. *Race, Ethnicity and Education, 13*(3), 383–408. https://doi.org/10.1080/13613324.2010.500846

Ladson-Billings, G. (2006). From the achievement gap to the education debt: Understanding achievement in U.S. schools. *Educational Researcher, 35*(7), 3–12.

Lesko, N., & Niccolini, A. (2016). Historicizing affect in education. *Knowledge Cultures, 4*(2), 19–35. Academic OneFile.

Love, B. (2019). *We want to do more than survive: Abolitionist teaching and the pursuit of educational rreedom* (Illustrated edition). Beacon Press.

Milner, H. R. (2007). Race, culture, and researcher positionality: Working through dangers seen, unseen, and unforeseen. *Educational Researcher, 36*(7), 388–400.

Morrison, T. (1992). *Playing in the dark: Whiteness and the literary imagination*. University of Chicago Press.

Petrovic, J. E., & Kuntz, A. M. (2018). Invasion, alienation, and imperialist nostalgia: Overcoming the necrophilous nature of neoliberal Schools. *Educational Philosophy & Theory, 50*(10), 957–969. https://doi.org/10.1080/00131857.2016.1198249

Ramlow, T. R. (2004). Bad boys: Abstractions of difference and the politics of youth "deviance." In S. Maira, E. Soep, & G. Lipsitz (Eds.), *Youthscapes: The Popular, the National, the Global* (pp. 229–251). University of Pennsylvania Press.

ross, kihana miraya. (2020). Black space in education: (Anti)blackness in schools and the afterlife of segregation. In C. A. Grant, A. Woodson, & M. Dumas (Eds.), *The future is Black: Afropessimism, fugitivity, and radical hope in education* (pp. 47–54). Routledge.

Soja, E. W. (1996). *Thirdspace: Journeys to Los Angeles and other real-and-imagined places* (1st Edition). Blackwell Publishers.

Sokolower, J. (2018). Schools and the new Jim Crow: An interview with Michelle Alexander. In D. Watson, J. Hagopian, & W. Au (Eds.), *Teaching for Black lives* (pp. 237–242). Rethinking Schools.

Solorzano, D. G. (1997). Images and words that wound: Critical race theory, racial stereotyping, and teacher education. *Teacher Education Quarterly, 24*(3), 5–19.

Squire, K. (2008). Chapter Seven: Critical education in an interactive age. *Counterpoints, 338*, 105–123.

Squire, K. (2010). From information to experience: Place-based augmented reality games as a model for learning in a globally networked society. *Teachers College Record, 112*(10), 2565–2602.

Steinkuehler, C. A. (2005). The new third place: Massively multiplayer online gaming in American youth culture. *Tidskrift Journal of Research in Teacher Education, 3*, 135–150.

Stornaiuolo, A., & Whitney, E. H. (2018). Writing as worldmaking. *Language Arts, 95*(4), 205–217.

Terlouw, K. (2011). From thick to thin regional identities? *Geojournal, 77*(5), 707–721. https://doi.org/10.1007/s10708-011-9422-x

Thomas, E. E., & Stornaiuolo, A. (2016). Restorying the self: Bending toward textual justice. *Harvard Educational Review; Cambridge, 86*(3), 313–338, 473.

Tuitt, F. A., & Carter, D. J. (2008). Negotiating atmospheric threats and racial assaults in predominantly white educational institutions. *Journal of Public Management & Social Policy, 14*(2), 51–68.

Vaught, S. E. (2012). Institutional racist melancholia: A structural understanding of grief and power in schooling. *Harvard Educational Review, 82*(1), 52–77.

Villenas, S. A. (1996). The colonizer/colonized Chicana ethnographer: Identity, marginalization, and co-optation in the field. *Harvard Educational Review, 66*(4), 711–731.

Villenas, S. A. (2019). Pedagogies of being with: Witnessing, testimonio, and critical love in everyday social movement. *International Journal of Qualitative Studies in Education, 32*(2), 151–166. https://doi.org/10.1080/09518398.2018.1533148

Woodson, A. (2020). Afropessimism for us in education. In C. A. Grant, A. Woodson, & M. Dumas (Eds.), *The future is Black: Afropessimism, fugitivity, and radical hope in education* (pp. 16–21). Routledge.

Zembylas, M. (2018). The entanglement of decolonial and posthuman perspectives: Tensions and implications for curriculum and pedagogy in higher education. *Parallax, 24*(3), 254–267.

Chapter 7

Academic Misfits

De/Constructing Academic Un/Belonging through Guardians of the Galaxy

Hannah Ruth Stohry, Miami University, Noella Binda Niati, University of South Carolina, and Jennifer Lynn Doyle, University of South Carolina.

GAMORA: "It's called Knowhere. The severed head of an ancient celestial being. Be wary headed in, rodent. There are no regulations whatsoever here."

GAMORA: "Hundreds of years ago, the Tivan Group sent workers in to mine the organic matter within the skull. Bone, brain tissue, spinal fluid. All rare resources, highly valued in black markets across the galaxy. It's dangerous and illegal work, suitable only for outlaws."

STAR LORD: "Well, I come from a planet of outlaws. Billy the Kid, Bonnie and Clyde, John Stamos."

DRAX: "Sounds like a place which I would like to visit."

STAR LORD: "Yeah, you should."

To: [16 Undisclosed recipients]
From: Jennifer Doyle
Date: Monday, April 6, 2020 @ 8:36PM EST
Subject: Holding Space Happy Hour Hangout -
             Freedom to Just BE

Hey friends! :)

As an educator trying (often struggling) to navigate these new virtual spaces, I have been pondering the following two questions:

How do we hold space for others?
How do we hold space for ourselves?

I've been holding these virtual spaces for fellow educators, and I figured it was about time to hold this space for friends, and not just on some work shit.

No pressure if you can't make it! Open invite. Come (or don't) for as little or as long as you'd like. It's just a deliberate space to come together in community, support & uplift one another, express how UGH this whole thing is, and just BE. Whatever we are, whatever we are feeling, however we show up. Just hanging out with one another for an hour. Holding space for one another. Connecting & loving during this time of social distancing. (Or even just being a silent participant hanging out in the space).

Plus, it's always great to link up with other amazing women across time / space. Spread the word, or don't :) Zoom link info is below. Do not feel obligated or pressured to join. No apologies needed if you want to back out last minute. I'm just holding space & extending the invitation.

Dr. Jen Doyle (she/her) is inviting you to a scheduled Zoom meeting.

Topic: Holding Space Happy Hour
Time: Apr 7, 2020 6:00 PM Eastern Time (US and Canada)

Join Zoom Meeting
http://www.zoom.us

Love you all!
Jen

Introduction:
There Are No Regulations Whatsoever Here

Sonya Renee Taylor (2018), in her book, *The Body is Not an Apology: The Power of Radical Self-Love*, stated that "there are times when our unflinching honesty, vulnerability, and empathy will create a transformative portal, an opening to a completely new way of living" (p. xi). During spring 2020, amidst the beginning of the global pandemic, the authors—three young womyn[1] scholars, assumed academic misfits—were brought together in such a rare portal, allowing for the de/construction of un/belonging in the academy during "Holding Space Happy Hour" every Tuesday evening from April–June 2020.

Drawing upon Boveda and Bhattacharya's (2019) perspective of love as a de/colonial onto-epistemology (ways of being and ways of knowing), along with Sonya Renee Taylor's (2018) call for radical self-love, we consider how popular culture comic/film franchises like *Guardians of the Galaxy* (Gunn, 2014) in the *Marvel Cinematic Universe* have opened our minds and imaginations to possibilities of futures that de/colonize and de/construct traditional notions of reality and productions of knowledge. Acknowledging the ways in which universities remain a place where "legitimate knowledge" is established and maintained (Córdova, 1998), function as hegemonic structure (dominant cultural body), an "apartheid of knowledge" is sustained (Delgado Bernal & Villalpando, 2002), and pop culture remains contained as other than/nothing but "legitimate" knowledge, we draw upon *Guardians of the Galaxy* as an active display of resistance to such notions. Utilizing the characters from the movie (as an unconventional yet worthy band of misfit superheroes) we as young womyn scholars co-construct a collective onto-epistemological understanding of becoming and un/belonging in our curricular bodies and in the academy writ large through our three interwoven narratives as academic misfits.

Our journey began each Tuesday night in spring 2020, during "Holding Space Happy Hour." Like the mining colony of Knowhere in *Guardians of the Galaxy*, it was a place for outlaws. For us to just be. There were no regulations whatsoever in Holding Space Happy Hour. For us to just be. Free. While there was a range of womyn who participated each week, all three authors were the only three womyn who attended consistently every week. While Hannah (Ph.D. student, almost Ph.D. Candidate at the time) had never actually met Binda (Ph.D. Candidate about to defend her dissertation at the time) or Jen (a recent Ph.D. graduate) in real life, we all spoke freely, openly, and honestly about our struggles during the pandemic and in our careers as professional womyn. We spoke deeply about self-care, the need to care for ourselves, and the foreign concept that self-care actually was to us.

"So, I did my nails and a face mask on Sunday; how the fuck am I supposed to self-care the rest of the week?!" Binda asked us in April.

We were all perplexed. We took care of everyone else. What did self-care even look like? Especially for us as academic misfits?

Framing Our Work:
Mining the Organic Matter

Academic institutional structures and cultural norms are not sustainable for the human souls of many; thus we move to blend our theoretical and methodological orientation. Our future success (measured on academic terms, since our professional lives surround the academy) is dependent on (not) conforming to 24/7 end-all-be-all academic onto-epistemology. As junior scholars, we question what is knowledge, and who gets to decide it? We situate the body and lived experience as curriculum in the fashion of Baszile's work (2006; 2009) on curriculum theorizing, in which we also situate our bodies and lived experiences as sites of legitimate knowledge.

We also rely on Baszile's (2006; 2019) refusal to have the mind, body, and spirit colonized through the scholarly act of writing. Referencing Indigenous scholar-activist Russell Means, Baszile (2019) framed writing "as a way of thinking, of narrating and of circulating ideas about the world—[it] plays a central role in colonization, and I would add enslavement and other forms of racial subjection" (p. 12). We understand writing and theorizing is a form of liberation, but "it fulfills this function only when we ask that it do so and direct our theorizing towards this end" (hooks, 1991, p. 2). Baszile (2019) further critically outlined how academic writing not only liberates but re-produces institutional scholarly standards of gate-kept meaningless colonial writing that requires re-writing. Our bodies and experiences are curriculum, and are read by others as evolving curriculum, or text. The bodies are different, but the process of accepting, negotiating, and being the "academic misfit" is very similar. The process and being of "academic misfit" shifts, but the desires to be (or not) also shift.

bell hooks' (1991) ideas of over-theorizing and under-theorizing, form our onto-epistemological perspective. What is the first thing that pops to mind when thinking about what a "misfit" means? What does the stream of consciousness of word association bring to mind? One is not like the rest? Doesn't fit? Outsider? Outlier? Outcast? *Out?* Transgressor? Traitor? Is it real? Is it projected? You get to decide. Being (and not being) academic misfits is our theoretical framework, within, and outside the traditional classroom, as "any theory that cannot be shared in everyday conversation cannot be used to educate the public" (hooks, 1991, p. 5). We struggle and trouble the notion that we HAVE to write (and be, and know, and do) in academic fashion, because we also understand that our work should be accessible and more reflective of the human (and not super-human, nor sub-human) experience, as *we* theorize/live.

We theorize that we as misfits conform to normative standards of living/being/knowing/doing, yet we do not conform. We reject and accept the proud moniker of "academic misfit," theorizing that by the act of rejecting/accepting, we are the theory, that our bodies *are* theory and produce theory; we are the theory and practice of academic and personal un-doing. We consider curriculum theorizing dangerous (Baszile, 2006), in that the ways in which we resist/negotiate our bodies as misfits, is un/belonging.

We situate comic books and superhero literatures as legitimate knowledge, and points of educational inquiry. Science fiction stories have significant potential in revealing the human condition and "has been used as a metaphor and as an illustration of human culture by researchers in fields that are not restricted to studies of science fiction literature...science fiction is employed as a lens through which human culture may be viewed to discover new interpretations" (Menadue & Cheer, 2017, p. 13). In this particular chapter, we are utilizing *Guardians of the Galaxy*, a Marvel movie based on comic books featuring multiple characters like Peter Quill (also known as Star-Lord) who is half-human half-god (spoiler alert, this is a truth we learn from *Guardians of the Galaxy Vol. 2*); Drax the Destroyer (intergalactic criminal); Gamora (assassin and adopted daughter of Thanos); Groot (large tree-like character); and Rocket (genetically modified raccoon-looking creature). Disney+ channel description of the movie describes the characters as misfits and we draw loosely personal comparisons to some characters in the following sections. We utilize *Guardians of the Galaxy* storyline content as based on our interpretations and *connections*, where a band of unlikely characters from multiple species brought together by Star-Lord trying to retrieve an orb (with mysterious worth, later revealed to be the Power Infinity Stone, powerful enough to kill any organic being). Rocket and Groot attempt to collect a bounty by capturing Star-Lord. Gamora tries to steal the orb from Star-Lord in order to prevent Ronan the Accuser (working for/with her father Thanos) from committing genocide on the planet Xandar. They are brought together by being collectively jailed, thus meeting Drax in Kyln (prison), who wants to kill Gamora for her father's influence on his family being killed by Ronan. These unlikely characters become a crew out of necessity, and (spoiler alert) eventually save the remainder of Xandar from Ronan's evil genocidal attempts.

The following sections outline how we each conceptualize our onto-epistemological understandings of being academic misfits (using social stratifiers like gender and race, as well as lived experiences), our un/belonging in the world and in academia, the apartheid of knowledge that exists because of the traditional notions of curriculum pedagogy, and our understandings of critical and radical love of ourselves, one another, and of our communities.

"You Said it Yourself, Bitch.
We're the Guardians of the Galaxy"

CUE THE MUSIC:

I'm an alligator, I'm a mama-papa coming for you

I'm the space invader, I'll be a rock 'n' rollin' bitch for you

Keep your mouth shut, you're squawking like a pink monkey bird

And I'm busting up my brains for the words

Keep your 'lectric eye on me babe

Put your ray gun to my head

Press your space face close to mine, love

Freak out in a moonage daydream oh yeah. (Bowie, 1972)

I, Hannah, orient to this project and life work as someone who is a fan (not quite worthy of the mainstream "nerd" status) of Marvel movies, or any superhero movies, as a "read as white[2]" female whose body (metaphorically?) invades spaces that makes others uncomfortable (Puwar, 2004). As an academic. And as a student of life in a broader curricular landscape. I view my body as full of stories, a body that likes to immerse in *music* (like I just shared—side note: the official soundtrack playlist for *Guardians of the Galaxy* is incredible), fictional stories and AfroAsian Imaginations (Stohry & Jackson, 2019); my body is one that theorizes and actualizes resisting bodies/brains like mine appearing and belonging in multiple storied universes and futures.

I have always *known*/felt, on some deep (mind/body/spiritual) level, that I didn't belong in most spaces. As a military kid, my norm was moving through time and space, weaving through multiple multicultural universes, not quite belonging in any of them. Still. This is quite a common embodiment for Third Culture Kids (TCKs) who grow up (during developmental years) outside of their passport country and live in a third culture that is described as one not fully owning the parent's nor the host's cultures, a shared cultural experience of *belonging everywhere yet nowhere* (Pollock, Van Reken, & Pollock, 2017) (like Gamora and Nebula, the adopted/captured daughters of Thanos being situated as useful for Thanos). It is what it is; this is my accepted reality. A perpetual state/feeling I have. As a multicultural, global, Third Culture Kid, mixed race Korean-American woman, I've navigated a lot of spaces and have had enough experiences to know this. It's so deeply and onto-epistemologically embedded in my ambiguous "read as White," sometimes olive skin. It's this idea that I don't belong, and even causes me to normalize this questioning of my onto-epistemologies (ways of being and knowing). For many, we know that it is a state of belonging, that may be imposed by others, and even ourselves.

> I constantly shift positions—which means taking into account ideological remolinos (whirlwind), cultural dissonance, and the convergence of competing worlds. It means dealing with the fact that I, like most people, inhabit different cultures and, when crossing to other mundos, shift into and out of perspectives corresponding to each; it means living in liminal spaces, in nepantlas. (Anzaldúa, 2015, p. 3)

Just as the nepantlera (shape-shifter) that Anzaldúa (2015) describes, young academics like us have adapted to be pliable for our own ethical pedagogy and practice. Or, some of us have adapted to merely survive, to our own detriment and at the risk of soul loss.

My favorite social worker Dr. Brené Brown (2017) theorizes/practices belonging, beginning from her process of understanding Maya Angelou's wise truths: "You are only free when you realize you belong no place—you belong every place—no place at all. The price is high. The reward is great" (p. 26). Brown's (2017) work moves into defining belonging (as a quest and paradox):

> True belonging is the spiritual practice of believing in and belonging to yourself so deeply that you can share your most authentic self with the world and find sacredness in both being a part of something and standing alone in the wilderness. (p. 40)

Brown (2017) further outlined that true belonging is not something that you negotiate externally; it's what you carry in your heart. (p. 41)

I struggled as an undergraduate, for SO many reasons. I struggled in both of my Master's programs for SO many reasons, coupled with monoracial people (despite multicultural and international contexts) projecting monoracial identity, meaning that I internalized that I didn't know anything (much less about myself). Some of the time I feel like an imposter, a fraud, illegitimate, invisible unless performing (Nebula's entire existence is to out-perform and defeat her sister Gamora...just to be seen). Much of this belonging process began in my second Master's program, with voluntarily going through a Mindfulness-Based Stress Reduction (MBSR) program, coupled with amazing bad@$$ Practicum mentors, leading into my professional life after the program, as a social worker being lovingly led by bad@$$ womyn teaching me about belonging, self-love, acceptance, in applicable ways that I had never experienced before, and *never* in the traditional classroom. Teaching me to be a good therapist taught me how to better care for myself, advocate for my self in ways that I had never done before. Because *I matter*.

I knew what I didn't like about the conditionality of collegiality and feeling a lack of academic support (positivistic and conditional, based on hobnobbing and "who do you know?" and "what can you do for me?") in both of my Master's programs (Gamora and Nebula had so much power they wielded by being associated with their "adoptive" father Thanos). Going into my Ph.D. program, I knew what I did(n't) want, and courageously and vulnerably asked for those things related to my interpersonal support and academic goals. In my initial "interview" with my now 3+ year assistantship relationship with my boss, and in my first Advising meeting, I finally had language to advocate for myself. Thankfully, both of these people have values that align with mine, that of collaboration and mutual trust. They helped cultivate my foundation for a reality of belonging, in ways that make sense for me, within my own limitations and potentials. This is not common, I am told, for most graduate students (nor for the Guardians of the Galaxy). I practice gratitude every day that I am supported, and challenged; my dissertation committee is a hand-selected group of bad@$$ womyn who help me reinforce that *my work is valuable and important*. As someone who is multiracial, I am finding that I must continuously and explicitly situate myself to justify my multiracial identity work, and how I show up in academic spaces. I am in flux, determining how to really queer that assumed White identity because I am read as White and the confusion surrounding mixed-ness as well as my Asian-ness. It has not been my experience that the academic majority can hold my Third Culture Kid-ness, or all of my overlapping boundary-crossing existence. Being it and experiencing it really solidifies the un-belonging. So, I work to belong within, and with others who "get it."

On the one hand, Brown (2017) gets me to think that "belonging to ourselves means being called to stand alone—to brave the wilderness of uncertainty, vulnerability, and criticism" (p. 32). I think that this is important when it comes to belonging within, especially in academic settings, where I (un)consciously push myself to exercise vulnerability in dominant spaces where belonging is not facilitated, and I am under-valued and under-estimated (Rocket is underestimated because of his size and inter-species hybridization). I feel a lot of courage, because I am supported by academic and personal support (and many of my colleagues tell me that this is uncommon to be as supported as I am). Any fear I have about my own skills, abilities, truths, are a result of socialization, internalization and embodiment of false truths, and systems maintenance (all Guardians internalized their own strengths and weaknesses as a result of their own lived experiences). So, I am in an ongoing process of internalizing my own un/belonging within myself, and in spaces I share with others (with other self-identified misfits or Guardians who call me in and out), and intentionally dis-connecting myself from toxic academic situations. I know that there is a lot of privilege that comes with being able to un/belong to dominant unjust structures and embodiments, because I know that so many communities do not have the option to resist without significant consequences. We still have agency, but there are levels. Just want to make that clear. The academy cannot and will not own my heart and soul.

I am and can be my own Guardian. I choose which galaxies I enter, and I choose when I leave. I connect this idealized state/trait of being to the definitions of belonging everywhere, yet nowhere that I mentioned above. This is a lens, and an embodiment of academic misfit or Guardian status. It is a theory and practice. It is a process and an outcome. And, I can choose to re-define on my terms, because like the Guardians, I have learned that this is not only safest for my survival, but the most life-giving ways in which I am allowed to be me. I have had the privilege of being able to explore my own onto-epistemological shift of being an intentional academic misfit and negotiating my own belonging, but I realize that this is not explicitly taught. The Guardians didn't have a guidebook for what it meant to address their own un-belonging as individuals and as a community that was brought together as a result. As scholars who have teaching experience, we must understand that "belonging in the classroom is not a Student Affairs issue, it is a pedagogical issue" (Baszile & Muhammed, 2020). During a global COVID-19 pandemic, racial uprisings in the U.S., universal chaos and unrest, we must consider and adapt ways of belonging for our selves and those around us, because we cannot survive alone. And, we are responsible for those around us, especially our students. Regardless of paeon status as rising scholars, we hold a lot of power in shifting what this means in our classrooms. In the classroom of life, we wield power to shift consciousness. Period. But, more specifically, we wield power to shift consciousness to shed light on the structures of power that relegate many graduate students, graduate students of color, women, and BIPOC graduate students (we see that no Guardians character holds the same identity and each has their own unique needs) to a purgatory of misfit un-belonging and not being good enough. We wield consciousness of belonging, as a deliberate move to un-belong to the norm of division, binaries, and dominant constructions of rigid onto-epistemologies. Through "Holding Space Happy Hour," we wielded un-belonging from the academy and fostered belonging amongst ourselves. We redefined "academic misfit" and joined forces to fill in the blanks that the academy cannot, does not, and will not. In many ways, we have talked about our educator experiences (with all learners in our lives) where we have infused our own un-belonging and efforts to connect and hold space, because our values are an extension of us.

As a graduate student (and person), I'm coming into my own when it comes to my own agency navigating and determining for myself what kind of a misfit I want to be (if I want to be one), and where/ when I want to belong (also understanding the privileges that come along with being a mixed-race person who is read as White). I represent almost every *Guardians of the Galaxy* character, but I will name a few: Rocket, hybridized machine/animal (I'm mixed race); Groot, a growing/living being who is eventually linguistically understood (I speak more than just English); Nebula, the rejected daughter of Thanos, robot machine pitted against her own sister Gamora; and Star-Lord (Peter Quill), half-human, half-god (I'm mixed Asian-White Korean-American), trying to make his way through the universes, trying to lead and be the author of his own life. I see myself in each character, and see how all of the characters band together, each whole and fit in their own right. As a whole, and especially in the academy, it is so easy to see people as parts of a whole, rather than whole. And, it's almost as if we make every effort to push people away, hungry for power and guardianship over work that is almost always collaborative. What we miss out on is true human connection and belonging by maintaining those systems. Therefore, we need to be our own superheroes, as cunning and crafty as the Guardians (before they even owned their moniker and knew they were a team) when they orchestrated a misfit prison break from planet Kyln, each character quickly improvising (relying on their unique strengths) in order to each achieve their goal of not being resigned to prison life. We do this to live. And not just survive.

As burgeoning scholars (and humans), we utilize methods of taking back power, but some have similar outcomes like Drax, when his attempts to avenge the murders of his family left him bruised and left for close-to-dead at the hands of Ronan. There are many mediating devices that promote a form of agency (and identity formation) that we utilize in our figured worlds (Holland et al., 1998). Let's consider belonging as a state, as a form of being, and trait, as a predisposition. I know it when I feel it. As my body moves throughout space. I know it as I intentionally facilitate this, as best as I can. I use this example to help us consider how we make sense of what it means to be an academic misfit, and how we know we do(n't) belong. State and trait inform each other. The Guardians' act of resistance in Kyln (and subsequent figured worlds), both as a state and trait, is what really solidifies their first (non-normative) team efforts. On many levels, I feel like I am very in tune and have such a deep self-awareness that I can sense when I am projected to be an academic misfit, and when I am intentionally owning my academic mis-fitting. I relate this to belonging, I *know* when I don't belong, and I *know* when I choose not to belong (especially in soul-sucking places). We facilitate this same thing with those that learn with us, including students we work with, and each other. We praise each other for asserting our agency, and conspire to keep up this academic naughtiness.

Who gets to decide if we belong (in academia) or not (whenever Star-Lord or Peter Quill tried to do his own thing, his Ravagers group pointed out the conditionality of his belonging, that he was Terran, or of Earth/Terra)? What are the conditions that determine this? How much of *me* goes into that process and structure of understanding my agency in knowledge, being, and doing? There is already an inherent truth that comes from being someone who navigates the world, much like a nepantlera, who understands that barriers and boundaries exist to keep people in or out, and people like us belong in all yet sometimes none of those spaces. There are inherent politics that come with transgressing boundaries, like what it means to act/be perceived as a race traitor (Ignatiev & Garvey, 1996). The problem is that we do not always agree on these constructed boundaries, and that the lines get re-defined dependent on context/interest convergence (Bell, Jr., 1980). So, becoming an academic misfit looks different for each person.

To demonstrate the power of a collective of academic misfits who denounce oppressive and hegemonic academic structures, I will share a scene from *Guardians of the Galaxy*. When the Guardians are able to thrillingly wrest the Infinity Stone from Ronan, Star-Lord catches the Infinity Stone and absorbs its full shock, hand-in-hand with Gamora, Rocket, and Drax.

> *Ronan stares in disbelief and says to Star-Lord "You're mortal. How?"*

> *Star-Lord squarely responds with: "You said it yourself, bitch. We're the Guardians of the Galaxy."*

The Guardians proceed to protect the Infinity Stone and save the remainder of Xandar's planet. Ronan underestimated Star-Lord and the fellow Guardians (and even mistaking Star-Lord as fully human, which resonates with lil ol' Korean and American me) and justice ruled in the end. Much in the ways that Binda and Jen and I (Hannah) came together over shared experiences of feeling like misfits, either by sharing Third Culture Kid experiences, womyn experiences, Marvel Cinematic Universe love, and academic experiences, we have been and are stronger together. While we are uniquely positioned as academic misfits in our own academic institutions, we each claim and re-position ourselves. We each facilitate our own inherent belonging within and outside the classroom, and model this as inspired by becoming our own and each other's Guardians of this galaxy in which we live.

We resist because we must. *We belong.* At the risk of sounding dramatic, soul loss at the hands of a colonial academy that insists owning our onto-epistemologies (ways of being and knowing), our belonging, and the ways in which we write, is a devastating consequence. We legitimate ourselves by owning the self-imposed label "academic misfit" because it frees us to come as we are, in radical acceptance. Our refusals (in my case) to perform to written academic standards (citation of every living idea, and the audacity to centralize science fiction storylines and characters) means that I am using writing to resist academic writing as playing "a central role in colonization" (Baszile, 2019, p. 12). In my personal scholarship, centralizing and bringing forth my biracial identity, and disrupting Whitened monoracial academic scholarship dominance, to disrupt the reproduction of "colonialized consciousness" (Baszile, 2019, p. 13).

After Ronan was defeated, the Infinity stone contained, and the warship Dark Aster was destroyed by the Guardians, Drax reflects, "It's really Thanos I need to kill." Drax's reflection inspires us to consider a perspective shift about bigger picture meanings we attach to the state/trait "academic misfit" and the state/trait of "belonging." This may be an ongoing assessment of how we navigate our assumed identities and how we embody/create belonging within, and with others. We can ask ourselves, "Who is the self that we bring to our work/life, and what academic self do we bring? Who is the resistant self, the resting self, the realistic self, the real self, the self? What does a perspective shift mean for the ways in which we learn, educate, belong, and *live*? In what ways have I already gained from a perspective shift?" hooks (2009) inspires me to consider belonging as a form of communion, not just with self, but with the people that we have in our community of care. These are the people that feed into us, not just as fellow junior scholars, but the people that are the connected extensions of who we are, and who we want to be. We have metaphorically agreed on our own strategic "the Dark Aster must not reach the ground. Locked in" collective anthem of belonging and community.

I have already internalized that I am only an (academic) misfit because I've recognized the ways in which learning/teaching/producing is not linear, and that I don't want to be linearly located. I have already internalized that I am worthy of not only being an academic misfit (in community with my chosen family of academic misfits), but that I am worthy of belonging, within and with others. It is both a process and an outcome. These are precursors to a larger conversation of apartheid of knowledge, apartheid of being, and apartheid of doing, perhaps calling on a larger Milano (Guardians' ship) full of other academic misfits in any universe, to facilitate belonging and co-construction of and growing agentive authors of our own living, being, doing, and *knowing*, because, "Bitch, we're the Guardians of the Galaxy."

"All Words are Made Up"

I thought by eliminating half of life, the other half would thrive. But you've shown me, that's impossible. And as long as there are those that remember what was, there will always be those that are unable to accept what can be. They will resist.

Thanos to the Avengers (Avengers: Endgame, 2019)

We live in constructs; function within constructs and elevate them (or not) to our hierarchical social structures...also constructed. On their way to Nidavellir, the Guardians are helped by our prototypical hero, Thor, God of thunder and lightning. "Nidavellir?" Drax implores, "that's a made-up word!" To which Thor responds, "all words are made up." Therein welcoming us to the constructed nature of power and privilege. If our token hero, the "right" hero, admits it's all made up... then how do we destroy the infinity gauntlet or rather, academic supremacy? Is it possible to destroy the master's house with his tools? This has been my (Binda) conundrum since entering academia.

Superheroes like womyn and, specifically, womyn of color are both known and unknown, visible and invisible in hegemonized institutions. Our identities, constructed and named in multiple ways, dominate our social realities; from hyper-sexualized images, submissive, aggressive tropes to invalidation and dehumanization because the status of womyn in history has been demarcated between the public and the private, womyn of color become the embodiment of the fusion of these two binaries. Their bodily lives are debased, sexualized, and/or animalized, while their economic and political lives are berated for treading on assumed masculine roles. In a word, womyn of color are misfits and, too, the *Guardians of the Galaxy*; their womanhood challenges and protects liberation, their color contextualizes feminism, and within academia, their scholastic output; sidelined, diminished, and/or co-opted.

In this sense, Womyn of Color (WOC) are the Gamoras and Rockets of the world. Unlike the accepted privileged superheroes to which we are accustomed, Gamora, kidnapped from her home planet and raised by a tyrant, is both daughter and prisoner, wanted and unwanted, seen and unseen. Rocket is viewed as a monster, trapped in a world that does not accept him. So he lashes out in unconventional ways; to be seen, to be heard, and to be respected (LeRose, 2019). Despite their positions, these two made do, persisted, planned, and dreamt. As women of color in academia, our presence in academia is both wanted and unwanted. We are good for certain statistics but irate our administrations (Jivraj, 2020). And yet...we persist. Our existence is resistance and, therefore, troublesome and troubling.

Womyn of color in academia are both visible and invisible. And for Black womyn in academia, this assumption is acute as they are made to be invisible within their departments and simultaneously made visible to support institutional diversification agendas. "Of all groups," Wilson (2012) writes, "as bona fide intellectuals, [African American womyn] are the furthest removed from society's expectations of their place, the least expected to succeed on merit, and the most vulnerable to insult" (p. 65). I am at once expected to serve and thrive in an institution that fails to appreciate and/or recognize my service (p. 71). The odds, it seems, are against me. Do I fall in line with accepted academic tropes and pray for tenure? Or, do I create space for misfit academic norms and pray for tenure? Is it not the point, as Dei (2016) asserts, that subversive work centering on decolonization is about radical inclusion (p. 29)?

Traditional superhero tropes usually present a White, cis-gendered man, who saves the world and gets the girl. Much as in academia, there are pronouncements of equality, democracy and centralized organization promoting all scholars. In practice, what we see in both the *Guardians of the Galaxy* and academia is a system that is "rigidly hierarchical and rarely democratic" (Beale, 1970, p. 102). Recent scholars writing about decolonizing academia (Dei, 2016; Mignolo & Walsh, 2018; Jivraj, 2020) consider how academia is oppressive, limiting and castizing, as such scholars of color must create "fissures, cracks" (Jivraj,

2020, p. 564) or safe spaces within the architecture as a means of re-defining and resignifying (p. 566). Educational institutions are places that both challenge hegemony and are also complicit in perpetuating inequality (McLaren, 2017). Delgado Bernal and Villalpando (2002) argue that an "apartheid of knowledge"—that is the segregation of faculty across institutions and academic departments, "marginalizes, discredits, and devalues the scholarship, epistemologies, and other cultural resources of faculty of color" (p. 169). This is due in part to a "Eurocentric epistemology" (p. 170) based on White privilege and ideals of meritocracy, objectivity, and individuality that are espoused in lieu of a non-majoritarian epistemology. Because institutions of higher education are founded on these ideals, the hidden hegemonic curriculum—that is, the "political, economic, and cultural system in which Whites overwhelmingly control power and material resources" (p. 171) reigns supreme as academics of color clamor for legitimacy and a seat at the scholastic table.

> STAR LORD: "I look around at us and you know what I see? Losers. I mean, like, folks who have lost stuff. And we have. Man, we have. All of us. Our homes. Our families. Normal lives. And usually, life takes more than it gives. But not today. Today, it's giving us something. It is giving us a chance."

> DRAX: "To do what?"

> STAR LORD: "To give a shit, for once, and not run away."

Karen Barad (2008) challenged us to understand how matter mat-ters, stating that "matter comes to matter through the iterative in-tra-activity of the world in its becoming…the issue is the conjoined material-discursive nature of constraints, conditions, and practices" (p. 140). Through this discussion, we hope to take pride in our unique-ness, womynness, and prowess…aka: we matter and we give a shit. And, recognizing our worth and giving a shit, that is, decolonizing academia, is an affronting declaration.

Decolonization, Fanon (1963) wrote, is almost always a violent process, one that leads to "total disorder…Decolonization is truly the creation of new men…The thing colonized becomes a man through the very process of liberation" (p. 2). Decolonization is both internal and external; the creation of new men, read: the liberated individual, can cause total disorder. Academia has for too long straddled a paradox that both uplifts and disempowers. Institutions of higher education pay lip service to diversity and equality, hiring faculty of color, Deans or C-list executives for newly created Diversity offices while simultaneously denying tenure to faculty of color or questioning their theoretical or methodological output as lacking rigour for a given subject. Academia, much like the *Guardians of the Galaxy*, exemplifies the many obstacles one faces in the quest for liberation. Though touting themselves as places of democratic and scientific expression, institutions of higher education continue to perpetuate racist, capitalistic systems that benefit few while harming most. How does a scholar of color navigate such a space? Is academia a suitable enclave for scholars of color? Seen as both fugitives and heroes, the Guardians of the Galaxy realized they could not live in one place and instead sought a life as freedom fighters. Once liberated from their oppressive space and state, the Guardians sought to liberate others, one planet at a time. Much like the Guardians, academics of color (be they rising graduate students or faculty), must undergo a double liberation; liberation from a European epistemology within the self and a liberation within the patriarchal and capitalist assumptions inherent within academia.

Society places value on certain types of knowledge; what is considered acceptable, rigorous and valid or true. And, universities function as a co-signer of what values are lauded or shunned. The "ghettoization" of faculty of color and their scholarship discredits and ignores the epistemologies of faculty of color and "isolates our contributions and scholarship, rendering our knowledge to the margins" (Delgado Bernal and Villalpando, 2002, p. 171). This ghettoization is a result of the "racialized double standard" inherent in Eurocentric epistemologies that privileges Whiteness as the norm. Thus, any discourse that departs from this norm is therefore devalued and subordinated (p. 171). Lastly, as tenure and promotion are significantly weighted on publications, professors of color risk their work being discredited if their work does not ascribe to accepted theoretical and methodological frameworks and is not published in the "right" journals and publishers.

Academia espouses liberal ideals while internally participates in the oppression of its faculty of color. Can we, like the *Guardians of the Galaxy*, choose to navigate within hierarchical mediums to find empowerment, dismantle these mediums, or leave? Are these the only option? How can academics of color liberate themselves from that which is rarely discussed among the supposed liberal faculty? If decolonization is always violent, then what sort of warfare must academics of color wage in order to liberate ourselves? Are we willing to do so? And, how do we go about leveling our position as womyn of color; misfits, and/or allies as a challenging body? Is this possible? Or, must we find our sources of support outside of academia? I end with Audre Lorde's (1984) anticolonial pronouncement as a means to illustrate our attempts to navigate and decolonize academia:

> Those of us who stand outside the circle of this society's definition of acceptable women; those of us who have been forged in the crucibles of difference—those of us who are poor, who are lesbians, who are Black, who are older—know that survival is not an academic skill. It is learning how to take our differences and make them strengths. For the master's tools will never dismantle the master's house. They may allow us temporarily to beat him at his own game, but they will never enable us to bring about genuine change. And this fact is only threatening to those women who still define the master's house as their only source of support. (p. 111)

Misfits, assemble.

"I'm no Family to Ronan or Thanos"

STAR LORD: "He was the only family I had."

GAMORA: "Not anymore."

My (Jen's) journey as an academic misfit differs greatly from my co-authors. Like Gamora, I am an assassin. I have been trained to kill by the academy and by institutions in my Whiteness. I have been trained to use my White skin, my White body, and my White womynhood in manipulative and deadly ways (Matias, 2020), similar to how Thanos trained Gamora and her sister Nebula to use their bodies in manipulative and deadly ways. I have never been society's definition of an acceptable womyn—which is why I am drawn so deeply to Audre Lorde's (1984) work—but I have always appeared to be. Yet, like Gamora, I feel deeply misunderstood. Ready to betray the system that

I have benefitted deeply from.

I remember so deeply, fighting back tears the first Tuesday in May during our "Holding Space Happy Hour." Hannah had just left. She stayed for the first hour. Binda joined in the second hour. It was just the two of us left. I felt like such a failure. So inadequate. Here was Hannah, a doc student, fully supported by her mentors. Encouraged to publish. Publishing SO MUCH STUFF! With the drive and ambition to do so. And what had I done? Two years since I graduated, and not one bit closer to accomplishing anything academic-related. I wasn't a scholar. I didn't belong in the academy. The academy didn't want people like me. I refused to conform. I said "fuck" a million times in my dissertation. But I was good at being in the academy. I remembered, faintly, how beautifully loved and aligned I felt when I was writing my dissertation. My own way. Not how the academy wanted me to do it. How I wanted to do it. How it came out of me. How I layered it. I had such critical love back then, that first half of 2018. Such critical self-love.

"Critical love means owning your shit, knowing you are the shit. Simultaneously," I wrote in chapter 6. I believed that. I felt that. I had written in my dissertation the importance of critical community. How blessed I felt to be part of a critical community. No one was really a scholar though. I didn't have scholar friends, really. The thought of reading academic papers and writing academically every day did not appeal to me. I had not met many academic friends I enjoyed, despite having been around for the last six years. I felt isolated in academia, yet so at home there in my own little world.

I remember May 5, that Holding Space Happy Hour, so vividly. I was going to apply for jobs. I was reading, for the first time, The Professor is In, and realizing how very unprepared I was to be an actual scholar. No one was guiding me or mentoring me. I had mentors along the way, but they more or less hazed me. They kept pissing on me and telling me it was raining. To be thankful for the rain. But I didn't feel thankful for the rain. My work was stolen, exploited, and used in ways that were not authentic to me.

Every time I wrote something to be published as a doc student, I would send it to a professor and they would change all of my words until I knew how to write like an academic. Well, I know how to write like an academic now. And I don't fucking like it. It is constraining.

Confining. Constricting. The academy was killing me. It nearly killed me as a writer. As a thinker. The academy, like Thanos, wanted me to think like it/him. I was trained to think in its syntax, using its diction, killing my cadence and flow. My rhythm. My me.

But I was good at it. I knew how to play the games of academia because they were the games of whiteness. I was trained for these deadly battles. Forced to fight my sister. Pitted against her, made to feel falsely superior, destroying families along the way. Until, like the *Guardians of the Galaxy*, I found myself in the prison of academia, Kyln, only to discover we had been imprisoned all this time. So, we got creative about survival. We banded together. Academic misfits.

I remember May 5th so deeply because it was coming up on my two-year anniversary of my graduation. I was in tears with Binda on Zoom. I couldn't even describe what I was feeling as imposter syndrome. It was this deep sense of unbelonging. I didn't belong here in academia. I was too harsh. Too angry. Too feeling. My words were too emotional. The way I wanted to write wasn't what the editors were looking for. I was tired of "playing the game" of Whiteness. I know how to be a "good White person," a "good daughter" to Thanos, what was expected of me. But it was killing me. And if Thanos and the academy are killing me, what are they out here doing to my scholars and friends of Color?!

These systems, they kill us all. But maybe they just damage me. Because in the end, I always look like I belong. If you don't know me, I look like I belong. And, now that I've found this community of academic misfits, I do belong. And it's carried into everything else—all of my other interactions as a scholar. I literally never felt like a scholar until we became these academic misfits, these Guardians of the Galaxy, these friends. And even now, sometimes though, I am not sure I belong in the same way. I know that I shouldn't belong in the same way. The apartheid of academia isn't a lived experience for me. I am a colonizer. A trained assassin. But, I'm no family to Thanos or the academy. My fellow academic misfits, we are family now.

We Are Groot

Collectively as a group over the next several months, we pondered how to care for ourselves, for others, for our communities, and for humanity. As the weeks went by, fewer womyn returned, and the conversations between the three of us bled into our academic lives as scholars who had grown up feeling a deep sense of unbelonging, difference, and unworthiness. Organically, each Tuesday, we held space for one another. We re/imagined a universe of academia beyond the traditional binaries and boxes of curricula. We de/constructed legitimate knowledge production in favor of a collective "academic misfit" both/ and onto-epistemological understanding of the world and our un/belonging in it. We fostered a nuanced un/belonging in a space outside of academia to consider a more humanizing approach to curriculum pedagogy and practice. We became Groot. A Groot that finds beauty in chaos, a Groot that gives what it can, at times growing a beautiful flower in its palm, for any little girl that needs it.

We came together in love, and really want to facilitate and teach communities of care and love, our own Guardians or academic misfits communities (Reyes, Radina, & Aronson, 2018) as active resistance to unjust academic (and life) structures. hooks (2009) remarked that "communities of care are sustained by rituals of regard" (hooks, 2009). Watching her parents age, hooks (2009) discussed the beauty of service and provision of comfort for them. Similarly, we have reached out to each other, have challenged each other on our own care, keeping each other accountable about academic workload and work/life boundaries. In many ways, our misfit community has exercised radical love, decolonized self (ves), and promoted community-building and caregiving in ways that mirror hooks' (2009) notions that "gratitude allows us to be blessings; it prepares the ground of our being for love. And it is good to see that in the end, when all is said and done— love prevails" (p. 230). We have been, and always will be stronger, as a group, a community of misfits. As Guardians.

Much like the Guardians of the Galaxy, we all started out as competitors. All competing for the Infinity Stone, looking out for ourselves, unbelonging to the academy, imprisoned in Kyln. Until we found out that we were really just a group of losers, folx who have lost stuff. Immortal because we banded together. Guardians of the Galaxy who critically and radically love ourselves, one another, and our communities. We know that "the work is to crumble the barriers of injustice and shame leveled against us so that we might access what we have always been, because we will, if obstructed, inevitably grow into the purpose for which we were created: our own unique version of that oak tree" (Taylor, 2018, p. xii). Academic misfits.

We have re/imagined a universe of academia beyond the traditional binaries and boxes of curricula, de/constructing legitimate knowledge production in favor of a collective "academic misfit" both/ and onto-epistemological understanding of the world and our un/ belonging in it. We understand belonging as a more authentic lived experience, generating from within and centered in critical love. We have fostered nuanced belonging in spaces outside of academia to consider more than humanizing approaches to curriculum pedagogy and practice—and we encourage our readers to do the same.

We ask our readers and fellow rising scholars to consider some of the concepts of academic un/belonging, academic misfit, and decolonization of the academy for the intentional purpose of engaging in more meaningful and humane onto-epistemologies. We invite you to also consider the following questions we wrestled with: What does it mean to re-design the academic misfit / superhero mold? How do we as junior scholars re-structure curriculum, literally and figuratively, to regard our very existence as "more than" what we have been reduced to? How do we actively and metaphorically hold space? We are active community members who step up for self and others, in meaningful ways; we offer gratitude for having been able to utilize science fiction like *Guardians of the Galaxy* to de/construct and de/colonize academic un-belonging, as re/constructed academic misfits. We "give a shit," and "own our shit." We mirror Groot, in a pivotal scene, where it grows its tree-like limbs to shield all the battered Guardians when all seems lost as they plummet to the ground.

Rocket screams, "No, Groot! You can't, you'll die. Why are you doing this? Why?"

Groot knowingly *replies "We are Groot."*

Middle fingers up. Linked hands. Absorbing the full brunt force of whatever life launches at us. All systems go. Cue your music jam playlists, because "there ain't no mountain high enough…" (Ashford & Simpson, 1966).

With that, we end scene with the Guardians' last conversation from the movie:

STAR LORD: "So, what should we do next? Something good? Something bad? A bit of both?"

GAMORA: "We'll follow your lead, Star-Lord."

STAR LORD: "Bit of both!"

Notes

1. We use the term "womyn" to center our womyn experiences, acknowledge and condemn patriarchy, and as an invitation to acknowledge the expansiveness of what it means to be a womyn.
2. The use of white instead of White is a deliberate choice in an attempt to decenter whiteness.

References

Ashford, N. & Simpson, V. (1966). Ain't no mountain high enough [Song]. On *Untitled* [Album]. Tamla.

Barad, K. (2008). Queer causation and the ethics of mattering. In N. Giffney, M. J. Hird, (Eds.), *Queering the non/human* (pp. 311–338). Aldershot, Hampshire, England Burlington, Vermont: Ashgate.

Baszile, D. T., & Muhammed, A. (2020, Oct. 28). Too much schooling, too little education (Session 6). In *Crucial conversations: Education in support of the movement for Black lives* [Podcast series]. #Educate2Liberate Initiatives. Retrieved from https://www.miamioh.edu/ehs/news/2020/07/educate2liberate.html

Baszile, D. T. (2006). Rage in the interests of Black self: Curriculum theorizing as dangerous knowledge. *Journal of Curriculum Theorizing*, 89-98.

Baszile, D. T. (2019). Rewriting/recurricularlizing as a matter of life and death: The coloniality of academic writing and the challenge of black mattering therein. *Curriculum Inquiry, 49*(1), 7-24.

Beale, F. (1970). Double jeopardy: To be Black and female. In T. Cade (Ed.), *The Blackwoman: An anthology* (pp. 166-176). Mentor: New York.

Bell, Jr., D. A. (1980). Brown v. Board of Education and the interest-convergence dilemma. *Harvard Law Review, 9*, 518-533.

Boveda, M., & Bhattacharya, K. (2019). Love as de/colonial onto-epistemology: A post-oppositional approach to contextualized research ethics. *The Urban Review, 51*(1), 5–25. https://doi.org/10.1007/s11256-018-00493-z

Brown, B. (2017). *Braving the wilderness: The quest for true belonging and the courage to stand alone.* New York, NY: Random House.

Córdova, T. (1998). Power and knowledge: Colonialism in the academy. In C.M. Trujillo (Ed.), *Living Chicana Theory* (pp. 17-45). Berkeley, CA: Third Woman Press.

Dei, G. (2016). Decolonizing the University: the Challenges and Possibilities of Inclusive Education. Socialist Studies/études Socialistes, 11(1), 23-61.

Delgado Bernal, D., & Villalpando, O. (2002). An apartheid of knowledge in academia: The struggle over the "legitimate" knowledge of Faculty of Color. *Equity & Excellence in Education: University of Massachusetts School of Education Journal, 35*, 169-180.

Fanon, F. (1963). *The wretched of the earth.* New York: Grove Press, Inc.

Gunn, J. (2014). *Guardians of the galaxy* [Film]. Marvel Studios.

Gutiérrez, M. G., Niemann, Y. F., González, C. G., & Harris, A. P. (2012). *Presumed incompetent: The intersections of race and class for women in academia.* Utah: Utah State University Press.

Haack, S. (2020). Not one of the boys: Memoir of an academic misfit. *Cosmos + Taxis, 8*(6), 92- 106.

hooks, b. (1991). Theory as liberatory practice. *Yale Journal of Law and Feminism, 4*(1), 1-12.

hooks, b. (2009). *Belonging: A culture of place.* New York, NY: Routledge.

Ignatiev, N. & Garvey, J. (1996). *Race traitor.* New York, NY: Routledge.

Jivraj, S. (2020). Decolonizing the Academy: Between a Rock and a Hard Place. Interventions, 22(4), 552-573.

Lorde, A. (1984/2007). The master's tools will never dismantle the master's house. In A. Lorde's *Sister outsider: Essays and speeches* (110-114). Ed. Berkeley, CA: Crossing Press.

McLaren, P. (2017). Critical pedagogy: A look at the major concepts. In A. Darder, R. D. Torres, & M. Baltodano The critical pedagogy reader (pps. 56-78). New York, NY: Routledge.

Menadue, C. B., & Cheer, K. D. (2017). Human culture and science fiction: A review of the literature, 1980-2016. *SAGE Open*, 1-15.

Pollock, D. C., & Van Reken, R. E. (2017). *Third Culture Kids 3rd Edition: Growing up among worlds.* Boston, MA: Nicholas Brealey Publishing.

Puwar, N. (2004). *Space invaders: Race, gender and bodies out of place.* New York, NY: Berg.

Reyes, G., Radina, R., & Aronson, B. A. (2018). Teaching against the grain as an act of love: Disrupting white Eurocentric masculinist frameworks within teacher education. *The Urban Review, 50*, 818-835.

Russo, A., & Russo, J. (2019). *Avengers: Endgame* [Film]. Walt Disney Studios Motion Pictures.

Solórzano, D. G., & Yosso, T. J. (2002). A critical race counterstory of race, racism, and affirmative action. *Equity & Excellence in Education, 35(2)*, 155-168.

Spencer, R. C. (2008). Engendering the Black freedom struggle: Revolutionary Black womanhood and the Black Panther Party in the Bay Area, California. *Journal of Women's History 20*(1), 90-113.

Stohry, H. R., & Jackson, J. J. (2019). AfroAsian imaginations: Autoethnographies of *Black Panther* in Korea. *Journal of Futures Studies, 24*(2), 29-36.

Section III

Place, time, and posthumanist curricular thinking

Chapter 8

A Curriculum of Conflation

Using Space and Place to tell "Big Little Lies"

Boni Wozolek, Penn State University, Abington College, Gabriel Huddleston, Texas Christian University

"I do believe, and I hope, that we can elicit change from the stories we tell and the way that we tell them. Let's keep the conversation alive."

Nicole Kidman, 2018

The economy of television drama often positions the consumer at intersections of witness and spectator (Storey, 1996/2010), of enjoyment and being enjoyed (Zizek, 1992); some place between looking and being looked at (Moten, 2003). Perhaps this is because drama often situates events and experiences as a binary—the best or the worst versions of ourselves, of the places we inhabit, or of the spaces we create (Tulloch, 2002). These binaries serve as a feedback loop of cultural (re)production, a "communicative event" (Hall, 1974, p. 9) that both encodes and decodes sociocultural and political norms and values. Dramas, like all forms of media, are therefore inherently generative, always biased, and a dialogue of unequal exchange between producers and consumers (Hall, 1997; Weaver, 2009; Williams, 1974/2003). The purpose of this paper is to discuss how posthuman exchanges—from those in the show, to intra-actions between the show and the audience, to those across sociocultural spaces and places—are in of themselves a form of curriculum. To discuss this, we argue that media is an enacted curriculum (Page, 1991), or what is learned from the process of making sense (Gershon, 2017) of the entanglements between human and nonhuman bodies such as media. This enacted curriculum deeply impacts the hidden curriculum (Apple, 1971), or what is learned through local and less local norms and values that are, in this case, co-constituted between the media, witness, and broader cultural bodies. Further, as we discuss below, this curriculum is explicit in terms of what the writers and directors seek to portray through their art. However, implicit messages are also taught in perhaps unintentional ways when the art is (re)conceptualized through the audience and (re)territorialized in broader cultural ideas and ideals.

Specifically, we use drama to underscore this curriculum. This is because drama, unlike other genres, has longstanding histories of (re) producing various forms of violence (Byrne & Taddeo, 2019; Gerbner, 1972; Sparks, 1992). Perhaps not surprisingly, violent events witnessed in television dramas and other forms of media have a disproportionately negative impact on marginalized people and communities (Gilroy, 1987; Nyong'o, 2018). In terms of gender—along with its multiple forms and expressions—despite a #MeToo and #TimesUp era that have driven positive change across several industries, narratives representing women still generally remain rather narrow[1]. Byrne and Taddeo (2019), for example, give an in-depth account on sexual assault as it is propagated by popular culture. They argue that some television narratives, like those found in *Outlander* and *Downton Abbey*, often seek to create a sense of "feminist empowerment [that]…provides a positive catalyst for debate, discourse and awareness" (p. 394) about rape culture. However, such series can also unintentionally reinforce sexual violence by, on one hand, expressing sexual assault as an isolated problem of an individual survivor rather than recasting it as a larger social, cultural, and political issue (Matthews, 1994). On the other, such programs do not prove a structured network for this conversation to take place outside of hallway dialogues or blogs that discuss the latest events on television (Byrne & Taddeo, 2019).

While sexual violence is particularly, and necessarily, evocative the same can be said of how violence against Black, Indigenous, People of Color (BIPOC) and queer communities are often reinscribed through drama series (Giroux, 1994; Peele, 2007). One only needs to think about the image of victimized queer people that is too often represented in crime shows such as *Law and Order: Special Victims Unit* that tends to recast a sociocultural norms of "queer as victim," rather than one focused on queer excellence.

Although not a direct parallel in terms of violence, schools and systems of schooling are also often either revered or demonized in drama series; with little room for other possibilities existing between this binary. While television has frequently offered pedagogical spaces in terms of children's programming (see, for example, shows like *Schoolhouse Rock, Sesame Street,* and *Mister Rogers' Neighborhood*), the Dickensian depiction of schools felt in dramas offer far less substance; frequently portraying schools as places of redemption for White, middle-class teachers who usually end up saving some part of themselves and a "star" student or two along the way while others are heartbreakingly lost to the system (Bulman, 2002; Dalton, 1995, 2006; Williams, 2014). As scholars have argued in the framing of dramas like *The Wire* or *Shameless,* while the representations of teacher–student–parent–community entanglements—what Nespor (1997) referred to as the "knot" of schooling—are sometimes accurate in their dramatizations, what's more, significant is what these programs can teach consumers about the normalized sociocultural and political views of schools (Potter & Marshall, 2009; Williams, 2014). In the end, dramas often prioritize ratings over the possibility of interrupting the tropes of schooling, leaving the image of the "damaged students and system" intact for audiences to enjoy (Weber & Hunt, 2020) as spectators.

The 2017 drama, *Big Little Lies,* is not much different in terms of these pitfalls and plotlines. For example, it is wrought with sexual and physical violence against women. It is similarly absent of adequate or complex representations of marginalized people, and is filled with White, cishetero and patriarchal privilege in terms of how schools remain (un)troubled in the sub-plot. Finally, the show continues a violent history of colonization as the place where the show was largely shot—Big Sur, California—is presented as a background character whose gentrification is silenced for the narratives of the (largely) White, wealthy families that inhabit it. Yet, as Kidman's quote in the epigraph above might suggest, the story does pry open spaces for many conversations and, possibly, for change.

Adapted from Liane Moriarty's (2014) novel, this seven-part miniseries is about the secrets and lies that the characters tell in order to keep up appearances. Starring Reese Witherspoon, Nicole Kidman, Shailene Woodley, Laura Dern, and Zoë Kravitz (with Meryl Streep joining as a leading character in the second season), this series tells the story of five women living in California who are embroiled in a murder investigation. Their husbands—played by Alexander Skarsgård, Adam Scott, James Tupper, Jeffrey Nordling, Kathryn Newton, and Ian Armitage—join the cast in supporting roles. Aside from the murder mystery aspect, the show mainly follows the lives of women who, much like the image of calm water, lead rather turbulent lives under the surface.

To think critically about this series, we have employed an intersectional representation analysis (Meyer, 2015). Intersectional representation analysis is one way to think deeply about a single source of media; in this case *Big Little Lies*. Meyer (2015) argues that this approach is significant in unpacking complex narratives, stating that:

> [T]he primary purpose of most media scholarship interrogating…is to examine representations (or lack thereof) for their implied cultural discourses of identity, ultimately suggesting that visibility is a crucial component… Intersectional representation allows television narratives to establish a logic whereby certain types of representations are ubiquitous yet surprisingly invisible simultaneously. Thus, the (visible) invisibility of identity politics maps a cultural landscape of post-difference onto the visual cultural terrain of popular media (p. 901).

Meyer uses intersectionality as a methodology rather than how it has frequently been used by critical race feminists in terms of representation and identity. Used methodologically, intersectional representation analysis seeks to critically examine a television text for questions of representation. While Meyer investigates the pattern of representation among bisexual and/or queer women that often deal with class disparities, this form of analysis is used here to think about how identities represented in *Big Little Lies*—from the identity of the town itself, to the school, to the ways of being, knowing, and doing of the characters that form and inform the plot—often function (un)intentionally as an erasure of difference. Meyer defines this as a kind of television "post-difference (post-racism, post-sexism, post-classism, post-sexuality) [that] is…layered to produce a commodifiable image" (p. 905). In the case of *Big Little Lies*, it is one that that both sparks dialogues about violence while reinforcing violent intra-actions (Barad, 2007) as normalized events.

Big Little Lies presents several implications for an intersectional representation. First, although the show presents sexuality as complex,

Zoë Kravitz's character, Bonnie, is quickly presented as the hyper-sexualized and exotic "Other". Scholars have consistently observed how this kind of representation reinforces Black women and girls as "Other" across sociocultural contexts, often capturing them as hyper-sexualized bodies focused on seduction and pleasure above all else (Hill Collins, 1990; Molina Guzman & Valdivia, 2004). This is most clearly represented in Season 1, Episode 3 ("Living the Dream") where Bonnie takes the dance floor at Renata Klein's (Laura Dern) daughter's birthday party, causing "erections," as one guest complains or in the opening scene of the first episode where Bonnie's eccentric dress is foregrounded as she notes that she made her own jewelry in Peru. As one of the few characters of color, Bonnie's character continues to be written throughout the first season as embodying the many tropes that Black women are expected to play among their mostly White co-stars. Second, the show is set in Monterey, California and was largely filmed in Big Sur, California. There is a significant argument to be made that while the place is rather visible—from the opening credits to consistent pans and flashbacks of the ocean—the politics of the land remain invisible. Namely that Monterey County, a place stolen from the Esselen Indigenous people by Spanish colonizers, had been without its people until 2020. It was not until this time that the Esselen Tribe of Monterey County was finally able to close escrow on a deal that acquired the land for both environmental conservation efforts and to give the people back to the space that was stolen from them over 250 years ago (Jackson, 2020). The show spends a considerable amount of time showing characters interacting with the land, as exemplified by Jane Chapman's (Shailene Woodley) relationship with the ocean as she replays, and runs from, flashbacks of being raped. It does not, however, address the colonization, and subsequent gentrification, of the area that, both in the show and in real life, is literally walled with private property disputes.

Finally, the school itself has an identity that might be associated with any district nested in a wealthy town—complete with rapidly passing images of the "right" kind of queer dads, White, fit men who are ready for a wine-tasting party with Madeline Mackenzie (Reese Witherspoon), to a few passing images of choice minorities dressed "appropriately" to be seen at school. In the second season, Renata is enmeshed in her partner's impending bankruptcy and her daughter,

Amabella (Ivy George) is deeply impacted by her parents' arguing and the fragile nature of the planet, a topic discussed by her teacher, Mr. Perkins (Mo McRae). While the episode (Season 2, Episode 3), focuses on parents' negative responses to the teacher's lesson, the school curriculum does not address any other "hot button" topics. This is especially surprising since both Dern and Woodley's characters address issues of consent and intimate partner violence. What becomes foregrounded is the teacher's execution of the lesson, essentially appealing to everyone, despite their position on climate change, while silencing what could have been a culturally significant point raised through the school curriculum. Meyer (2015) argues that this kind of catch-all narrative allows for shows to be more "economically successful than those lauded as more progressive...speaking to our cultural willingness to accept (in)visibility" (p. 914) of certain people, places, spaces, and stories.

As an act of engaging in an enacted curriculum across layers of scale, this paper will now present a series of letters written between the authors that capture our reactions to the show and our analysis of the points above. Rather than a traditional textual analysis of the show, we believe this is important for at least the following reasons. First, we wish to foreground ourselves as we exist at the intersection of enjoyment and being enjoyed, of looking and being looked at, through the consumerism that is engaging with the show. Second, although our own identities as scholars are very much knotted due to sharing academic fields and coming from a close intellectual family "tree," our personal identities are rather distinct. It is through this process of writing and responding that we seek to let our own positions and positionalities speak to each other while analyzing the content of the show. After these letters, we will conclude with a brief dialogue about the process and our findings.

Letter 1:
Place and Space of Big Little Lies

Dear Boni,

Maybe it's the confessional overtones of *Big Little Lies* that has prompted me to write this as a personal letter (don't get too excited, I don't think I'm going to express any scandalous revelations) or maybe it's because I'm not exactly sure how I want to approach dissecting this show. Whatever the reasons, here we are, a letter. In other work, I have discussed using popular culture as an apparatus of diffraction, a move inspired by the work of Barad (2007), so the letter format is an experimental addition to this line of thinking. As you can see in my previous citation, I'm not comfortable enough letting go of the demands of academic writing, so the letter is an attempt to write through those entanglements, not around them.

As a fellow curriculum theorist, I know you understand that in addition to thinking of popular culture as an apparatus of diffraction, my work applies a curricular lens as well. As Schubert (2006) and others (e.g., Dimitriadis, 2015; Huddleston, 2017; Huddleston & Helmsing, 2020) have noted, curriculum theory is not only for spaces deemed educational, but also to ask curriculum questions of any unit of analysis, "How is this designed to teach?", "What is it trying to teach us?", and "What knowledge does it posit as of most worth?". Thinking of *Big Little Lies* (BLL) as a curriculum shifts my perspective on this show that I mainly saw as a master class in acting. Stemming from my days as a high school theatre nerd wherein one of my highlights was seeing the movie "Heat" with my castmates (It was the first time I went to a movie with others to study the craft of acting, in this case, the "gods" that were Pacino and DeNiro) I initially saw BLL as a chance to see some wonderful actors plying their craft well. The plot? I can take it or leave it. But Meryl Streep going toe-to-toe with Nicole Kidman while Reese Witherspoon artistically pouts and Laura Dern shouts, "I will not *not* be rich"? Sign me up. That said, given our area of study, applying a curricular frame forces me to pay attention to other elements of the show beyond those I take a guilty pleasure in viewing. This is obviously the point of any theoretical frame, but in the case of curriculum theory I believe *Big Little Lies* reveals some interesting points of knowledge production.

Given these frames, my analysis has to start with that damn bridge. Do you know the bridge I'm talking about it? It's featured prominently in the montage that opens every show. Characters, especially Reese Witherspoon's, are often filmed driving back and forth on it while they drive their kids to school or meet the person with whom they are having an affair. I was always fascinated by that bridge, to the point that it became my favorite recurring character, and I would often say out loud, "Oh look, it's the bridge!" Apparently, I wasn't the only one. The bridge is the Bixby Bridge located in Big Sur, where much of the show was filmed and it has become a tourist destination, thereby raising the ire of Big Sur residents[2]. Big Sur was seeing an increase in tourism before BLL hit and the show has further fueled it. The bridge, which is on the two-lane State Highway 1, has become a popular site to capture selfies—leading motorists to stop and cause traffic jams. As a response, a group of local residents hung a sign on the bridge that read, "Overtourism is killing Big Sur". This lead me to an Instagram account called "bigsureducates"[3] which reposts tourists' photos engaging in illegal activity (i.e., stopping in the middle of Highway 1 to take pictures, stopping on the side of the road to do the same, hanging out of their cars as they cruise around town, and hiking or walking in areas that are fenced or partitioned off for safety). This feed's intent seems to be public shaming of the tourists and calling attention to the problem tourism is causing in the community. Another website, www. bigsurpledge.org, notes, "The recent increase in the number of visitors is challenging the safety and wellbeing of residents, visitors and the fragile natural environment" and asks visitors to agree to some basic principles.

I'm not going to pretend to know enough to take a definitive stand on the issue of tourism in Big Sur, but since this is a private letter, let me tell you what I really think. Don't get me wrong here, I'm all for protecting the environment and I'm sure the rule-follower in me would curse the various cars parked where they shouldn't be parked. I'm sure that stopping on the side of a road that was never designed to accommodate selfies presents a traffic safety hazard. My adopted "leave no trace" ethos would shutter at anyone walking past roped-off areas as it could result in the destruction of fragile ecosystems, but these concerns belie a deeper fear. Much of the property of Big Sur is held by public land trusts with 84% of the total land restricted for development. As a result, the little bit of private property available is highly valuable to the point of being priceless. While tourism can often lead to overdevelopment and gentrification, in the setting of Big Sur this fear seems to be somewhat misplaced. Instead, the fear of tourism is maybe less to do with protecting the environment and more about protecting private land. This protection, in turn, relies on a foundation of colonial violence and literally stands on stolen land.

That capitalist and White supremacist ideology, in which the protection of private property is paramount, is foundational to understand any conflicts in and around Big Sur obviously goes without saying. However, taken in conjunction with an analysis of *Big Little Lies*, there is a level of complexity that is akin to the work of Anna Lowenhaupt Tsing. Tsing (2005) points out in *Friction* that critical cultural studies and ethnographic research often reify a dichotomy of the monolithic dominant global hegemony pitted against the nuanced, heterogenous, inherently resistive local or native. Instead, this work should focus on the friction created between these two spheres. In later work, Tsing (2015) pushes this line of thinking even further by asking what is left in the wake of capitalism's destructive path. Tsing's work is influential for me, especially in terms of ethnographic work, but I haven't really considered her in relation to studying popular culture. In *Big Little Lies*, the opportunity presents itself as a process to add depth to the superficial elements of the show by plunging more deeply into the societal issues it attempts to address. Tsing does something similar in the areas she studies, but such a process is not simply about examining something more deeply, it's about finding points of friction between what we've come to assume are two sides of a dichotomy.

In the case of *Big Little Lies* and the location that serves as its settings, what happens when we apply Tsing's concept of friction and/ or the possibility of life after the death and destruction created by capitalism? I am inspired to do so because of the storyline surrounding one of the main characters, Bonnie. Her character arc in Season 2 focuses mainly on living in the aftermath of death. Bonnie, as others have noted (Bastién, 2020; Bradley, 2020; Ibrahim, 2019) is a highly problematic character on the show. Played by Zoë Kravitz, she is the only major character of color in the show. It is these two elements, the protection of White property in Big Sur and the character of Bonnie that I want to examine.

As McKittrick (2006) notes, the ways in which privilege and racism work spatially is powerfully resonant for those living at specific historical periods and for those of us who tread those spaces subsequently—Big Sur, both the real and fictional version portrayed in the show are no exception. More specifically, the process by which spaces become marked as either places of freedom or places of oppression is extremely important to understand any present moment. When combined with Tsing, we can also think in terms of how space and place transform in capitalism's destructive wake. Yes, there are barren wastelands leftover and such devastation creates barriers and blockades where there were none previously, leaving us all to navigate sometimes as the edge of a precipice. However, life exists and, in some cases, thrives in spite of such destruction. This type of maneuvering and survival is most evident by the character of Bonnie. In the second season of BLL, she is told by her mother, "You are out here surrounded by people who don't get you. They don't look like you. I haven't even seen one other Black person since I've been out here." Bonnie's mother (played by Crystal Fox) represents a point of entry into of Bonnie's backstory and adds a little more depth to a character that felt shallow in the first season. Angelica Jae Bastién (2020), writing for *Vulture*, noted that the Bonnie character in season one was severely underwritten to produce "the moneyed version of the Carefree Black Girl archetype come to life" as a means to simply be a "counterpoint to the vicious, hypercompetent mothers who define the Monterey, California-set show".

By the time Bonnie's mother drops the aforementioned line on Bonnie, she is grappling with feelings of anxiety, grief, and guilt in the wake of her actions at the end of season one resulting in the death of another character's husband. The killing of the husband and its subsequent coverup is interesting here because Bonnie, the only person of color involved in the scandal, is isolated in her grieving with no real connection to the other characters, symbolized by her long runs through the woods. This isolation is seen mainly as one of her own doing, but in reality, it is the result of the other characters feeling no real obligation to her and the definitive lines of privilege and racism they must navigate, but also maintain. By positing Bonnie as aloof and distant, the characters have no real responsibility to explore how their Whiteness is the actual cause of the isolation and they (or the show's writers) refuse to really examine how Bonnie confessing to the accidental killing of a White businessman is fraught with peril. Their outreach is superficial, ignorant, and thoughtless, demonstrated best when Madeline says to Bonnie, "I'm so tired of taking care of you and your fucking feelings". If the writers of the show really wanted to develop the character of Bonnie and interrogate racism and Whiteness, they would have created opportunities for them all to explore the ways in which the spaces and places they inhabit are designed to isolate, marginalize, and maintain privilege. Instead, the show offers Bonnie as a static being that can only be defined temporally by the events that preceded her, not as someone with a more complicated spatial relationship with her surroundings that includes both her struggle and her survival. In other words, Bonnie deserved to be a character with multiple points of friction to the context that surrounded her.

Bonnie, as a problematic element of the show, is far more interesting than the way schools and education is portrayed. Schools and teachers are only considered insomuch as they further the major plotline and are therefore even more superficial than how Bonnie is depicted. Throughout the show, teachers are presented as perhaps well-intentioned, but ultimately inept. Administrators are seen as so beholden to the parents that every decision is made to appease or passively-aggressively annoy them. I've remarked several times while watching the show, "A teacher at that school wouldn't do that!" True, this feeling is based on my conceptions of a fictional town and a fictional school, but the BLL elementary school is one with an abundance of resources and, from what little we see, a curriculum based on a progressive, political liberal view of the world where issues such as social justice and climate change are at least touched upon. In the day and age of school choice, the BLL is a public school of which the characters on the show seem willing and proud to choose. Given the tax base, this school would serve, the type of ineptitude on display is hard to believe, especially when most of the characters' wealth would allow them to choose a private option. But I digress as the choice of school is obviously done to serve the plot. Without the children attending a public school, the interaction between characters coming from various economic classes wouldn't exist and without ineffective teachers, most of the drama would be absent from the main storyline. In this way, which is similar to Bonnie, the school and those within are only considered in relation to events of the main character's lives and not examined in terms of their spatiality and so they need to be seen as buffoons and idiots. I would love to see a version of the show in which teachers are shown with a keen sense of the Big Sur community, fully aware of the complexities that obscure the White privilege of most of their students' parents.

To return to Tsing and McKittrick, what *Big Little Lies* forces me to consider is that if we are to move beyond White supremacy built on simplified dichotomies, which presents humans in a static relationship to their geographic surroundings and is defined mainly by temporal events, a critical spatial analysis that looks for points of friction is necessary. This is especially true when it comes to education. The status quo, as seen in *Big Little Lies*, is a fictional ineptitude of teachers that furthers the narrative of public-school districts being frontiers of inefficiency and decay demanding reform. This obscures the spatial structures of Whiteness that are really to blame for the inequities in our schooling systems. In *Big Little Lies*, by ignoring the spatial context as it relates to either Bonnie or the school, presents Big Sur as simply a pretty place with a pretty bridge.

Best,
Gabe

Letter 2:
Capitals of shame in BLL

Dear Gabe,

When you texted and asked if I wanted to watch *Big Little Lies* and write something about the curriculum of the show, I remember thinking to myself, "Well, at least engaging in this will give me a chance to take part in some much-needed selfcare." The more I thought about it, the more I struggled with the thought of a "working-break." While pretending to escape the COVID world by binge-theorizing a TV show did not exactly sound like indulging, I came to appreciate quiet moments of sipping wine and thinking about how pop culture both forms and informs our ways of being, knowing, and doing. I'll be honest; this show was difficult for me. As a queer, Brown woman who has survived (and recently worked hard to come to terms with) personal experiences of sexual violence, watching the constant dramatization of assault that was peppered with essentialized messages about bodies of color and queer people, was hard. As a mother of two children that I love deeply, thinking about all the things we do to protect our children, even in the face of violence, was more difficult—like a two-season punch to the gut with which I both identified and cringed to watch play out on the screen. Separating out personal experience, this show left me with many other thoughts about what I learned by watching it and, as you might guess, I have thoughts. Since you've seen *Big Little Lies*, I imagine you know much of this analysis—complete with questions of shame, toxic masculinity, racializing and heteronormative content, and, of course, the slightly derivative undertones of the show in its Stepford-esque noir. In short, from my perspective, *Big Little Lies* is a strong curriculum of late-stage capitalism.

By late capitalism, I am invoking Jameson's (1991) characterization of the cultural rupture that accompanies the emergence of late-stage capitalism as it intersects with Hennessy's (2018) work on sexual identities in late capitalism where she explicates social reproduction through Marxist feminist discourse of sexual politics. There are a few specific dialogues from these scholars that relate to "Bit Little Lies" that I wish to unpack. First, I am interested in Jameson's dialogue on "late," where he conveys this as a "sense that something has changed, that things are different" (p. xxi). One of the elements of late capitalism that he addresses in this "change" is through the intra—to borrow from Barad (2007)—the relationship of media. Jameson describes this entanglement as integral to the capitalist normalization of culture, perspectives, and their subsequent realities and I think that Barad might agree on the co-constitutive nature of subjectivities that arise from media events like the production of *Big Little Lies*. Second, Jameson describes Munch's "The Scream," where he discusses the disconnections between aesthetic expression while the subject remains imprisoned in it. Jameson describes this painting as a moment when "vibration becomes ultimately visible as on the surface of a sheet of water, an infinite regress which fans out from the sufferer to become the very geography of a universe in which the pain itself now speaks and vibrates through the material" (p. 14). I believe that this is significant in terms of how one might understand the tones of shame that are punctuated by violence in this series.

Returning to Hennessy's work, I would like to focus on two aspects. First, her definition of late capitalism, which in includes an argument that late capitalism is an "array of contradictory global and local structural adjustments in the organization of production and consumption that are altering the way life is lived" (p. 5). This is not unlike Jameson's dialogue on media above that, as Hennessey writes, "repeatedly invokes the icon of the traditional family as the cure-all for a host of social ills" (p. 3). She continues by explaining how non-nuclear family structures are too often vilified, noting specifically that marginalized families are more acceptable if they are classified as "middle class" across forms of media. Second, her dialogue on social reproduction strikes me as particularly significant. Specifically, her description of social reproduction as it "joins the material sustenance of bodies to how bodies matter and which bodies matter" (p. xxii) is resonant with the show. I am therefore arguing that within the mattering of bodies, the curriculum of *Big Little Lies* is one of the norms found in late capitalism that impacted the emotional labor of m/others whose ways of being often existed within what I call *agentic contingencies* (Wozolek, 2021)[4] that are, in this case, heavily constrained by *capitals of shame*[5] (Wozolek, 2019).

While there are many rich examples in the show that demonstrate this claim, here I will predominantly rely on Nichole Kidman's character, Celest, who is a stay-at-home mom, raising two boys, and in a complex and abusive relationship with her husband, Perry, played by Alexander Skarsgård. This is because the relationships within that family dynamic are a clear indication of the agentic contingencies that limited Celest's ability to remove herself from an abusive situation but were also instrumental in the way her son was able to escape persecution when he ended up assaulting his classmate.

Here I'm using agency in both Barad's (2007) sense of intra-actions, where agency emerges from relationships, and Ortner's (1996) dialogue on agency as it is entangled within a set of individual intentions and power relations. Both Ortner and Barad's frameworks are significant to the show. The second season, for example, tacks back and forth between the current/future investigation of the murder as it is layered with the past/present context of the women's experiences that are formed and informed by their pasts; notably the sexual and physical violence Celest endured and her son's growing awareness of domestic violence. Toward Barad's theory of intra-actions, in this case the apparatus is the murder that is pulled into layers of scale through intra-actions of relationships. Similarly, Ortner's focus on intention and power is equally significant. Citing the Gramsci-derived notion of hegemonies that are strongly controlling but never complete, Ortner argues that agency is power but that such agency still exists within systems that are socio-politically and culturally controlled. Enacting agency is, therefore, an act of intention, like Celest's decision to remove herself from domestic violence. Yet, even in moments where we exercise agency, we are left like "The Scream" in that the pain often takes over the once peaceful façade, often leaving the survivor trapped by the conditions of the event.

While the women in this show exercised agency in their jobs, families, and, most notably, within the school, they were all subject to agentic contingencies, or the sets of circumstances that impact one's ability to enact agency. Much like Ortner's dialogue on power and Barad's framing of agency within relationships, each character moved within limiting factors. One of the most prevalent limitations that women were portrayed as experiencing in *Big Little Lies* was often the use of shame. As I have discussed in other places (Wozolek, 2021), shame can be understood as a form of capital. Capitals of shame are used like all social capital as a means to maintain oppressive structures. What is new here is that a capital of shame is not a form of power that one wishes to gain, as opposed to cultural or financial capital, for example, but is instead the ability to use one's available wiggle room to shame others. As with all forms of capital, those with less power can still use their agency to shame the powerful either individually or as a group, as seen in the way that teachers in the show received shame from both parents and students as to their pedagogical abilities. However, and significantly, it is most often the case that those with capital are much more likely to shame others and to understand those actions as normal and socioculturally appropriate. Shame ran consistently through the show. It was used in a group, like mothers shaming each other for their work status, and out group, like adults shaming children for their actions. Celest expressed several degrees of shame that she eventually articulated in therapy, including feeling torn about leaving a sexually consenting relationship that was adjacent to an extremely physical and psychologically abusive relationship where she felt concerned about her sons losing the relationship with what she perceived to be a "good father".

By this point, Gabe, I'm betting you're thinking to yourself, "Dammit Boni, I pitched something about schools and the curriculum observed in the school, will you ever return to the pitch?" The answer is, "No." I find the context of the school in *Big Little Lies* to be utterly banal as it demonstrates the racial segregation of wealth in public schools while ignoring the possibility of sexual and class diversity. What I'd rather attend to is how the ubiquitous shaming of adult characters seeped into the school, making moments like when Jane's son is shamed in front of his class and their parents for allegedly committing a crime that Celest's son had done as a response to exploring the violence he witnessed at home. Further, the victim, the daughter of Renata, played by Laura Dern, endured a public display where she was forced to reveal her assailant, something that is never discussed in the show. While this show boasts feminist undertones, in moments like this where the "shame" explored through Jane's son's humiliation and not Renata's daughter, it becomes clear that this is yet another exercise in a hidden curriculum that normalizes the oppression of women. Meanwhile, women in the show continue the emotional labor that is key in feminist dialogues on late capitalism. The labor of raising children, keeping up with the Joneses, and working within a limited set of agentic possibilities that is all-too-often governed by capitals of shame.

Anyway, Gabe. Here's what I'm thinking. Next time, can we pick a show with perhaps a less star-studded cast that invests more into paying strong writers than it does into big names. It's like hiring police officers over school psychologists and counselors; when the flash wore off, I feel the show was left with no more than a broken system that reified oppressive norms and values and was utterly unhelpful to interrupting harmful ideas and ideals of either the woman-victim or Madonna-whore complex that remains all-too-familiar in antiquated plot-lines written to be evocative through the abuse of women. I look forward to your thoughts and, of course, the next show recommendation.

Your Scholarly Sister,
Boni

Letter 3:

Big Little Veneers

Boni,

Your letter was so wonderfully rich, complex, and theoretically provoking that it has me thinking on all different levels, so apologies if I don't address all the insightful points you raise. The thread I want to pick up is ultimately methodological, which, given our research interests, shouldn't come as a surprise. More specifically, your letter has pushed me further on a question I've been exploring as of late. Which is: How does popular culture scholarship risk reifying the very hegemony it seeks to critique? Such a danger as always been at the heart of good Cultural Studies[6] work, I think best typified by Stuart Hall, but as Mark Helmsing and I (2020) point out, such work has now been subsumed by the means of production and repackaged as "smart" popular culture criticism. In other words, mass media popular culture critique is the super glossy version of Cultural Studies more nuanced look at the cycle of cultural production. What makes it more dangerous, as evident of my willingness to cite such work, is that these critiques can be damn good. So, your letter has left me wondering: What's the difference?

The answer, I think, is ultimately a methodological one. It starts with your discussion of Jameson and late capitalism. We must be on the same wavelength as I've recently started reading some Jameson inspired mainly by Razmin Keaucheyan's (2013) discussion of his work. In reading your letter and your discussion of superficial agency, Keaucheyan's interpretation of Jameson's concept of depthlessness seems most apt. He writes:

> 'Depthlessness' is to be understood here in the literal sense of the lack of any depth or substance or of what is found on the surface. To illustrate the point, Jameson stages a comparison between Van Gogh's *Old Boots* (1887) and Andy Warhol's Diamond Dust Shoes (1980). The first painting represents a peasant's boots. Although they take up the whole canvas, they indirectly refer to the whole peasant world, which viewers are invited to reconstruct imaginatively. Warhol's shoes, by contrast, are superficial in the sense indicated above. No perspective or spatio-temporal markers referring to any world appear in them. Everything happens

> as if objects have been stripped of their very capacity to be represented. In this respect, Jameson evokes 'death of the world of appearance' and introduces the concept of 'simulacrum' (drawn from Baudrillard) to explain the aesthetic regime in which we now find ourselves. (p. 247)

As you deftly point out, *Big Little Lies* presents its characters stripped of any real capacity to represent the issues of which they portend to address. In other words, the creators of the show rely on imagery and superficial identities as a simulacrum to a real investigation of domestic violence, racism, and Whiteness. In doing so, the show ignores the structures of shaming that force us into positions we consider to be full of agency. Or as Keaucheyan (2013) says of Jameson, "Late capitalism generates not only a culture, but also a new range of emotions, which conditions the type of subject formed today" (p. 247). This begs the question, does our analysis also double as a superficial investigation because our source material lacks depth? Your letter, I think, is evidence that this is not the case for two reasons.

The first is, much like Jameson's examination of Warhol, you use BLL to make a larger point about the postmodern condition we all find ourselves in, more specifically that our perceived agency is a dangerous illusion that disguises deep structures of inequity and oppression. This is a perfect example of Hall's (1998) directive to treat popular culture only as serious as its ability to examine the locus between hegemonic and the resistant. This type of analysis tickles all of my theory nerd bones but, taken in conjunction with other elements of your letter, hits me emotionally as well, which leads to another distinction between pop culture critique and Cultural Studies work involving pop culture.

I tend to agree with Grossberg (2010) that Cultural Studies is, at its core, the work of saying "yes, and…". In other words, it works against the typical academic move of making points to discount ones previously made and recognizes that objects of analysis can be many things to many people. I've always interpreted such a call as inherently positive and constructive, which I think it still is. However, by examining your own positionality in relation to BLL you demonstrate that such work should contain an element of vulnerability. Added to this is in signing off your letter as "Your Scholarly Sister", you acknowledge that our relationship is more than simply as colleagues, but as graduate students who became Ph.D.'s together, sharing academic lineage in the form of our advisors, and our shared theoretical foundations. In this way, Grossberg's insistence to do the work of "yes, and…" means that it's not just building on academic points, but it should be academic, personal, emotional, dangerous, and…—it needs to be all the things that our current societal state of depthlessness is not.

Your academic brother,
Gabe

Letter 4:
Unpacking Whiteness and other Curricula

Dear Gabe,
Like any scholarly friend whose ideas both challenge and support your own, your letter has had me thinking. Specifically, I'm wondering what we learn in moments of silence. Moten (2003) and I (Wozolek, 2018), among others, have thought about how silence has movement in that it can teach us as much about what is present as that which remains (un)heard. I've been wondering: What do we learn when the curriculum in the "school" serves a plot line and not larger social issues? What is learned through the (in)visibility of marginalized people in shows like *Big Little Lies*? What is heard in the silence of the cars as the mothers shuttle their children to and from school and other activities? As a parent, I know you are likely familiar with this feeling—both being lost in your own thoughts while wondering what is flickering through your child's mind as the road rumbles as loudly as the ideas in your mind. Finally, how do the characters become "larger than life" through what is presented as "everyday events" gone awry?

While my first letter focused on a curriculum of late capitalism—one punctuated by capitals of shame—in this letter I would like to briefly take up your points about the school. Specifically, your indignation at the reality, or lack thereof, portrayed in fragments during the first, and more pointedly, during the second season. I think it's worth thinking about this as it relates to Bonnie's aloof character that, as you said allows "the characters have no real responsibility to explore how their Whiteness". You go on to connect this to the school, noting that the context demands "intervention by nice White parents".

I suppose it begs the question, "What is the curriculum of shame?" in the show, and how does Whiteness deploy shame in ways that colonize everything from the bodies, to the ways of being of characters, to the land, to the normalization of assault? I wonder if the show's producers and writers were motivated by shame in a contemporary context where the Black Lives Matter movement and the prevalence of critical race theorists in the United States would reject Bonnie's character. I wonder how they were similarly motivated by the empowerment of the women's movement and #MeToo to broach the topic of assault so clearly. From Kidman's Golden Globe acceptance speech, it's clear that they foregrounded assault, but they missed some of the nuances of this all-too-common violence that are significant. For example, I believe there is a parallel drawn between Kidman's wealthy character and Woodley's less-privileged character in that they both face forms of sexual violence. Perhaps this is to show viewers that it can happen across class contexts. While this is true in that no one— despite genders, class, races, sexual orientations, or ability, to name a few—is exempt from these concerns, I remained unimpressed that they had an opportunity to think deeply about the topic of consent in the school and questions of solidarity as people are far too often shamed into silence about this topic. It took a murder for the women to identify with these common threads. Perhaps if they had replaced climate change with consent, they could have touched more deeply on these issues.

In the case of Skarsgård's murder, I wonder about the decision to have Bonnie be the person who pushed him down the stairs. Does this fit another trope of the "angry Black woman," or does she become the "savior," the person whose quiet nature was set aside to rush in at the right moment and interrupt the violence? What does it mean that she falls apart in season 2 because she feels compelled to silence her confession? In this case, the decision not to confess, along with the context of the school, was a blanket intervention by "nice White ladies". While I am not able to answer all these questions, I suppose what is learned, perhaps what is reinforced, is a curriculum of Whiteness whereby shame is a consequence of not falling in line with the expectations of White identities. So, how do you feel about watching *Little Fires Everywhere* next? I think there might be some interesting parallels that we might explore over drinks at a conference, whenever COVID calms down.

Your Socially Distanced but Academically Close Friend,

Boni

Concluding Analysis:
Lessons of Big Little Lies

There are several entanglements presented in the letters above. Among them are the ways that scholars and scholarship are knotted, consistently being de-and-re-territorialized (Ares, Buendía & Helfenbein, 2017; Deleuze, 1983) across contexts. Further, and perhaps more significant here, both authors explicated the enmeshed nature of bodies, both human and nonhuman, that engender and maintain forms of oppressions (Braidotti, 2017; Puar, 2007; Weheliye, 2014). This last point is important for at least the following braided reasons. First, as Barad (2007) argues, within the entanglements of bodies through a phenomenon, subjectivities become co-constituted. As with all forms of media, the body that is *Big Little Lies* is in constant intra-action with the witness' being, as well as with broader bodies of culture. What emerges from the knotted and nested layers of intra-action are new, co-constituted ontoepistemologies that form and inform the bodies as they are sewn together and pulled apart. In other words, like a person moving kaleidoscope to respond to the light, as reviews on the show are surface, production editors and directors might adjust the focus. As images from the show emerge, the witness responds within the feedback loop.

Second, and related to this loop, as ontoepistemologies shift, the bodies of cultural norms and values are impacted. As Goffman (1959) argues, we all participate in forms of multistage dramas. Scholars like Meyrowitz (1985) and Berger (2017), among others, have longstanding dialogues that argue the role of electronic media as a co-constituted actor that deeply impacts sociocultural norms and values; an imbrication of on-screen dramas with the performances of people and cultures. The balance between drama and reality can, in fact, skew cultural norms (Serrone et. al., 2018). In the case of "*Big Little Lies*," the authors' concern are the cultural values that are made and unmade through these intra-actions through relatively untroubled notions about salient topics such as intimate partner violence, relationships to colonized spaces and places, and racialized ways of being and knowing.

Finally, woven within the points above are the curricula that emerge from such intra-actions. Like all forms of curriculum, the enacted curriculum between bodies folds into larger hidden curricula, territorializing sociocultural and political norms and values. The significance in shows like BLL, then, is not just in the boundaries they might push but in the way that they are witnessed, interpreted and, many times, accepted. The pitfall of key moments—like the schools portrayed in the show not addressing topics such as consent or colonization—often aides in messages that devalue roles of solidarity with survivors of and across forms of oppression. Such unabated violence engenders sociopolitical aggressions connected to things like shame and agentic contingencies that emerge from and are buttressed by the performances and intra-actions among and between bodies.

What is learned, then, in this curriculum of conflation between bodies? Returning to Kidman's quote in the epigraph, what conversations are ultimately "kept alive" through the show and the curriculum that emerges from it? As discussed here, *Big Little Lies* and other pop culture artifacts, are only as powerful as their ability to heighten our focus on root causes of injustice and oppression and they can't be counted on to do that work on their own. It is in our collective conversations as scholars that we must bring that potential to its fullest by doing work that is collaborative, but also lays bare vulnerability in our own positionalities. That responsibility is ultimately a methodological one in which scholars not only look to popular culture as a place of academic excavation, but one deserving a thoughtful methodological approach beyond simply critiquing it.

Notes

1. It is important to pause and note that this paper will discuss topics such as sexual assault and intimate partner violence. The authors would like to remind those who are in, out, and between violent contexts that they are not alone. Help is available through national organizations like RAINN (800.656.4673).

2. For more on the dialogue on this bridge in the media, see: https://www.huffpost.com/entry/big-little-lies-bix-by-creek-bridge-tourism_n_5d27899fe4b02a5a5d57ef8a

3. To view this Instagram page, please go to: https://www.instagram.com/bigsureducates/?hl=en

4. By agentic contingencies I am referring to the circumstances that impact a person's ability to use her agency. This conceptualization of what has and can use agency is not unlike Barad's (2007) conceptualization of agency that is co-constituted and fluid and, like Ortner's (2006) dialogue on power or Bourdieu & Passeron (1977) talk about fields, is controlling but not all-encompassing.

5. By capitals of shame I am referring to the many ways that those with privilege and power negatively employ sociocultural norms and values that at once cultivate criteria for shaming, then utilize those criteria as a

means to declare people or groups publicly noticeable in their incompetence or impotence across all manner of interactions, possibilities, and/or ways of being, knowing, and/or doing. What is argued here is that shame, unlike other forms of capital, is not someone that one wants to gain. However, in the case of garnering power, the ability to shame can be collected through lines and lenses of privilege and then using that shame against a person or group can provide the person enacting shame with degrees of social mobility.

6. I capitalize Cultural Studies to make a distinction of the line of research emanating from the Birmingham School in the 1960s (Wright & Maton, 2004).

References

Apple, M. W. (1971). The hidden curriculum and the nature of conflict. *Interchange, 2*(4), 27-40.

Ares, N., Buendía, E., & Helfenbein, R.H. (Eds.). (2017). *Deterritorializing/Reterritorializing: Critical Geography of Educational Reform.* Sense.

Barad, K. (2007). *Meeting the universe halfway: Quantum physics and the entanglement of matter and meaning.* Durham, NC: Duke University Press.

Bastién, A. J. (2020). Why Bonnie, *Big Little Lies'* Most Underwritten Character, Deserved More. Retrieved from https://www.vulture.com/2017/04/big-little-lies-bonnie-deserved-more.html

Berger, A. A. (2017). *Manufacturing desire: Media, popular culture, and everyday life.* New York, NY: Routledge.

Bradley, L. (2020). Big Little Lies: Why Bonnie's Big Moment Was Both Wrenching and Disappointing. Retrieved from https://www.vanityfair.com/hollywood/2019/07/big-little-lies-bonnie-confession-celeste-mary-louise

Braidott, R. (2017). Four theses on posthuman feminism. In R. Grushin (Ed.), *Anthropocene feminism* (pp. 21-48). University of Minnesota Press.

Bourdieu, P., & Passeron, J. C. (1977). *Reproduction in education, society and culture.* London, UK: Sage Publications.

Bulman, R. C. (2002). Teachers in the'hood: Hollywood's middle-class fantasy. *The Urban Review, 34*(3), 251-276.

Byrne, K., & Taddeo, J. A. (2019). Calling #TimesUp on the TV period drama rape narrative. *Critical Studies in Television, 14*(3), 379-398.

Dalton, M. M. (1995). The Hollywood Curriculum: who is the 'good' teacher? *Curriculum Studies, 3*(1), 23-44.

Dalton, M. M. (2006). Revising the Hollywood curriculum. *Journal of Curriculum and Pedagogy, 3*(2), 29-34.

Deleuze, G. (1983). *Anti-oedipus: capitalism and schizophrenia.* University of Minnesota Press.

Gerbner, G. (1972). Violence in television drama: Trends and symbolic functions. *Television and social behavior, 1*, 28-187.

Gershon, W.S. (2017). *Curriculum and students in classrooms: Everyday urban education in an era of standardization.* Landham, MD: Lexington Press.

Gilroy, P. (2013). *There ain't no black in the Union Jack.* Routledge.

Giroux, H. A. (1994). *Disturbing pleasures: Learning popular culture.* New York, NY: Routledge.

Goffman, E. (1969). *Presentation of self in everyday life.* New York, NY: Doubleday.

Grossberg, L. (2010). *Cultural studies in the future tense.* Durham: Duke University Press.

Hall, S. (1974). Encoding and decoding in the television discourse, *Education and Culture, 25(1),* 8-14.

Hall, S. (1998). Notes on deconstructing "the popular". In J. Storey (Ed.), *Cultural theory and popular culture: A reader.* Pearson/Prentice Hall.

Hall, S. (1997). Culture and power. *Radical Philosophy, 86(2),* 24-41.

Harvey, D. (2009). *Social justice and the city.* University of Georgia Press.

Hennessy, R. (2018). *Profit and pleasure: Sexual identities in late capitalism.* New York, NY: Routledge.

Hill Collins, P. (1990). *Black feminist thought: Knowledge, consciousness, and the politics of empowerment.* New York, NY: Routledge.

Huddleston, G. (2017). The zombie in the room: Using popular culture as an apparatus. In N. Snaza, D. Sonu, S. Truman, & Z. Zaliwska (Eds.), *Pedagogical matters : new materialisms and curriculum studies.* New York: Peter Lang.

Huddleston, G., & Helmsing, M. (2020). Pop Culture 2.0: A Political Curriculum in the Age of Trump. *Handbook of Theory and Research in Cultural Studies and Education,* 543-557.

Ibrahim, S. (2019). What Big Little Lies Got Wrong About Bonnie. Retrieved from https://www.theatlantic.com/entertainment/archive/2019/07/big-little-lies-season-2-question-of-bonnie/594457/

Jackson, A. (2020). After 250 years, Native American tribe regains ownership of Big Sur ancestral lands, *CNN Travel,* Retrieved from: https://www.cnn.com/travel/article/native-american-tribe-big-sur-ancestral-landstrnd/index.html.

Jameson, F. (1991). *Postmodernism, or, the cultural logic of late capitalism*. Durham, NC: Duke University Press.

Keucheyan, R. (2013). *Left hemisphere : Mapping critical theory today* (G. Elliott, Trans.). New York: Verso.

Kidman, N. (2018). Limited series at the 2018 Golden Globes. Retrieved from: https://www.youtube.com/watch?v=BsHx2dclkLE

Matthews, N.A. (1994). *Confronting rape: The feminist anti-rape movement and the State*. New York, NY: Routledge.

McKittrick, K. (2006). *Demonic grounds: Black women and cartographies of struggle*. Minneapolis, MN: University of Minnesota Press.

Meyer, M. D. (2015). The "other" woman in contemporary television drama: Analyzing intersectional representation on Bones. *Sexuality & Culture, 19*(4), 900-915.

Meyrowitz, J. (1985). *No sense of place: The impact of electronic media on behavior*. New York, NY: Oxford University Press.

Molina Guzman, I., & Valdivia, A.N. (2004). Brain, brow, and booty: Latina iconicity in US popular culture, *The Communication Review 7(2)*, 205-221.

Moriarty, L. (2014). *Big little lies*. Sydney, Australia: Pan Books.

Nespor, J. (1997). *Tangled up in school: Politics, space, bodies and signs in the educational process*. Mahwah, NJ: Lawrence Erlbaum Associates Inc.

Nyong'o, T. (2018). *Afro-Fabulations: The queer drama of Black life*. New York, NY: New York University Press.

Ortner, S. B. (2006). *Anthropology and social theory: Culture, power and the acting subject*. Durham, NC: Duke University Press.

Page, R. (1991). *Lower-track classrooms: A curricular and cultural perspective*. New York, NY: Teachers College Press.

Peele, T. (2007). *Queer popular culture: Literature, media, film, and television*. New York, NY: Springer.

Potter, T., & Marshall, C. W. (Eds.). (2009). *The Wire: urban decay and American television*. New York, NY: Bloomsbury Publishing.

Puar, J.K. (2007). *Terrorist assemblages: Homonationalism in queer times*. Duke University Press.

Schubert, W. H. (2006). Focus on the BIG CURRICULUM. *Journal of Curriculum and Pedagogy, 3*(1), 100-103. doi:10.1080/15505170.2006.10411585

Serrone, R. O., Weinberg, J. A., Goslar, P. W., Wilkinson, E. P., Thompson, T. M., Dameworth, J. L., Dempsey, S.R., & Petersen, S. R. (2018). Grey's Anatomy effect: television portrayal of patients with trauma may cultivate unrealistic patient and family expectations after injury. *Trauma surgery & acute care open, 3(1)*, 1-4.

Snyder, J. (Producer). (2020, 2020-07-23). *Nice White Parents* [Retrieved from https://www.nytimes.com/2020/07/23/podcasts/nice-white-parents-serial.html

Sparks, R. (1992). *Television and the drama of crime: Moral tales and the place of crime in public life*. Berkshire, UK: Open University Press.

Storey, J. (1996/2010). *Cultural studies and the study of popular culture*. Edinburgh, Scotland: Edinburgh University Press.

Tsing, A.L. (2005). *Friction: An ethnography on global connection*. Princeton, NJ: Princeton University Press.

Tsing, A. L. (2015). *The mushroom at the end of the world: On the possibility of life in capitalist ruins*. Princeton University Press.

Tulloch, J. (2002). *Television drama: Agency, audience and myth*. New York, NY: Routledge.

Weaver, J.A. (2009). *Popular culture primer*. New York, NY: Peter Lang Publishing.

Weber, J.B. & Hunt, P.M. (2020). *Shameless sociology: Critical perspectives on a popular television series*. Newcastle, UK: Cambridge Scholars Publishing.

Weheliye, A.G. (2014). *Habeas Viscus: Racializing assemblages, biopolitics, and Black feminist theories of the human*. Duke University Press.

Williams, L. (2014). *On the wire*. Durham, NC: Duke University Press.

Williams, R. (1974/2003). *Television: Technology and cultural form*. Philadelphia, PA: Psychology Press.

Wozolek, B. (2019). Mothering redoux: Agency and joy in negotiating capitals of shame. *Journal of Gender Studies, 28(8)*, 873-882.

Wozolek, B. (2018). In 8100 again: The sounds of students breaking. *Educational Studies: A Journal of the American Educational Studies Association, 54*(4), 367-381.

Wozolek, B. (2021). *Assemblages of violence in education: Everyday trajectories of oppression*. New York, NY: Routledge.

Wright, H. K., & Maton, K. (2004). Cultural studies and education: From Birmingham origin to global presence. *Review of Education, Pedagogy & Cultural Studies, 26*(2/3), 73-89. doi:10.1080/10714410490480359

Zizek, S. (1991). *Looking awry: An introduction to Jacques Lacan through popular culture*. Cambridge, MA: MIT Press.

Chapter 9

Curricular Disruptions

Signifying Nigeria through Africanfuturisms

Sandra J. Schmidt, PhD, Teachers College, Columbia University

"Wakanda Forever". Those words echoed across Black communities young and old four years ago. *Black Panther* brought from comic books to the big screen the imagination of a technologically advanced, un-colonized African homeland. Less a story of what could have been, it features some imagination of what Africa is and can be. Dashikis, lion robes, spears, and tribal art/adornments were reassigned from symbols of darkness or backwardness to symbols of an advanced society that integrates its history, culture, and connection to the physical world. As Wakanda rose, Blackness was expanded and celebrated. Wakanda's greatness was insular and throughout much of the film and comic series, the place sits invisible and disconnected from Africa and its descendants. Backlash reflected the deep discomfort Wakanda offered to the narrative of Africa and Blackness that circulate freely in European/White-dominated societies (Strong & Chaplin, 2019). And yet, Wakanda itself is an invention that arises from US authors for a largely US readership/viewership. The most recent comic books and film were written by Black Americans. This complicates the supposed African-ness of the film but also frames this chapter -how is/does Africa come into being, by whom and for whom, and how do African ways of seeing contribute to a curriculum of space, temporality, and the continent.

What is Africa? Oyewumi (2005) argues, "Africa is used merely as a vehicle for articulating Western preoccupations and modes of understanding." (p. xiii). Soyinka (2012) contributes,

Every so-called nation on that continent is a mere fiction perpetrated in the cause of external interest by imperial power, a fiction that both colonial rule and post-independent exertions have struggled and failed to turn into an enduring, cohering reality. It is a gross fiction whose exposure continues to exact penalties in hundreds of thousands of lives...one that only a few governments, such as Ethiopia, have had the courage to stand on its head and creatively interrogate. (p. 45).

African writers and scholars have been arguing the words of Oyewumi and Soyinka for decades, acknowledging that the manner in which Africa is shared tells us the history and politics of colonizers and not the intricacies of the continent. While Oyewumi, Soyinka, and others bring African ontologies into US scholarship, there is no retrieval of the African (Appiah, 1993). These authors themselves, both tenured in US universities, reflect a postcolony of interacting knowledges (Mbembe, 2001). But, we can do more to elevate and evaluate work that centers Africa rather than the US/Europe.

The question "what is Africa?" is necessary to pose in US social studies classrooms wherein Black, White, and African immigrant youth form economic, political, and sociological views of the continent. Africa is a minor subject in most history/social studies classrooms. Research finds that textbooks and curricular materials demonstrate a failure to incorporate significant topics in African history, focusing almost exclusively on ancient kingdoms (relegating contributions of the continent to the distant past), slavery, and colonialism (Davis, 2005; Waweru & Ntarangwi, 2013.) Wildstein (2018) reviewed world history standards and textbooks used in 7 states and found that only three states required teaching West African kingdoms. Her study noted that the most common topics presented in the standards today are European imperialism, African nationalism after World War II and contemporary human rights violations and AIDS crises (Wildstein, 2018). These selective topics reinforce more qualitative findings about manners of othering, misperceptions, danger, and lack of agency assigned to Africa in classrooms (Awan, 2011; Dei, 2010).

Combine school curriculum with the presentation of Africa in US films and media and we are not surprised by a survey that finds young Americans travelling to Africa expected to find a place that was "poor, dangerous, hot, underdeveloped, violent, tribal, and spiritual" (Keim, 2014, p. 15). In a recent interview with author Tochi Onyebuchi (featured in this chapter) he takes as inspiration for his writing the need to re-inform people in the US that Africa is not a country but a continent of countries and to re-depict images of poverty and huts (Breakfast Club, 2019). As many problematic representations of Africa as there are in media, there are also new works, largely written/produced by people of African descent, that are transforming and critiquing these representations. Social media sites such as "Africa is a country", "OkayAfrica", and "Omenana" disrupt narratives and re-frame the continent and where we turn for sources of knowledge. New mediums, produced across the diaspora that re-center the geography, spirituality, and lives on the continent are important to critique as curricular materials.

This chapter engages with contemporary works of Young Adult fantasy and futurisms from authors of African descent. I borrow from an African ontology of storytelling as sharing the past and engaging with the present in how I situate and examine these novels. As such, the authors are elders using the novels as curriculum to educate Black and non-Black youth about the continent, themselves, and Blackness. My analysis explores how these elder-authors present the continent, and specifically Nigeria, to young readers. I pursue this as a means to think about how the past, told in the future, may disrupt problematic and pessimistic narratives of a continent.

History/Futures

'But Africans don't do speculative fiction!' … However, this is a claim that anyone who has ever sat down to listen to tales of spirit husbands, mermaids and forest dwarfs, whose mats have the ability to make one rich, knows to be false. In our folktales animals talked and the gods walked among men; what is called fantasy today was as real as night and day. But, we have lost the immediacy of those stories and have been reduced to trafficking in borrowed images that vilify our heritage. This is a tragedy because stories do more than entertain us, the best stories hold up a mirror to the world. They show us not just what is, but what could be, if it chose. Omenana

Omenana is an online journal of speculative fiction from the African continent and diaspora. This quote comes from their website as an invitation for writers from Africa and its diaspora to join this community. The editors simultaneously recognize the utterances that have cast African and Black writers out of speculative fiction realms and the resonances that make it a genre of possibility for liberating postcolonial storytelling and conceptions of the continent.

"Baba, tell me a story…" are the opening lines of *Black Panther* (Babb, 2020). This invitation to tell a story is fitting for a film about Africa. Storytelling is an oral tradition that distinguishes African societies (Bisschoff, 2020; Bryce, 2019; Rutledge, 2001; Tamale, 2020). The oral tradition I call upon is akin to written scholarship and not only literature in Western, modernist societies. The African story is a means of transferring knowledge from elders to youth and is the pedagogical counterpart of the history lecture in US schools. Whereas Western scholars tend to develop rational arguments that approach truth (Rutledge, 2001), storytelling in Africa is non-linear. Tamale (2020) embraces Ourka's philosophy that youth should "seek wisdom from traditional sages, male and female, who possess unique insights on fundamental human themes such as the nature of time, freedom, death, education, and the existence of God" (p. 273). Storytelling engages the past through spiritual ideas, not through historiography and truth. The African epistemology embedded in storytelling already has a resonance with the imaginations of speculative fiction/Africanfuturisms and posthumanisms. It contains mythologies that cohere the animal, human, and physical worlds, and it allows play between gods, magical figures, and tricksters (Bisschoff, 2020; Burnett, 2019).

The work of futurisms is a complement to these African ideologies. Eshun (2003) writes, "The field of Afrofuturism does not seek to deny the tradition of countermemory. Rather, it aims to extend that tradition by reorienting the intercultural vectors of Black Atlantic temporality towards the proleptic as much as the retrospective" (p. 289). Eshun importantly resignifies the "future" in Afrofuturisms by acknowledging the intra-action of past, present, and future (Guthrie, 2019). It does not try to apologize or undo the past but to reckon what has happened with what is still possible. The genre bends space and time, merging history with future possibilities (Strong & Chaplin, 2019). This allows Afrofutures to recover Black histories that recognize the greatness of African empires and cultures (Yaszek, 2013). For example, authors may present a world where the legacies of slavery are re/solved (Babb, 2020) or wherein a mystical/dis-bodied Middle Passage allows authors to wrestle with slavery's trauma (Eshun, 2003).

Through a reexamination of the past through African eyes, we can endorse different futures; we are freed from continuing the linear progressive march in which binaries and oppression are expected and recognizable (Eshun, 2003). Afrofutures are not written to comfort Whites but to empower Blacks/Africans to reprogram the present (Burnett, 2019; Eshun, 2003; Guthrie, 2019). Okorafor (2019) repositions her own work as Africanfutures rather than Afrofutures in an effort to re-center Africa in a futuristic genre. She responds to writers of African descent whose work centers Blackness or the diaspora but not Africa. Her language in important in this chapter as I turn to novels that center the continent as curricular texts in the US.

African oral storytelling is a source of knowledge on the continent. Writers in the diaspora use the related genres of speculative fiction, Afrofuturism and fantasy to represent knowledge of the animal, human, spirit, and physical worlds of past and present that was shared by their elders to readers in the US and on the continent. I turn to these written works as curricular and pedagogical in a manner akin to how storytelling has been used to tell the lineages of the past and to share lessons of the world. What do these stories teach young readers about the continent?

Positionality and Curriculum Inquiry

In this chapter, I follow the work on popular media critics, literary critics, and cultural studies writers. I do not seek to replicate their work, but to consider these ideas as an educator, particularly a social studies educator. I am a teacher and a teacher of teachers. As a spatial theorist, I think about curriculum as the multiple ways that concepts are encountered in the nested layers of a school, including its material forms and written subject matter and disciplines, and are embodied as young people navigate relationships with authorities, with adults, with peers, and with social norms. This means that in the social composition of the curriculum in schools, there are many points at which Africa is formed for young people. The racial position of the youth matters in these encounters. White youth are more likely to try to build Black as deficit and Africa as doom, while Black youth may be seeking the language and the validation of home narrations that refuse those productions. Youth read different texts and see themselves mirrored in those texts based on race and gender. Bodies are regulated based on race, further fostering the curriculum of race, Black, and Africa.

As an educator, I turn to Africanfutures texts to explore them as social studies curriculum. I am concerned with both the texts teachers pick up to frame the continent as well as those materials they give young people. Each has an influence on the worldviews of young people. In social studies education, we tend toward history textbooks as the "correct" texts through which to think about the past and how that past informs the present we might deconstruct. Africafuturisms and their connection to the past present a rupture with the historical tools we accept. It is for this reason that I turn to stories categorized as fiction to think about a curriculum of/about Africa. The use of African stories as history challenges Western scientific knowledge and reflects a willingness to sit in different epistemological spaces that break with racial and knowledge hierarchies and erasures.

My inquiry engages with three young adult novels from the traditions of African/futurisms/speculative fiction that are widely available in the US. I want to wonder with these texts about the production of an Africa, specifically how they educate about common social concepts. Unlike a literary critic, I look less at the nuances and richness of content, writing, and literary devices but focus on the substance, the text as a curricular encounter for young people. I specifically think of these novels as the work of elders who are also Black, Nigerian American and seeking to tell stories to young readers that were passed through their own elders as they maneuvered this complex postcolony.

I am a White educator, who has lived on the African continent, but not in the area where these materials (scholarly and literary) are set. I am not mirrored nor searching for mirrors in these texts. I am not implicated by the presentation of Africa and Blackness in these novels. I am drawn to these books and to this project as part of ongoing academic work on the continent and with young people that are bound in the relations of and with Africa and how Africa is taken up in schools. My research with African youth and African youth immigrants to the US demonstrates the need for materials that disrupt the stereotypes of the continent that are placed on these people and are so rarely refuted in the materials available to teachers who believe that they are teaching about Africa. My view is limited but I try to use this position to reach other White teachers and interrogate our work and thinking.

The Selected Works

I have drawn from contemporary works as a response to the energy for more writing by African diasporic authors that participate in reclaiming the continent. The novels are *War Girls* by Tochi Onyebuchi (2019), *Children of Blood and Bone* by Tomi Adeyemi (2018), and *Akata Witch* by award-winning writer Nnedi Okorafor (2011). The Young Adult works of fiction are each the first novels in a series by the author, set in Nigeria as a lived and/or imagined space, and share young female protagonists. *War Girls* and *Children of Blood and Bone* are some of the newest series that share these characteristics, but I felt it important to also feature Okorafor as she is a widely awarded author in this genre. Each of these authors is Nigerian American and has lived much of their life outside the continent but has used their writing to connect back to the continent. Okorafor and Onyebuchi are of Igbo heritage and Adeyemi of Yoruban. They are themselves positioned in this space between—raised Black in the United States (the space of the colonizer) and oriented through their lineage to Nigeria. Their work, then, arises from these spaces of African knowing and being that is set off the continent.

Introduction to *Akata Witch*

> An ugly, sickly color for a child of pure Nigerian blood. Everything about you is "wrong"—your eyes, your hair, your skin. Otherwordly... They say your kind has one foot set in the physical world and one foot in the wilderness—that's what we call the spirit world. (p. 116).

Sunny, our young leader in *Akata Witch*, is Nigerian (Igbo), but her albino skin is the color of the sun. She was born to Nigerian parents in the US who returned with her older brothers to Nigeria. We learn at the conclusion that her mother initiated the return to Nigeria because something needed to happen to Sunny there. The book is situated in present day Nigeria and familiarizes a Nigerian world wherein Sunny plays soccer (after the sun has set) with her brothers, is ridiculed for being smart in school, and has lawyer and doctor parents.

Sunny sees a premonition in a candle that sets off the story of magic. It is discovered by a classmate, Orlu, and his out-of-school friend, Chichi, that Sunny shares their magical powers as Leopard people. Unlike Orlu and Chichi, Sunny is a free agent meaning she is not born to and raised by Leopard parents. They are joined by a fourth teen, Sasha, who has been sent to live with Orlu's family when he used magic with classmates in Chicago. Magic becomes the connective thread of the novel—it connects the animal, human and spirit worlds, it connects elders and young people, and it is shared by Leopards of varying race, ethnicities, and nationalities living around the globe.

The children sneak off at night to their teacher Anatov who helps each young person find a mentor. The mentors are elders, sharing their knowledge so that their mentees may turn their riddles and experience into wisdom. As readers, we are introduced to the magical world through its books, social structures, spells, celebrations, and community, and finally through battle. The elders have ultimately convened the four youth into a coven that will defeat a criminal recking havoc in the Lamb (non-Leopard) and Leopard world before he can invite evil into their world.

Introduction to War Girls

> The battles are getting easier and easier. She suspects it's because they've heard of her by now. The warrior on the front lines. The inhuman pilot who destroys Nigerian mechs as though they were flies to be swatted out of the sky. And who has no fear of death. With her mechanized eye, the outlet at the base of her neck, and the tech that covers half her face running down her shoulder and back to her augmented right arm, she barely looks human. She looks like something much more evil. The Demon of Biafra. (Onyebuchi, p. 119-120)

Onyii, the Demon of Biafra, adorns the front cover of the novel, *War Girls*. Onyii is presented to us with her mechanical arm and dark eyes staring back. Her young face expressing emotion belies the body ready for war. Behind her rise, tall buildings and smoke contrasting post-apocalyptic Nigeria beset by the technological advances that perpetuate war and the grave destructions those technologies make possible. The novel begins in 2172 and while much of the White world has fled to space colonies, Africa remains inhabited, its borders still reflecting colonization and war. The novel uses futuristic imagination to re-articulate the Biafran War, a period that Onyebuchi argues does not receive due attention outside of Nigeria. The war between Nigerians and Biafrans has separated young girls and their families. In one of these camps where young girls are being trained as war leaders, a sisterly bond is formed between Onyii and Ify. They are separated in battle, and their journey back to one another reveals the lines that are drawn between groups and through people and the ravage war takes on land, animals, and people.

Introduction to Children of Blood and Bone

> Creation swirls before my eyes, the birth of man, the origin of the gods. Their magic crashes into the room in waves, a rainbow of every vibrant hue. Magic shatters through every heart, every soul, every being. It connects us all, threading through the shell of humanity. (p. 518)

Tomi Adeyemi's *Children of Blood and Bone*, culminates in a connection between diviners and non-magical kosidan. Adeyemi draws inspiration from *Harry Potter* and Suzanne Collins, but she attempts to position her story in the magical tradition of Yoruban ethos and geography. Set in fictional Orisha whose geography borrows from Nigeria, *Children of Blood and Bone*, engages the magic of Orisa. In sharing with a Western and African readership, Adeyemi exemplifies much of the theory Wole Soyinka takes us through in *Of Africa* (2012). Soyinka takes us into the deep spirituality of a continent that carried across the oceans in bodies of enslaved Africans but whose integration of body, soul, place, and past does not induce proselytizing. Adeyemi is critical of the social divisiveness used to oppress people along with race and class. She uses magic to write her Orisha through and past this history.

The youth of Orisha are the protagonists tasked with saving the country from itself. Adeyemi's central characters capture the complicated divisions. Zelie is a fighter and a diviner. She is featured on the cover where readers are introduced to the white hair, dark skin, and piercing eyes that mark her as a diviner and place her father and brother in harm's way. Her mother was one of the diviners who was killed eleven years earlier when King Saran took away magic. Zelie is cast aside with the marks of her legacy but not its powers. Her powers come from her courage, her desire to protect her father, her connection to her mother, and her strength as a fighter. She forms a contentious friendship with King Saran's daughter, Amari, who has fled the castle with a sacred/magical scroll after watching her father kill her diviner servant. Amari appears in need of saving but throughout the novel, grows in her strength, knowledge, and facilitation skills. Tzain is the kosidan brother of Zelie. When they set off to restore magic, Tzain mediates Zelie and Amari. Amari's brother is largely the antagonist as he battles with Amari and Zelie. Early in the novel, he realizes that he is a diviner. He attempts to resist the magic he can feel building in him. His hatred for magic and its resultant cleavages, but also for his father's rule, impel him to help the others but ultimately fall victim to his own vision for united Orisha without magic.

African Resignification and Liberation

This section provides curricular/pedagogical inquiry into selected fiction. After writing initial descriptions for each novel, I have identified four concepts that are substantial lessons across the texts. In each of these, I explore the novels, sometimes in conversations and sometimes independently advancing lessons about youth, gender, indigeneity, and conflict. I conclude each section in trying to summarize what I have taken away as a reader and the lessons, through me, I am allowing these novelists as elders to share with other readers as we think about this place of Africa.

Youth Protagonists

The young people's strength and societal roles invite us to consider the books as part of the elder system and simultaneously comment on it. Onyebuchi, Okorafor, and Adeyemi were each raised by Nigerian immigrant parents in the US who either shared their Nigerian upbringing in their home and/or with travels to Nigeria (Durosomo, 2017; Locus, 2020; Wabuke, 2018). Each author is now sharing knowledge or provoking other Black youth to gaze into these stories as mirrors into their world.

Each book is young adult fiction and thus employs youth characters to appeal to young readers. The books share the agentive possibilities of youth while trying to be a mirror for the injustices Black youth experience among peers and elders. Each novel presents youth who are crucial to resolving social conflicts that far exceed their lived experience. They become entwined in battles and unresolved issues of their elders. This seems mimicked in much youth experience today where unresolved problems are inherited by the next generation. In these books, the youths similarly do not end the war but fight one of the battles that will embed them deeper into the sources of problems in future novels. But youth are not left to fight alone; the novels do not replace the elder system. Elders are the holders of wisdom and memory. In *Children of Blood and Bone* and *Akata Witch*, elders are sages and invoke stories and metaphors to give young people the knowledge they need to carry out their missions. In *War Girls* , most of the warriors and their abd[1] are young people because the war has taken many elders or at least cast them to the periphery in the story. This wisdom of the elders through which youth understand their social positionings and the causes and consequences of war are not disseminated through elders in human forms but through technologies into which the characters plug themselves to acquire knowledge and memories. This is why Xifeng, the Chinese aid worker, is collecting memories of adults left in the ground when young people were taken to war—to have records into which future generations can plug themselves. The importance of stories transmitted across time remains. The task, as with storytelling, is for young people to turn this knowledge into wisdom with which to control their worlds.

Each novel has a significant focus on larger social problems, but each also has individual moments of struggle through which young people learn and relate. In *Akata Witch*, Sunny is taunted by a classmate who singles her out for her differences—her albinism, her American accent, and her studiousness. When physically knocked down, Sunny brings forth her spirit face, violating an important Leopard law not to reveal this world to Lambs. Situations of individual differentiation based on race are common encounters for Black youth. Each author writes into their novel these relatable moments that are part of the whole story but also connective moments for readers, and sometimes memories for the authors.

The notion of un-wanting heroes arises in each of these novels. The label of an un-wanting heroine seems particular prevalent in fantasy novels with female protagonists. The un-wantedness of the social position tends to dissipate across the trilogies, but in these first novels, Zelie, Amari, and Sunny question their skills and position. Zelie shifts from confident fighter at Mama Agba's school to uncertain leader when Mama Agba tells her of her mission. There are many times in the subsequent pages where Zelie tries to pass the leadership to others. It also takes Amari most of the novel to find her way from a runaway, hiding princess to the compassionate, warrior queen she will become. Teacher Anatov tells Sunny of the powerful heritage of her grandmother and her albinism, but Sunny largely experiences the Leopard world as an outsider. As a free agent, she is relegated a differentiated position even though she is essential as the fourth corner of the youth coven. The one time she is confident is with the soccer ball at her feet. The lesson on the unwanting hero is perhaps a mirror to young girls in the US struggling with social positioning and the refusals of a singular hero. Onyii is the character who most willing takes control of her position as she searches for Ify and the answers of war. The coming into a hero form hinges on learning the world and experiencing their own power. Zelie learns from her elders and other diviners about the magical world. The more she knows, the better she is able to trust her instincts and participate in the resistance. Sunny listens carefully to her teachers, her magic teachers and her mentors to understand her strengths and their belief in her.

The youth in these novels are their own agents, even as they respect their position within the Nigerian elder system. In centering youth, the stories become relatable, connective, and educative to their audience. I see these writers as elders sharing their knowledge so that young readers, re-signifying the continent through novels, are informed in their actions.

Relational Feminism

The feminist trickster embodies an African womanist sensibility counter to the gendered binary/hierarchy often thrust upon African women from their Western saviors (Burnett, 2015). Within Nigerian culture and language, the biological boundaries of gender and sex are refuted. Oyewumi (2005) argues, "the category women cannot be used as a synonym for gender given the fact that in many African societies social roles are not necessarily biological roles...social roles and sexual roles are understood to be separable" (p. xiii-xiv). From Yoruban society, she writes of females who assume the roles of ruler, mother, diviner, husband, and offspring. Through language, she refutes the hierarchy of male and female foist onto African women. Amadiume (2000) provides a similar critique through Igbo society. With Africanfuturisms, human alterations and magic further gender disruptions (Bisschoff, 2020; Bryce, 2019). My Western gaze, attempting to engage African feminisms, reads gendering curriculum in these novels. The centrality of the female character alone is insufficient to identity these as feminist projects; it is what the authors do with their female characters.

The sisters of war and the magic-employing girls defy Western tropes of female bodies and social positions (Oyewumi, 1997). Onyebuchi's war girls are physically and intellectually powerful. Ify has superior intellectual abilities, yet she still fits herself with an Accent that enhances her digital processing capabilities. After being rescued/captured by the Nigerians, her scheming capabilities allow her to lure her captors into battle, producing a means of escape for herself. Onyii, leader Chinelo, and the other war girls comprise a sisterly tribe. They are gifted with superior physicality and warrior instincts and augmented with technology. Among Biafran warriors, Chinelo's camp produces the most sophisticated battalion. The Nigerians argue that Biafrans devalue women because they serve in war but Ify recognizes that Biafran women are the fiercest defenders of the Biafran nation. Sunny, the albino witch, excels in the classroom and on the football pitch, even though she occupies a body/skin that is often perceived as weak due to its light sensitivity. Okorafor rewrites the albino body out of fragile margins into an esteemed position within the Leopard coven. Zelie is also physically strong; the novel opens with her defeat of a more experienced fighter. She and other diviner-girls are being prepared to defend their community against the king. These girls stand out because they take up positions assumed to be reserved for male bodies and yet each novel makes clear that it is not gender that is the central social division.

The feminist tropes engage a relational frame. Women's relationships with others are central to their power and resistance. The war sisters are a closeknit countersociety; as family, the women fight for and protect one another. The sisterly relationship at the center of the novel is that of Onyii and Ify, the young girl Onyi took as a sister after she killed Ify's parents in the act of war. It is this bond for which Onyii will eventually leave her war sisters; she departs to search for and re-rescue Ify. When they enter into a battle, the war girls fight for one another as much as for Biafra. There is a difficult and exemplary scene when the war girls enter into battle and become trapped during the battle that Ify facilitated from her place of capture. But rather than leading to the death of her captors, it is the Biafran war girls who are placed in a precarious situation. One war girl has to be sacrificed so that the others can escape. There is an intimate good-bye and a promise by the others that they will look after the lover of the girl being sacrificed. But care is complicated when emotion and expression are difficult. Chinelo and Ify are lovers at times, but in others, Chinelo's desire to be without emotion/care/affect cause passion to surface as violence. As warriors, Chinelo designs an abd program in which each warrior is paired with a synth (more to follow) who acts as slave-defender. The abds are quick studies and are trained to do anything to protect their warrior, lessening the need for the sisters to be one another's primary protectors in battle. Because the synth is not human, these pairings should remove the emotional ties of protection. But ultimately, lines of caring emerge between abd and warrior and the synths become little brothers or part of the family. When Chinelo concludes that the abds have become unstable after failing to protect their warriors in battle, she orders them killed. Onyii is unable to kill Agu, playing on the senses of emotion and relation the characters confront. The relational work is central in defining sister society although Onyebuchi provides complicated manners in the act of care. He suggests that repeated acts of caring can produce feelings that approach bonding.

Children of Blood and Bone and *Akata Witch* rely on a cast of characters to enact the mission. They break from the individualist notion of a hero to feature communal sensibilities. In *Children of Blood and Bone*, the female characters are pushed into action when their relationships are threatened. Amari flees her father and his reign when her girl-servant is put to death. The loss of this relationship gives Amari an understanding of wrong-ness in the rule of her father. Zelie is forced into action when those closest to her are attacked and threatened. She has been secretly training with other diviner girls to protect their community when the prince invades. She was persuaded to carry out a mission against the king because her father's life is at stake. Emotional connections are central to characters finding their inner strength and convictions. The crusade into which Zelie, Amari, and Tzain are thrust is successful when they trust one another and employ connections with other diviners. Each test—winning the aquatic games, the ceremony (and escape) from the bandit camp, breaking Zelie from jail, and finally reaching the Holy Temple—requires a community of co-conspirators who are brought together around the heroine's goal. Strength rests not upon the individual but upon matriarchal ideas. The patriarchal form of power exuded by King Saran over his subjects, set by fear and totality, is contrasted with the leadership that forms around Zelie. *Akata Witch* develops this feminization the least but shares a similar de-individualization trope with *Children of Blood and Bone*. Sunny's magic is developed quickly because she is essential as the fourth corner of the coven. Individuals cannot alone destroy the power of an evil criminal determined to revive dark figures of the part. The novel develops the characters, their coven, and their relationships with one another, but through magic, even the coven does not work alone. The magic they draw upon brings in ancestors, spirits and memories of the past to build an "army" that defeats evil.

As the author-elders share lessons of the world, we see them disconnect the gendered body from social positions. These authors assign strength, fierceness, and intellect to the female characters/bodies that take up a multitude of roles. Through these readings, matriarchal lines of power are promoted as desirable and powerful. It is not that "the future is female" but that the evils are better confronted utilizing the relational bonds. Perhaps, the leaders will be women, but the more important lesson is to see what feminized relationships make possible.

Indigenous Ontologies, Ancestral Worlds

Centering Africa engages Indigenous and ancestral ideas that critique Western humanism. Indigenous ontologies depict a world in which animal, land, humans, and spirits are interrelated rather than distinguishable. Mythical creatures or diviner-rulers embody this hybridity/interconnectivity. *War Girls* positions technology in the human-land-animal flow. As such, it raises questions about what it means to be human, in body and in spirit. Ify is red-blooded or the most biologically human. She gives herself an Accent that enhances her digital intellectual capabilities. Onyii and the other war girls are Augments, meaning they have robotic/machine augmentations to their physical body, but their minds are biologically "human". Synths, like

Agu, are "synthetic"—the combination of machine and repurposed bodies. These classifications become blurred on the physical bodies, thus raising an ongoing theme about whether human-ness relates to body, mind or soul. At some juncture, Onyii and her abd/synth are not so distinct in their bodies and minds. Each body contains significant technology and struggles with feeling. Onyii is so programmed for war that she knows no other way. When she loses Ify, she feels that loss and finally acts on it. But through most of the novel, feeling is something that is not part of her being. In contrast, we encounter Agu attempting to learn feeling:

> It is good, what you are telling me. I am a synth. I am a soldier. I am doing horrible things but Xifeng tells me I am also boy and that, once upon a time, I am having mother and father and they are loving me... When I am telling her what is going on inside my head, she is looking at me with water in her eyes, and I am feeling like old man because I have seen so much war...but she is tells me I am little boy, so I am trying to be little boy" (p. 328).

These plays with Onyii and Agu as they question their bodies and existence exemplify the blur between human and machine.

Onyebuchi seems to offer a critique of Western humanisms. The classifications, a modernist product, do little to our understanding. Instead, we see similar desires emerging for freedom across distinguished bodies. They become interconnected when they can feel. The mechanized, human bodies are not a future construct. How different is the spear held in the hand that gives identity to a warrior of the past from weapons Onyii can launch from her body in 2172? The weapons are all extensions of the body and produce one's identity. Ancestral values focus on the interplay of the spirit, human, physical, and animal kingdoms. This novel seems to extend this to the mechanical world. Liberation does not arise from the form one takes, but in the hope that emotion or connection to others can stop these differentiations and violence.

Adeyemi shares in the critique of the West, specifically efforts to hide the ancestral world. Adeyemi reclaims this by using fiction to educate about Orisa/Orisha. The ancestors are not people of the past, but spirits who live in the present and share their wisdom to guide others. The form of spirituality/magic that comes to life in the novel features the architecture of Orisa and the various gods people rely on to support and guide them in life. Adeyemi offers the readers a map of the maji clans. We see how the world is organized in Orisa belief—life/death, spirit/dreams, water, fire, air, earth/minerals, dark/light, health, time, animals. Each clan has a deity and domain and each diviner in the novel traces through a specific clan that gives them their powers. Though distinct, each is required. Together they comprise the wholeness of the world. The human may stand at the center, but that life experience is comprised through the interdependencies of these domains. The bringing back of magic is ultimately the rejection of the Western forms that presume humans have control over the others. When Adeyemi brings back magic at the end and gives it to all Orishians, not only the diviners, she offers a solution to social divides that is not about just eliminating distinctions but embracing an Orishian worldview.

Sunny is a shape-shifter and Okorafor's novel allows us to see that literally and metaphorically. Sunny's mentor, Sugar Cream, gives the language to Sunny because her ghost-like appearance allows her to change her shape to move across planes and to physically take herself through keyholes so that she can leave her house unnoticed. She is someone through whom the ancestral world takes form and creates remedies in Nigeria's physical world. But her parents, having lived in the US, do not shape this spiritual world with her. The shape-shifting idea is also a manner of understanding how a person like Sunny can re-form herself to be visible in each of her social contexts (Cox, 2015). In negotiating the world, Sunny also comes to value the array of creatures—human, insect, animal—and physical forms that help her navigate the magical realm.

These novels engage with Indigenous and ancestral ideas differently but collectively teach that the world is improved upon when spirits are heeded, land is protected, and people feel connection to one another and the world. There is indirect critique of the remnants of humanism and other Western ideologies that have become invasive species in Africa. Although damaging, these novels reveal that even when magic (ancestral values) are suppressed, they are not extinguished.

War and Social Conflict

These novels provide commentary but little resolution on the co-lonial project of classification for political purposes that lingers in group conflicts today. Onyebuchi is most deliberate and explicit in his re-telling of the Biafran War, a war arising from imperialism but little acknowledged beyond Nigeria, and yet a war that has marked the ethnic distinctions central to Okorafor and Adeyemi. As Onyebuchi writes near the end, how does one stop war when advancement and the economy have become dependent on it. This is his critique.

Onyebuchi offers us insight, a reflection on the time past, to chal-lenge us to think about the complexities and unnecessary construc-tions we rely on to perpetuate conflict rather than peace and its impact on humanity. There is a play with the geography—Africa remaining intact with its colonial cities and boundaries while the rest of the dev-astated planet has "colonized" space. The political and physical geog-raphy of Nigeria remains intact, perhaps an educative tool about Bi-afra, the fight over a new mineral found largely under Igbo lands, and religious/cultural/identity divides that led to Biafran nationalism and resulted in a war between Biafra and Nigeria that remains. Is Biafra Nigeria? The characters reflect this tension. By the end we learn that the reason for Ify's light skin is that she is not Onyii's sister by shar-ing a birthparent but because Ify was raised by Onyii when her birth family was killed. It is specifically, though, Ify's shifting identity from Nigerian to Biafran to Nigerian and finally un-belonging that posi-tion identity as cultural, linguistic, nationalistic, and political. Ngozi explains to her sisters Chinelo and Onyii that there is no option but war, "We have tried peaceful protest. We have tried marching. You do not meet hate with love" (p. 234). The "we" in her statements are the Igbo. The Igbo feel their minority status and that inability to control the resources beneath their land. The Igbo share geographic and his-toric distinction from the Northern Hausa and Fulani whose live-lihoods and identities were formed through interactions with Arab traders and ethnic groups on the periphery of the Sahara. The Igbo formed relationships through connections on the coast. And then slave-trading turned into colonialism, and Nigeria came into existence as a political-economic entity and new attachments were needed. "I am a Nigerian because a White man said so. I was Igbo because my tribespeople long ago said so. And I am Biafran because I say so" (p.

237), said Chinelo. She is positing the relationship between a cultural/tribal locale and nationalist language. At the heart of the war is the struggle over just this: If Biafra and Nigeria are independent national ideologies, can the need to share resources and political geography allow a cohered living. In the end, Onyebuchi is pessimistic. Ify, who became Nigerian, walked back across the border once the ceasefire was enacted only to express that her Nigerian rescuers/captors never accepted her as truly Nigerian, not because of her ethnicity but because of her wandering nationalist sensibilities. Even though she is released to wander as independent, an indication of a ceasefire, her captor/rescuers embed in her a tracker that will help them find Onyii and reignite the war. The war is too profitable and too much a part of the mind/body of warriors such that they cannot resign themselves to accept peace. The costs are humanity. Children are many of the actors, taught to hate and trained as machines of. The children, raised as warriors do not know another way of being.

The recovery of the Biafran War and its critique on social divisions that need redress in Nigeria today implicates colonizers. The Igbo-Fulani-Hausa-Yoruba distinctions predate slave trade and colonialism but oppressive colonial systems played on those divisions. Hence, Onyebuchi offers critique of outside powers. Most of the outside influence occurs through the Colonies that migrated to outer space. White people fled the devastated world and left Africans to survive on lands rotted by war and other degradations. It is unclear whether the Chinese aid workers reside on Earth or elsewhere and thus their racial-social position. The colonies produce desire and distrust. At the end of the novel, this is where Onyii and Ify want to travel; it is the only way to escape the capture that will send them to a tribunal or be returned to war. The colonies offer the allure of a better, peaceful life alongside distrust. Colonialism created the Nigeria that is embattled throughout the novel. There is also a short reference to a Truth and Reconciliation process as something the colonies brought to Nigeria to resolve war. Onyii and Chinelo discuss the unfairness of this process; the colonizer/outside world categorizing people as either perpetrators or victim without understanding that all Nigerians and Biafrans were victims in some way. They do not understand the people on whom they enact their policies.

Adeyemi's Orisha is not at war, but trapped within an authoritarian rule that exacts random violence on diviners and their families. This is not so different from the police violence Adeyemi sees around her as a Nigerian American living in the US. There are consequences of that violence. Families are torn apart. Zelie and Tzain lose their mother and later their father in the physical realm. Prince Inan is killed by his father-king and Amari kills her father-king, although perhaps these deaths are an ending and new beginning. These losses are just those among the lead characters. The king attacks Zelie's fishing village and many lives are lost in the search to rid the area of diviners. The struggle is not only the loss of life, but a society organized to defend that authoritarian regime.

Orisha is geographically organized to divide people. We learn much of the landscape as we follow Zelie, Amari, Tzain, and Inan across the country to collect their magical elements. Around the capital of Lagos, there is the walled city that supports the function of the government. In nearby Ilorin where Zelie lives in a fishing village, people live independently but in constant fear of the king. It is for this reason that Zelie and her classmates train with Mama Agba but hide their fight training within a sewing school. Lagos, Gombe, Ibeji, and Jimeta—the places they travel to collect the magical elements— are separated from one another by uninviting mountains, forests, and bodies of water. These divides and distances allow communities to form beneath the watch of the king. A community of diviners banded together in Calabrar where they had been able to sustain themselves beyond the gaze of the king. In Gombe, even further from Lagos, the diviners, non-politicized, and kosidans seem to live divided but harmonious. A system of taxation also places a burden on the trust and activities of the people. We experience this most harshly in Ibeji, where games of death are essential to raise the remittances people need for taxes and survival. But even in Ilorin, people lived in daily fear of being asked for remittances. The lives that battle to the death and the voyeurs who benefit reflect the social divides of the country. The authoritarian gains financial and political strength from keeping people divided, making kosidians fear the diviners, and suppressing belief systems that may threaten his form of governance.

In *Akata*, Okorafor examines the interpersonal and local conflicts and seeks to demonstrate how communalism can redress divide. Sunny sits in for a variety of contested positions in Nigeria—she is Akata or African American, she is Albino, she is female, and she is a Leopard, but a free agent Leopard. She is constantly set apart from others and yet never beaten down. Her strength arises, as argued before, from the human and spiritual connections that cease her individualistic needs. The simple lessons from Okorafor, speaking to young people, is that we are better when we embrace our difference. Sasha encourages Sunny to play in a football match. When the other boys first glance at her, they try to push her away. Sasha insists that she be allowed to test and they are able to witness her athletic gift. Although her green team ultimately loses a close match, it is her skill that allows them to keep a close match against an older team. The boys are better as a team when they set aside their sexism. Similarly, the Leopard network is built across an array of differences—different creatures, people of different sizes, shapes, ethnicities, and nationalities, and age—living and spirits. This diverse but cohesive group with a common goal of learning and preserving magic unifies them across the globe. The Leopards see themselves as distinct and outside of but these insular community needs to embrace one another to thrive.

These are stories of how we got this way as a world and the consequences of colonialism, imperialism, and racism. The remnants of these systems—modeled in the Leopards—connect the experiences of people around the world. The novels for young people allow these social critiques to be offered in ways they are "safe" to readers; the engagement with magical worlds simultaneously embraces these African ideas while allowing the Western critique to form indirectly. But looking to futures or imagined spaces, we can ask questions about our world without offending one another. Afterall, these are fictional or imagined people, places, and time, even if they are not. The novels do less to create blame but, in trying to think through peace and conflict, ask critical questions about the consequences of a maintaining a divided world. If the coven of youth Leopards are not successful next time in containing Ekwensu, will the consequence be dangerous war games that the war girls cannot escape? Or might these encounters with conflict and the reconnection with emotion, land, and spirit produce a different path?

Black Mirrors, White Gazes

Binyavanga Wainaina's (2005) satirical piece, "How to write about

Africa", commented on the stereotypes a writer must incorporate – the acacia tree, naked warriors, diviners and seers, monkey-brains and grubs, starvation and conflict, and personified animals. He wrote this as social commentary and yet there is something revealing in how some of these condescending images are differently signifying when they are positioned in the works of Africanfuturists. Wainaina critiqued these features for the manners in which White authors depicted and justified an imperialist and savior orientation toward Africa. Onyebuchi, Adeyemi, and Okorafor incorporate some of these images—warriors/conflict, diviners, ancestor—to depict the context from which they were formed or to turn the gaze and provide social critique. In considering my analysis through a curricular lens, I want to imagine the "unimaginable" or what these texts might mirror for Black youth in their encounters and how these novels contribute to Black double-consciousness and separately, how these texts are situated to disrupt a White gaze.

The mirror has been used to question the reflection between self and society. Often in schools, especially in social studies classrooms/curriculum, Black youth in the US do not see themselves and their history mirrored. Africanfutures offers possibilities for mirroring and recovering. Oyewumi (1997) argues that one problem with the West is it epistemically over-relies on a world*view*. This also incorporates the categorizations and divisions that arise from it. She contrasts this to a Yoruban worldsense with an encompassing spirit. This spirituality and interconnectedness have travelled the world through slave systems but sit in opposition to the project of modernity. These Africanfuturist texts contribute to an imagined Africa that embraces interconnective spirituality. The futuristic settings add technology to the intertwined human-animal-land-spirit world. The synths in *War Girls*, Leopards in *Akata*, and diviners and their animals in *Children of Blood and Bone* force a conversation about the independent human long-reflected in the opposition between modernity and indigeneity. They invite Black readers outside Africa to rethink their relationship to this spiritual place. The novels also take up the form of African-storytelling. Storytelling is a powerful tool of recognizing ancestors, sharing morality, maintaining community, and passing history. Perhaps these books will themselves be the history that is passed along to future Black youth, but within the books, in their contemporary position we see each of these themes. The books bring the ancestors into the lived world of the main characters. These main characters each resist Western ideas. But these are not simply books of colonial resistance; they are young books with complex protagonists. Readers who see themselves in Onyii must confront how she kills and rescues; in Zelie we see her doubt and her strength. More importantly, resistance is not an individual trait. Each of these resistors works with/in a community, often of women, who give them power and knowledge. The stories themselves resist by retelling certain pasts—either confronting colonialism or trying to situate oneself outside of it. They do not romanticize the continent but rather produce stories in which African ways of seeing and being in the world, particularly for women, are important ways to work through conflict.

Positioned as a White woman raised amid Western worldviews, it is still difficult to predict how reading these texts and accompanying analysis will disrupt the White gaze. We have seen that curricular interventions are not always sufficient to challenge position. While writing and reading texts that re-create Africa and allow the continent to speak back to colonizers may be an important de-colonizing act for Africans, these same encounters may not destabilize the colonizer's position. That these exist as futuristic and fictional, enable a viewer to leave the texts in that space. In their genre, they are designed to play between the what is and the what if. None of these texts has a White character. The texts refuse the disempowered Black subject, and they refute patriarchy. Racial hierarchies and patriarchy are refuted as desirable social structures. They are either absent or their dismantling is called for in the text. For the White reader who is willing to travel with these Africanfuturisms, one acquires a sense of the spirituality, the interconnectedness, and the strength of the continent. Burnett (2019) writes, "If Africa and Africans are left out of our imagined futures, a form of epistemic violence is being carried out by the collective Western imagination against Africa and its people" (p. 121). But, we must also consider the epistemic violence that occurs when only the West imagines/produces Africa and Africans. Within these texts and this genre, we are presented the opportunity to move into new worlds that are unfamiliar to most White westerners. We are invited to see the importance of the wisdom of the ancestors, to believe in magic, to understand the values of ubuntu, Egungun, and the collective power of matriarchal systems, and to glimpse how African ontologies create peaceful co-exitance. Most importantly, we can allow our worldviews to be disrupted and to listen to African rewrite its past and see differently in the present.

Notes

1. Abd is an Arabic word for Slave

References

Adeyemi, T. (2018). *Children of blood and bone* (Vol. 1). Henry Holt and Company

Amadiume, I. (2000). *Re-inventing Africa: Matriarchy, religion and culture*. Zed Books.

Babb, V. (2020). The Past is Never Past: The Call and Response between Marvel's Black Panther and Early Black Speculative Fiction. *African American Review, 53*(2), 95-109.

Bisschoff, L. (2020). African Cyborgs: Females and Feminists in African Science Fiction Film. *Interventions, 22*(5), 606-623.

Breakfast Club. (2019, December 9). *Author Tochi Onyebuchi creates an alternate look at the Nigerian conflict in his novel 'War Girls'* [Video]. YouTube. https://www.youtube.com/watch?v=kgv5FbQHv-4

Bryce, J. (2019). African Futurism: Speculative Fictions and "rewriting the great Book". *Research in African Literatures, 50*(1), 1-19.

Burnett, J. Y. (2015). The great change and the great book: Nnedi Okorafor's postcolonial, post-apocalyptic Africa and the promise of black speculative fiction. *Research in African Literatures, 46*(4), 133-150.

Burnett, J. Y. (2019). "Isn't Realist Fiction Enough?": On African Speculative Fiction. *Mosaic: an interdisciplinary critical journal, 52*(3), 119-135.

Cox, A. M. (2015). *Shapeshifters: Black girls and the choreography of citizenship*. Duke University Press.

Davis Jr., R. Hunt. (2005, January). Teaching African History in an Era of Globalization. *History Compass*, Vol. 3.

Dei, George J. Scfa. (2010). *Teaching Africa: Towards a Transgressive Pedagogy*. Toronto: Ontario Institute for Studies in Education.

Durosomo, D. (2017, March 29). This 23-Year-Old Nigerian Author's Afrofuturist Novel Has Been Picked Up By Fox Studios. *OkayAfrica*. https://www.okayafrica.com/tomi-adeyemi-children-of-blood-and-bone-movie-deal/

Eshun, K. (2003). Further considerations of Afrofuturism. *CR: The New Centennial Review, 3*(2), 287-302.

Guthrie, R. (2019). Redefining the Colonial: An Afrofuturist Analysis of Wakanda and Speculative Fiction. *Journal of Futures Studies, 24*(2), 15-28.

Keim, C. (2014). *Mistaking Africa: Curiosities and Inventions of the American Mind*. Westview Press.

Locus. (2020, August). Tochi Onyebuchi: Power systems. https://locusmag.com/2020/08/tochi-onyebuchi-power-systems/

Mbembe, A. (2001). *On the postcolony*. Univ of California Press.

Okorafor, N. (2011). *Akata Witch*. Speak.

Okorafor, N. (2019, October 19). Africanfuturism defined. Nnedi's Wahala Zone Blog. http://nnedi.blogspot.com/2019/10/africanfuturism-defined.html

Onyebuchi, T (2019). *War Girls*. Razorbill.

Oyěwùmí, O. (1997). *The invention of women: Making an African sense of western gender discourses*. University of Minnesota Press.

Oyěwùmí, O. (2005). Visualizing the body: Western theories and African subjects. In O. Oyěwùmí (Ed.), *African gender studies: A reader*, pp. 3-22. Springer.

Rutledge, G. E. (2001). Futurist fiction & fantasy: The racial establishment. *Callaloo, 24*(1), 236-252.

Soyinka, W. (2012). *Of Africa*. Yale University Press.

Strong, M. T., & Chaplin, K. S. (2019). Afrofuturism and black panther. *Contexts, 18*(2), 58-59.

Tamale, S. (2020). *Decolonization and Afro-Feminism*. Daraja Press.

Wabuke, H. (2018, February 23). Nnedi Okorafor Is Putting Africans at the Center of Science Fiction and Fantasy. *The Root*. https://www.theroot.com/nnedi-okorafor-is-putting-africans-at-the-center-of-sci-1790862186

Wainaina, B. (2005). How to write about Africa.

Waweru, F. N. & Ntarangwi, M.. (2013). Amending Eurocentric Narratives of African History in the U.S. Classroom: A Popular Culture Approach. In *The Pedagogy of Pop: Theoretical and Practical Strategies for Success*. (pp. 143-158). Lexington Books.

Yaszek, L. (2013). Race in Science Fiction: The Case of Afrofuturism. *A Virtual Introduction to Science Fiction*.

Chapter 10

More Human Than Human?

Transformational habitus, capital, field and the implanting of memories in school curricula

Prof. Phil Wood and Dr. Aimee Quickfall, Bishop Grosseteste University, Lincoln, UK

Introduction

Deckard: *She didn't know?*

Tyrell: *Memory implant. She was programmed. But I think she transcended her conditioning. I think she was beginning to suspect.*

Memory is a core issue in both of Ridley Scott's *Blade Runner* films, a topic that has already gained attention and been written about specifically in relating the nature of memory to identity within the films (Shanahan, 2014; Heersmink & McCarroll 2020). At the core of the films is the complex relationship between humans and replicants, genetically engineered "beings" which are created to fulfil dangerous and undesirable roles in society, such as sex work and frontline military posts; implanted memories act as a buffer to help them understand and accept their assigned roles. Thus, memory and its foundational role in the development of identity are crucial to creating stable, coherent replicants who can take on their roles in society without question.

The links between memory, identity and social contexts are explored in the work of Pierre Bourdieu, through his development of the concepts of habitus, field and capital. In this chapter, we consider these concepts in relation to the experiences of the replicants in the *Blade Runner* films; how do memories and identity impact how the replicants understand their place in their social contexts? What is the role of memory implantation in creating capital, and to what extent do the replicants transform their own capital and habitus to create social roles different from those set out for them?

These reflections will lead to the final part of the chapter, which takes what has been learned from this critical consideration of the *Blade Runner* films and the evolution of habitus and capital to consider the nature and process of the National Curriculum in England (2013) and its role in shaping the experiences, memories, capital and social roles of the children exposed to it.

Memory and Identity in Blade Runner

The original *Blade Runner* film was released in 1982, a story set in a post-apocalyptic world, caused by unspecified events. The Earth is a dying planet, ravaged by environmental breakdown and overpopulation; the film is set in the decaying city of Los Angeles. There are constant reminders that those who can have left the planet for colonies on other planets. What is left is a world caught between the bureaucracy of agencies such as the police, and the power of corporations, physically embodied by the huge ziggurat of the Tyrell corporation that towers over the urban skyline. As Park (2012, p. 96) suggests,

> In the post-nuclear context of 2019, the film depicts the future as "a totally administered world"...The corporate and administrative power regulates the city of Blade Runner. Social control is set up by the complete combination of the police with technology.

Exploration and colonisation of new worlds is a dangerous process, and this has led to the development of replicants, genetically engineered humanoids based on human DNA, which are "built" by the Tyrell Corporation. As the beginning credits of *Blade Runner 2049* state,

"Replicants are bioengineered humans, designed by the Tyrell corporation for use off-world. Their enhanced strength made them ideal slave labor."

The development of replicants means humans have been spared from undertaking dangerous and unsavoury tasks, such as fighting and sex work. But what underlies the film and its narrative, therefore, is the question of what it means to be human, and how identity is formed and plays a role in constituting who and what we are. When five replicants illegally return to earth wanting to meet their creator in an attempt to increase their lifespan, it is the job of a Blade Runner, Deckard, to find and kill them.

Blade Runner 2049 continues the story (and is bridged by three short aminations which chart the trajectory between the two films, *2022 Black Out; 2036 Nexus Dawn and 2048 Nowhere To Run*). By the second film, the Tyrell Corporation has been taken over by Niander Wallace, a synthetic farming expert. The film, as with its predecessor, centres on the boundaries between humans and replicants and Wallace's wish to develop replicants who can reproduce so that he can increase production of the replicant workforce. The main protagonist, K, a replicant working for the police department as a Blade Runner, is forced to question his identity as he perceives his memories in different ways as the story line unfolds.

Park (2012) highlights that replicants, despite their identical DNA with humans, appear to be distinct from them in three main ways, empathy, memory and the fact they are made rather than born. Here, we focus on memory, its role in both films, and how this then relates to the formation and practice of identity and the roles of replicants within society.

The replicants in Blade Runner, as bioengineered humanoids, are made rather than born, their temporal point of creation labelled as their "incept date". The replicants are implanted with a set of memories to ensure that they can function as humans, to give them a history and identity. As Norris reflects (2013: 21)

"To function as it does in the world, each Replicant must have a sense of being a temporally extended being, one whose enduring relationships and future prospects concern an identity which has already been established."

Memories are crucial to creating a history for each replicant to make them more accepting of the environments to which they are assigned and the tasks they are responsible for carrying out. If the replicants have a history and the potential inherent in a future, they are more likely to fit within societal norms. In addition, memories give them a notion of their identity and who they are. As Tyrell explains to Deckard,

"If we gift them the past, we create a cushion or pillow for their emotions, and consequently we can control them better."

Hence, memories act as a form of control over the replicants, and create human-like responses to situations, whilst also creating more complex and authentic identities (Heersmink and McCarroll, 2020)

The most explicit example of this in the original *Blade Runner* film is the character of Rachael, a replicant living at the headquarters of the Tyrell Corporation. She has been implanted with the memories of Tyrell's niece, and these *"[are] the most intimate, unmediated, and powerful source of her sense of identity."* (Shanahan, 2014: 66). However, by completing a Voight-Kampff test (which measures empathy in the respondent) on her, Deckard leads her to question her identity as she begins to understand that her memories might not be her own.

In *Blade Runner 2049*, K, a replicant who is employed as a Blade Runner goes through a process of calling both his memories and his identity into question. Heersmink and McCarroll (2020) go as far as to argue that the whole film centres on his journey to gaining a different identity, as he discovers that his memories are implants created by a professional memory-maker called Dr. Ana Stelline.

But whilst the replicants are given "artificial" memories their existence over time means that they overlay these with their own experiences, and hence new memories. The active role of memory in the first film is emphasised by the regular inclusion of photographs as sources of memory on which the replicants rely. Rachael has a photo of "her" as a child; in fact, it is a photo of Tyrell's niece, whilst Leon has a collection of photos he has found which he uses as a source of memory.

Memory plays a crucial role in creating an identity for us. As Shanahan (2014) suggests, based on Locke's Consciousness Theory, memories are what link our past to our present and give us coherence. This is what makes Rachael think that she is Tyrell's niece, her memory implants explicitly and strongly linking her apparent past to who she is now. But consequently, Deckard's involvement in her memories being called into question as "genuine" leads to a breakdown in her identity.

Memory, and particularly working memory, play a key role in education and learning theories. Working memory is defined as a "system responsible for temporarily storing and manipulating information" (Alloway, 2006, p. 134). As Rachael grapples with whether she can trust her memories, we see that a false memory results in a degradation of identity; how information has been manipulated, connected and understood is affected, as well as a sense of self that endures through time.

The films present implanted memory as central to the formation of replicants who are stable and who will take up their assigned place in society, secure in a given identity based upon those memories. However, this simplistic process becomes inherently problematic as both films unfold, and as the replicants begin to call into question both their memories, and their identities as a consequence. But why do their identities and memories fall into question? Here, we can use the work of Pierre Bourdieu to begin to understand both how memories help to form the individual, but also how the social structures around those individuals in turn impact on their identities and how they understand and experience the world.

Bourdieu:
Habitus, Field and Capital

Pierre Bourdieu was a French sociologist and philosopher who focused on sociological theory and the sociology of education. Much of his work centred on how social groups function and relate to each other. Underlying this is an interest in power and how some groups appear to be the arbiters of taste in society and are seen to set cultural and social agendas in wider society. His work is conceptually rich, with *habitus, field* and *capital* sitting at the centre of his writing (Bourdieu, 1990). These concepts can help us understand the role of memory and identity amongst the replicants in *Blade Runner*, and further explain how and why they begin to deviate from the expected behaviours which have been set out for them by their creators.

Bourdieu used the metaphor of a game to explain the complex construct of the social world (Bourdieu, 1990; Lahire, 2011). The game itself takes place within "the field", or a social space; the number of fields we "play in" are multitudinous as they reflect the number of social categories we are part of. The way in which individuals play the game is the result of their habitus and capital.

The "field" is essentially a social space in which interactions between individuals occur. Fields related to particular social processes, for example, a professional sphere, educational activities, or art gallery events. Within these specific social spaces, individuals interact, interactions which are generally competitive and hierarchical, but which are not static, allowing for change and agency over time. They are hierarchical in the sense that the position of each individual within the field is the result of the rules of the field (rules some individuals will understand well, and some will not), each individual's habitus (explained below but linked to individual experience) and the capital (economic, social, symbolic, cultural) they bring to the interactions. Hence, those individuals who understand the rules well, have a habitus which aligns with the nature of the field, and who bring high levels of the most valuable capital, will dominate, feeling at ease, and understanding the "rules of the game". However, those who are unsure of the rules, who have a habitus misaligned to the social space and who have little relevant capital may feel ill at ease and may feel to some extent alienated from the "game" being played on the specific field as they have a lack of understanding of the rules. For example, two junior legal executives are invited by their boss to a dinner party; one is at home in this situation and knows what to wear, what gift to bring and what topics of conversation are appropriate. The other has never been to a dinner party and is nervous, awkward and does not seem to fit in. In the field of the social group, and more widely their legal profession, one is at a distinct advantage. By focusing on both the social and individual, the field and the processes which play out within it are an attempt to overcome simplistic systemic, agent dichotomies. Von Rosenberg (2016: 1490) highlights the complex nature of the field by stating,

"Each field comes with codes that are reproduced in accordance with the intrinsic logics that determine the implicit and explicit rules of the field and are continually passed on and transformed."

In *Blade Runner*, the field and its hierarchical nature are clearly apparent. In the original film, Rachael believes she understands the field within the Tyrell Corporation. Her implanted memories have acted to create a particular habitus and identity which lead her to be at ease when Deckard first encounters her at the corporation headquarters. Her social and cultural capital within that particular social space are both high, and her (implanted) past experiences means she is at ease in that environment, confident that she understands how to play the game. In *Blade Runner 2049*, K, as a hired replicant Blade Runner working for the police, conversely has little social capital. He is constantly reminded of his low status within that field by his human superior, Lieutenant Joshi. Whilst he understands the game very well, his lack of capital means he is forever at the bottom of the hierarchy. Likewise, the replicants in the first film who return to earth do so from fields they have been "built" to operate within, their memories and identities ideally suited to the roles of soldier, sex worker and manual labourer.

At the level of the individual, habitus is a crucial concept to explain how people interact in social settings. Habitus is a concept which attempts to characterise a network of dispositions or tendencies that shape the way we perceive the social world, and can be shaped by factors such as sex, position within a family, position in a social field, and trajectories through social space over time (Cronin, 1996). Maton (2014:51) summaries this complex concept thus,

"Simply put, habitus focuses on our ways of acting, feeling, thinking and being."

Hence, habitus is shaped through both individual and social processes. It includes aspects of hexis, such as posture, accent and tendencies of the body as well as mental habits, perceptions, appreciation, feelings and action. These are aspects of an emerging and evolving tacit knowledge of how to act as a competent social agent (Haugaard, 2002). At the same time, the experiences we are most likely to be exposed to relate to the social structures of which we are a part. These various processes shape our perceptions and experiences and help to determine how we will react to various events. As a consequence, our habitus is shaped continually by our experiences and in turn, our experiences shape our habitus. However, our habitus is neither static, nor in constant flux; instead, our dispositions evolve over time. Haugaard (2002) identifies a loose cycle of the habitus, with our place in society leading to a set of particular experiences, which become internalised and evolve our habitus leading to the structuring of future behaviours and resultant views of place in society. Haugaard theorises that this process is cyclical and tends to reinforce a person's original place in society, as our perception of our position leads us to have certain experiences, which become internalised as a habitus, which then structures future behaviour, which finally reinforces our perceptions of our place in society (Haugaard, 2002).

Similar dispositions tend to be shared by people of similar backgrounds and reflect the lived experience of socialisation; "the set of symbolically structured and socially inculcated dispositions of individual agents" (Cronin, 1996) have commonalities with others. Children who grow up in the same neighbourhood, and hence have similar experiences will tend to share similar outlooks, perceptions about how society works, and interests, e.g., football. However, whilst there might be some similar dispositions and hence common features of habitus, an individual's habitus evolves over time, and hence has a temporal structure (McNay, 1999) creating a "system of durable, transposable dispositions that mediates an individual's actions and the conditions of production" (Bourdieu 1990). However, whilst habitus is evolutionary in nature for any individual, movement into new social fields can be difficult as,

> The attempt at advancement usually culminates in failure because the newly acquired habitus, the new manners and meanings, do not form part of the actor's deeply internalised habitus, the habitus of childhood, which is what renders action easy and natural to perform (Haugaard, 2002, p. 226).

A major element in our evolving habitus must be the experience and hence the memories on which we draw to understand and engage with our social world. Hence, when Tyrell comments to Deckard that the replicants have been "gifted a past" this can be understood as implanted memories creating an artificial habitus which in turn allows the replicants to feel at ease in certain fields. Pris is given the role of a "pleasure model", with a habitus that shapes her expectations of treatment and behaviour and allows her to make sense of that social space. Likewise, Roy has had implanted memories that allow him to operate successfully in a conflict-oriented field. In this way, as Tyrell states, the replicants become more easily controlled. There are particular fields in which they feel assured and confident, and by extension, if they were to step out of these fields, then their habitus would lead to conflict or a feeling of not belonging. It is interesting that both Zhora and Leon, having successfully returned to Earth, find jobs in the same fields for which they were created off-world. By doing this, they are less likely to stand out as they will feel comfortable; as Haugaard (2002) suggests, to operate in other, unfamiliar fields will lead them to have to operate using newly acquired habitus, which will not be easily or totally internalised and may lead to them being suspected as not belonging.

Using the examples above, we can begin to understand how the implanted memories of the replicants begin to mediate their experiences and decisions within the social spaces which they encounter and inhabit. The same processes are apparent in *Blade Runner 2049*, except that the expected positions of replicants within society are much more explicit, with K being allowed to act as a Blade Runner, and Mariette a sex worker. Here, memories are still important in the film, but capital and laws ensure that replicants fulfil specific, given roles and remain within defined fields. To attempt to transcend these fields and operate in other social spaces is not allowed.

When we play the game within a field, we bring "capital" in various forms (Bourdieu, 1990; Haugaard, 2002). These include economic capital, the financial resources an individual can call upon in support of their activity, social capital, the family and friendship networks which can be called upon, e.g. "the old school tie", cultural capital, the knowledge, tastes, and cultural dispositions we have developed over time, and symbolic capital such as qualifications and honours we have received. An example of this is in the education field where middle-class mothers can draw upon cultural and social capital when complaining to a teacher about the education of their child, thereby reproducing class structures by more successfully and confidently navigating the field for their children than other parents might be capable of doing (Bourdieu, 1990; Reay, 1998). As Haugaard (2002: 228) once again argues,

> Education institutions reflect the habitus of the bourgeoisie and as a consequence those to whom this order of things is taken for granted: in this instance, it is not nature which disguises the perception of cultural arbitrariness but academic knowledge which is validated by the state and by a link to the truth.

In both films, replicants have little capital, another process in the attempt to control them. However, capital is not consistent across fields. Roy has a great deal of social capital within his group of replicants, and it becomes obvious through the course of the film that he has gained a great deal of cultural capital. He is able to beat Tyrell at chess to gain access to him before discussing the genetic engineering problems involved in giving the replicants a longer life span. These are examples of how the replicants begin to build their own experiences over their life courses, leading to shifts in their capital and shifts in their habitus, which begin to transcend the boundaries and social spaces identified for them.

von Rosenberg (2016) explores the role of education in attempting to overcome the potential for fields, habitus and capital to retain social inequalities. He sees education as having the potential to allow children to change their habitus, and hence to engage in the game in different and equal ways with others who may have greater capital and a better understanding of the rules than they initially do. However, adolescents may choose to transform their habitus in ways not designed by schools.

Helsper et al. (2013: 130, cited in von Rosenberg, 2016: 1488) see habitus as evolving as a part of growing up. They argue that children will take the orientation and interests of their immediate family, but as they reach adolescence, they may not transform their habitus from that of adolescent to adult in keeping with their parents' habitus but instead "generate their own models of adulthood as distinct from those of the preceding generation." Thus, habitus can be transformed not only through formal processes such as education but through the agency of individuals who choose to develop a different habitus for themselves. This may involve conscious decisions about the worth of different forms of cultural capital, and/or the networks they see as offering social capital with currency in the fields on which they choose to play. What this demonstrates is that the individual agent has the power to evolve their habitus in ways important to them and not as passive automata serving a predetermined role in society in keeping with their initial position. However, it has been argued that changing one's habitus significantly, to move upwards in the hierarchy of fields, is unlikely. Habitus continues to work "long after the objective conditions of its emergence have been dislodged—for example, women's entry into the workforce has not freed women from the burden of emotional responsibility" (McNay, 1999: 103). Whilst what may be considered sideways moves into fields (such as Zhora's move from sex work to exotic dancing) are possible, accessing higher fields is made difficult; "The dominant class is so successful in imposing its domination because it can count on the complicity of the dominated, which is extorted through the state-sanctioned inculcation of the norms of the dominant culture" (Bourdieu, 1992). One may consider how quickly Zhora would have been identified had she attempted to secure a role like the ones Rachael and Luv (Niander's personal assistant in *Blade*

Runner 2049) fulfil. With growing awareness of the fields that are accessible and those which are clearly not, questioning, indignation, resentment and anger may follow.

And this is a crucial feature in understanding how the replicants in both *Blade Runner* films begin to act in ways other than that expected of them from their "programming". As argued above, the implanted memories of replicants give them a ready-made, artificial habitus. But the mistake made by the Tyrell Corporation is in thinking that this will be a single, static "once and for all" process. Once the replicants are sent out into the world, they begin to build their own experiences, they begin to act and reflect on their positions in society. And as this happens, they begin to question their assigned roles. As Helsper et al (2013, cited in von Rosenberg, 2016) explain, adolescences might begin to transform their habitus in unexpected ways, and ways not in keeping with the parents who have helped them understand their social world and the fields within which they operate, so the replicants do not remain accepting of the artificial habitus implanted into them. The original, scant and disparate memories that were adequate at their incept date no longer sit comfortably with their acquired memories and understandings. This leads to changes in their identities; as Pris says to Sebastian, *"I think therefore I am."* reflecting the idea that Pris can be assured of her existence, as Descartes theorised, beyond the potential implanted memories of evil demons or dream-makers.

The replicants in both films transform their habitus, and to an extent their capital, as they engage in social practices and develop their own understanding of the world. They break out of the deterministic roles set for them. In *Blade Runner*, it might even be argued that the replicants act in an adolescent way in the early part of the film. But by its climax, Roy, the one remaining replicant appears to have transcended adolescence altogether, and in a field which he understands and operates in far better than Deckard, finally appears to be "more human than human", not only physically but also emotionally and ethically. And yet, it is only by changing the nature of the fields in which they operate that the replicants can succeed. In both films, there is no evidence that by transforming their habitus and adding to their capital with the associated changes in their identities which result, that they would be accepted as equals in the fields inhabited by the powerful and the human. The slogan that helps to sell them as a product; that they are "more human than human," points to their lifelike responses, whilst overlooking the lack of humanity in their treatment. When it suits the rich and powerful, they are suggested to be equivalent to human—when it does not, they are a resource to be exploited for commercial gain, then disposed of. They can only become more human than human, or perhaps more humane than humans, by subversion and criminality, due to the hierarchical structures of their world.

Being a replicant in the English education system

"The accumulation of cultural capital—the acquisition of knowledge—is the key to social mobility."

"The lack of ambition evident in those figures [the percentage of children gaining the English Baccalaureate[1]] was reinforced for me recently when we launched an initiative—open to every state school in the country—to enable their students to visit a top university, see for themselves how welcoming and exciting such places could be—and tempt them to apply.[1]"

Both of the quotes above are from a speech given by Michael Gove in 2013 when he was the Secretary of State for Education in the UK Government. His four-year tenure (2011-2014) in that position heralded a major turning point in English education. He was determined to break with what he saw as a 20-year experiment in "progressive" approaches to schooling. He argued that children had been starved of knowledge, that they had had their potential for social mobility taken from them by previous governments, particularly those headed by the New Labour party in the late 1990s and the early 2000s. But both his speech in 2013, and a previous speech made in 2011, soon after he had been appointed to his post, set this critique in the context of an attack on the working classes as being uneducated. The underlying narrative which he began to develop was one of the need to give children a "core curriculum" of traditional disciplines and "the best that has been thought and written." (Gove, 2011). This movement was further boosted by the inclusion of cultural literacy (Hirsch, 1987) as a framework for thinking through the knowledge which needed to be included in the curriculum and even the order in which it ought to be taught. These shifts in focus and emphasis led to the rewriting of the

English National Curriculum.

What is interesting in both the resultant curriculum and the arguments which led to its creation are the soft demonisation of the contemporary working class, the middle-class nature of the curriculum, and the ways in which Gove berated "progressive" academics and "do-gooding" middle-class politicians, who he blamed for undermining the poor and leaving them ignorant through the development of fundamentally misguided policies. At the same time, he positioned his own policy initiatives as being focused on reinvigorating social mobility; by creating a traditional, academically driven curriculum and pedagogy, children would become well-read, informed and intelligent individuals who, regardless of their backgrounds, would be able to rise up in society and take the roles and careers he argued are often reserved for those from the upper-middle and upper classes.

At first glance, this might seem attractive, as it paints a picture of children from all walks of life, but particularly those from poor backgrounds, being able to rise in society as a result of the new approach to education. But are the children from these poor backgrounds really being treated as equals, as full humans, or are they the replicants of the English education system? As Rachael points out in *Blade Runner*, "I can't rely on my memories," a sentiment that may be echoed by those who do not see the parallels with their own cultural and social experiences and memories with the content delivered in school.

An example of the insidious nature of the curriculum reforms, in building a cache of essential knowledge that would shape children's views of the world and their place within it, was the proposed History curriculum. Historians railed against Gove's plan for their subject, which was reduced to "memorising the feats of imperial heroes" (Watson, 2019, para. 2). Gove's project was not just to give children a knowledge-rich curriculum, which would give them a basis for building concepts and skills; he proudly explained that he was upholding "the right to learn why Britain has always been an exceptional country and a beacon of hope for the rest of the world" (Watson, 2019, para. 3). The role of memory here becomes clear, the memorisation of selected "facts" that uphold an ideology and sense of place in a hierarchy, in addition to the wider retelling of history, of our cultural memory, to suit the current political agenda. The project has rolled on without Gove at the helm, as recent developments at the Department for Education illustrate. "Schools should not use resources produced by organisations that take extreme political stances on matters" has appeared in the latest guidance on teaching Personal, Social and Health Education (DfE. 2020). Examples of extreme political stances include; "a publicly stated desire to abolish or overthrow democracy, capitalism, opposition to the right or freedoms of speech, or organisations that promote victim narratives that are harmful to British society" (DfE, 2020, London-Miyo, 2020). Even if the victim narratives are true, we are not to teach them. Whilst there is a clear difference between curriculum subject knowledge content, and memory as implanted in a replicant, the difference becomes less distinct when cultural memory is being rewritten to suit political ends and "implanted" to give a shared understanding that minimises questioning, criticism and debate. Gove and many of his outriders in the wider education sector regularly passed comment on the "dumbing down" of the education system, and the examples they used were almost exclusively focused on popular, working-class culture. The not always implicit message was constantly one of the inadequacies of a working-class habitus, of the need for children to inhabit different fields and foster capital other than in their own communities and families. As a result, the curriculum has become a process of implanting a whole new set of beliefs and experiences, of uploading a set of memories that are destined to create a habitus fit for the desired set of roles in society. An individual example of this in action comes from Rousmaniere's autoethnographic exploration of the connection between curriculum and memory, where she describes the different experiences of education that she and her friend, Jessie had been through. Jessie did not have the advantages of class, social and cultural capital and struggled with a curriculum that never felt authentic to her. As Rousmaniere comments; "that I was successful in school says more about tracking and classism in education than about my own individual accomplishments and abilities" (Rousmaniere, 2000, p. 87). Chiming with *Blade Runner*, the idea that emotion, curriculum and memory are all tied together is explored by Rousmaniere, illustrating that our experiences of curriculum, our feelings towards it, and our beliefs about our future in education and life are intertwined. As Dr. Ana Stelline in *Bladerunner 2049* points out, "They all think it's about more detail. But that's not how memory works. We recall with our feelings".

It is important to emphasise that we are not suggesting that a curriculum with elements of traditional academic knowledge is a bad thing, it is not, but the deliberate extinguishing of a wider cultural spectrum, as well as the loss of certain subjects, such as technology, and increasingly the arts, for example music and visual art, leads to a narrowly defined set of experiences and hence memories. At the same time, clashing elements of subject knowledge, such as Britain's colonial past, are erased to fit the chosen narrative. As these new memories are implanted into children from disadvantaged backgrounds, there then becomes an issue concerning their identities. As they begin to take on a new habitus, as they are exposed to new fields in highly mediated ways, their identity may also begin to shift. There is nothing inherently wrong with this, but like the replicants in *Blade Runner*, will they eventually be consigned to a position where they are in a constant liminal space? Will they never understand the game of the new fields to which they might become a part, whilst no longer fitting into the fields of their own communities? Using our example of the history curriculum, what are Black and ethnic minority children to make of a curriculum that makes no mention of the shocking abuses of their ancestors and seeks to glorify colonial heroics that their communities tell in very different ways? Roy, Pris, Leon, and Zhora all decide to leave the fields which have been assigned to them, in which they have an aligned habitus and a large store of capital. But on reaching Earth, they are unable to find security and contentment as they do not fit into the fields now open to them without others playing games they are not good at responding to. It is only the coming of the finale of the film and the duel between Roy and Deckard when the former once again inhabits a field he is naturally comfortable in.

Tyrell abdicates responsibility for his part in the replicants' bleak future by asserting that "You were made as well as we could make you." What he means is that they were made to perform a service, and designed to do this as well as they could for the end consumer. The rewriting of the National Curriculum has been argued to give all children the chance of social mobility, of allowing them the opportunity to thrive in society, and by implication, to become middle-class too, but this can be argued to point to the same view that Tyrell holds. Michael Gove (2103) himself makes the point that,

Wherever you look—Cabinets or Shadow Cabinets—newspaper editorial conferences or FTSE 100 boardrooms—the nation's galleries or bishop's palaces—the positions of power and influence are overwhelmingly held by the privately-educated or the children of middle-class professionals. The social differences which existed in our society before the Nineteen-Sixties have—in all too many cases—not just been perpetuated but crystallised.

This is implicitly the goal all children should be aspiring to, as the working-class and disadvantaged backgrounds from which they come are characterised as being hellish and benighted. The best that we can hope for our working-class children is that they are "made as well as we could make you" in terms of escaping the perceived horror of their communities, and being of value to a future employer. Kulz (2017: 45), undertaking an ethnographic study in an inner-city school in England that aligned itself to the emerging Govean philosophy, quotes a teacher commenting on the biometrically triggered front gates of the school as,

"[N]ot allowing the bad elements of the community to come into the school gates. So once they [students] come into the school gates, anything that's not wanted is left outside. It's another set of rules once they enter....and all of that must be left behind."

This all points towards a system which treats children from disadvantaged backgrounds as somehow different and in need of being reprogrammed to allow them to take up a useful role in society, through the uploading of wholly different experiences and memories, truly the replicants of the English education system. And as with the replicants in the *Blade Runner* films, even the symbolic capital of good school examination results and degrees will not lead them to be true "humans" as those who have been brought up in middle-class households will not only have been exposed to the same school curriculum, but their greater economic capital will have given them access to much more cultural capital, to social capital which emerges simply through their place in society and hence they will be able to play the games in the academic and corporate fields with far greater confidence. They will have had parents who talk about their work in boardrooms, they will have met their parents' bosses; they will have been introduced to editors or will have been exposed to the rites of the church from an early age. This capital cultural and social capital can never be part of a curriculum, however well-conceived.

At the same time as middle-class humans are building their capital, the replicants will have been constantly told that the knowledge and cultural reference points of their own communities are somehow deficient, that their artificially fostered habitus and new identities are the better way of taking up their roles in society. However, there is a genuine possibility that some children from these backgrounds will begin to question and critique what they have been given as a diet in school as their manufactured habitus not only does not give them true access to the professional fields they have been inculcated to strive for but will also begin to close off those positive fields which go to make up their communities. Their options could be theorised as subversion or to accept their place in society, having seen "the best of what has been written and said" and knowing this does not represent the best of their own communities, and playing the game as imitation middle-class players, complicit in their own subjugation.

There is a potential paradox here, however. Is it fair to suggest that giving working-class children a diet of traditional, academic knowledge is somehow wrong? Why should they not have the experiences and memories with the shifts in identity this might bring? Whilst Niander Wallace in Bladerunner 2049 acknowledges the need for a vast and disposable workforce; "Every leap of civilization was built off the back of a disposable work force. We lost our stomach for slaves, unless engineered. But I can only make so many", perhaps the new curriculum represents a revolution and a move away from a system that generates low-skilled wage slaves. Quoting Michael Gove (2013) once more,

> A 1944 survey of unskilled workers showed that almost half had grown up in homes with substantial libraries.

> And these working-class readers were not only reading widely—they were reading deeply.

> As Rose points out in his work, housemaids read Dickens and Conrad and kitchen maids saved up money to attend classical music concerts. The servant girl Dorothy Burnham, who grew up in care, "found herself in Keats, Tennyson and Arnold."

There is no reason why all children should not have exposure to a wide range of educational experiences, and be able to engage with classic literature, and foreign languages. However, in the current model, this is all they are exposed to. And this implicitly states to them that their own cultural reference points, their own fields and habitus are somehow deficient. If we are to encourage the development of humans as opposed to replicants, then we need to ensure that they are able to engage with a full spectrum of experiences. In his example of the working-class readers, what Gove apparently forgets is that they are reading in the context of wanting emancipation, of being secure in their own fields, in evolving their habitus with agency rather than because they are being told they have to.

Whilst we acknowledge that a curriculum that is based on the best that has been written and said is a worthy idea, what seems to be missing from the current debates is a consideration of who judges what constitutes "the best". Unsurprisingly, as has been pointed out, ministers, advisors and consultants tend to come from the culturally and socially rich, privileged backgrounds that Gove suggested should be open to all, and yet these are the decision-makers who build the curriculum based on their own habitus and understanding of the game. Middle-class and public school education ideals reproduce the conditions for success in the field, whilst working-class identities are either perpetually considered "lesser", or adapt to become imitations of middle-class identity, inauthentic, insincere, and with all the challenges that come with being an imposter.

The assumption that working-class culture is lesser, or the ignorant blunder of omitting working-class culture from the curriculum, means that middle-class ideals will be reproduced and a levelling of the hierarchy will never be achieved. There are underlying and unspoken theories that are the foundations of this implanting of cultural capital into the working classes; that working-class culture is less valuable, that everyone should aim to be middle class, that there is room for everyone to become middle class. In our society, as on the Earth of *Blade Runner*, if working-class work was held in higher regard, if working-class culture was valued and individuals protected from dangerous and unsavoury working conditions, if the economic rewards of skilled and traditionally working-class jobs were comparable with skilled and traditionally middle-class jobs, there would be no need to programme replicants to do the work, and no need to implant a particular habitus to make this social position palatable. The working classes would not need to be placated or duped into "knowing their place".

In *Blade Runner*, Roy Batty asks, "Can the maker repair what he makes?" and our fear is that the results of the curriculum that values a particular classist experience of the world, together with a narrative that excludes negative (yet true) accounts of a society, not only "implants" a certain way of being on a generation of children that is not easily repaired. When curriculum becomes memory of true events, sections of the population are alienated; other sections are validated, all are cheated of the opportunity to debate, discuss, question and connect their own community and lived experience with what they are learning at school.

Whilst education alone will not "level the field" or dismantle our class system, a curriculum that values all of British culture and the specific communities that children build their habitus in from birth, would certainly seem like a good start in compressing a hierarchy that limits not only the economic value of our habitus, but also which fields we perceive as open to us.

Notes

1. The English Baccalaureate is a school performance indicator. Examinations are sat by children at the age of 16 in England, called General Certificate of Secondary Education (GCSE). The English Baccalaureate is an academic measure, and to attain it, a student must pass English Language and English Literature, Mathematics, Combined Sciences OR three subjects from Chemistry, Physics, Biology or Computer Science, a Modern or Ancient Foreign Language and either Geography OR History.

References

Alloway T. (2006). How does working memory work in the classroom?, *Educational Research and Reviews*, 1 (4), Art. No.: 475D3083412], pp. 134-139.

Bourdieu, P., Passeron, J.-C., Nice, R., Bottomore, T., & Richard Nice with a foreward by Tom Bottomore (1990). *Reproduction in education, society, and culture.* London: Sage in association with Theory, Culture & Society, Dept. of Administrative and Social Studies, Teesside Polytechnic.

Bourdieu, P., & Wacquant, L. J. (1992) *An invitation to reflexive sociology.* Chicago: University of Chicago Press.

Cronin, C. (1996) Bourdieu and Foucault on power and modernity. *Philosophy & social criticism*, 22(6), 55-85.

Department for Education (2013) *The national curriculum in England: key stages 1 and 2 framework document.* Available at: https://www.gov.uk/government/publications/national-curriculum-in-england-primary-curriculum

Department for Education (2014) *The national curriculum in England: complete framework for key stages 1 to 4.* Available at: https://www.gov.uk/government/publications/national-curriculum-in-england-framework-for-key-stages-1-to-4 (Accessed: 21st December 2020).

Department for Education (2020). Planning your relationships, sex and health education curriculum. Available at: https://www.gov.uk/guidance/plan-your-relationships-sex-and-health-curriculum (accessed 13th March 2021).

Gittinger J.L. (2019). Defining Personhood in a Posthuman World. In: Personhood in Science Fiction. Palgrave Macmillan, Cham. https://doi.org/10.1007/978-3-030-30062-3_2

Gove, M. (2011) Michael Gove at the Durand Academy. 1st September, 2011. Last accessed on 30th December, 2020 at https://www.gov.uk/government/speeches/michael-gove-to-the-durand-academy .

Gove, M. (2013) *Michael Gove speaks at the SMF*. February 5th, 2013. Last accessed on 30th December, 2020 at https://www.smf.co.uk/michael-gove-speaks-at-the-smf .

Haugaard, M. (2002) *Power: A Reader*. Manchester: Manchester University Press.

Heersmink, R. & McCarroll, C.J. (2020) 'The best memories: Identity, narrative and objects.' in T. Shanahan & P. Smart (eds.) *Blade Runner 2049 A Philosophical Exploration*. Routledge: Abingdon. 87-107.

Helsper, W., Kramer, R.-T., & Thiersch, S. (2013). Orientierungsrahmen zwischen Kollektivität und Individualität - ontogenetische und transformationsbezogene Anfragen an die dokumentarische Methode [Orientational frameworks between collectivity and individuality—confronting the documentary method with questions of ontogenesis and transformation]. In P. Loos, A.- M. Nohl, A. Przyborski, & B. Schäffer (Eds.), *Dokumentarische Methode. Grundlagen - Entwicklungen - Anwendungen* (pp. 111–140). Opladen: BudrichLahire, 2011

Hirsch, E.D. (1987) *Cultural Literacy, what every American needs to know*. Boston, MA: Houghton Mifflin Company.

London-Miyo, C. (2020). I didn't become a teacher to ban independent thought. Anti-racist education should not be up for debate. *The Independent*, August 2020. Accessible via: https://www.independent.co.uk/voices/education-dfe-schools-victim-narratives-capitalism-blm-racism-b737415.html (Accessed 10th March 2021).

Maton, K. (2014) 'Habitus.' In M. Grenfell (Ed.) *Pierre Boirudieu: Key Concepts*. Routledge: Abingdon. pp. 48-64.

McNay, L. (1999) Gender, Habitus and the Field: Pierre Bourdieu and the Limits of Reflexivity. *Theory, Culture & Society*. 1999;16(1):95-117. doi:10.1177/026327699016001007

Norris, A. (2013) "How Can It Not Know What It Is?': Self and Other in Ridley Scott's *Blade Runner*.' *Film-Philosophy*, 17:1, 19-50.

Park, S.H. (2012) 'Dystopia in the Science Fiction Film: *Blade Runner* and Adorno's Critique of Modern Society.' *International Journal of Contents*, 8:3, 94-99.

Reay, D. (1998) Rethinking Social Class: Qualitative Perspectives on Class and Gender. *Sociology*. 1998;32(2):259-275. doi:10.1177/0038038598032002003

Reay, D. (2019) in W. Mansell, 'Ofsted plan to inspect 'cultural capital' in schools attacked as elitist' *The Guardian*, 3rd September 2019.

Rousmaniere, K. (2000). From Memory to Curriculum, Teaching Education, 11:1, 87-98, DOI: 10.1080/10476210050020417

Shanahan, T. (2014) *Philosophy and Blade Runner*. Palgrave Macmillan: London

von Rosenberg, F. (2016) 'Education as habitus transformations.' *Educational Philosophy and Theory*. 48:14, 1486-1496.

Watson, M. (2019). Michael Gove's war on historians: extreme whig history and Conservative curriculum reform. *London School of Economics blog*, accessible here: https://blogs.lse.ac.uk/politicsandpolicy/michael-goves-war-on-historians/ (Accessed 13th March 2021).

Chapter 11

The Refugeetude of Lady Trieu

Pedagogies of Displacement in HBO's Watchmen

Van Anh Tran, Teachers College, Columbia University

The word ["refugee"] tends to suggest vulnerability: someone in need, someone who needs to be saved. I think it's more beneficial to think of a refugee as someone defined not by their need but by their desire. The desire to protect themselves and those they love. - Vu Tran (2018)[1]

Lady Trieu steps into the world of HBO's *Watchmen* (2019) at the outset of the fourth episode entitled, "If you don't like my story, write your own." A character not found in Moore & Gibbons' (1986-87) original *Watchmen* comic, Lady Trieu asks, "So, what have you heard about me?" when she appears on our screens for the first time. The Clarks, Oklahoman farm owners who are awoken by Lady Trieu at their door in the middle of the night, identify her as "the billionaire building the big clock down the road" (Lindelof et al., 2019). We learn from their interaction that Lady Trieu is a determined and brilliant trillionaire (not billionaire, as Lady Trieu is quick to correct) who obtained her wealth through advancements in pharmaceuticals and biomedical technology; moreover, the audience knows from previous episodes that Trieu Industries had acquired Veidt Enterprises at approximately the time that its founder, Adrian Veidt, went missing. Lady Trieu declares her intentions of obtaining the Clarks' house and the forty acres on which it sits, although they say that the land is not for sale. Lady Trieu replies, "Right, I get it. It's been in your family for generations. Legacy's a big deal." "Legacy isn't in land," she counters. "It's in blood, passed to us from our ancestors and by us to our children." Lady Trieu warns the Clarks, "You two have no children...your legacy will be extinct" (Lindelof et al., 2019).

The theme of legacy, entwined with memories and past traumas, and the implications of what we inherit weave through Lady Trieu's arc on the series. While not explicitly named as "refugees" within the world of *Watchmen*, the effects of displacement and generational remembering undergird the storylines of various characters within the series, including two of its central characters: Angela Abar/Sister Night and Lady Trieu. Subedi (2013) explains, "The pedagogy of displacement asks that learners unlearn how they have come to understand the category of refugee and to question how refugees are represented and received locally and globally" (p. 297). Within a series that opens with the 1921 massacre of Black Wall Street in Tulsa, Oklahoma and reimagines a United States in which the nation and its peoples attempt to come to terms with its violent, racist, and dehumanizing legacies, the subjectivities produced through this universe are multilayered and complex—extending an invitation to broaden the boundaries of temporality, agency, and relationality. Claiming this space of possibility, *Watchmen* engages pedagogies of displacement that demonstrate how such visionary narratives can move us toward freer worlds (Imarisha, 2015) and offer opportunities to push us even farther.

Building on decolonial frameworks within education (Grande 2004; Santos 2014) that aim to "challenge exploitation and domination globally...at the level of epistemology and ontology" (De Lissovy, 2019, p. 421), this chapter will engage specifically with the character of Lady Trieu in HBO's *Watchmen* through a combined conceptual framework of refugeetude (Nguyen, 2019) and a feminist refugee epistemology (Espiritu & Duong, 2018) to explore how notions of legacy surface a pedagogy of displacement that engages both movement and emplacement. What can we learn both from Lady Trieu's failed journey to "save humanity from the traumas of its past and move it 'gloriously into the future'" (Simek, 2020, p. 390) and the way that her subjectivity as a Vietnamese woman refugee was produced in relation to other characters? What are the implications of understanding the refugeetude of Lady Trieu for pedagogical thinking? Lady Trieu's arc in *Watchmen* invites an exploration of the intersection of identity, lineage, memory, and power and provides opportunities to consider pedagogies that not only recognize, but disrupt the production of certain subjectivities as "irregularities" (Nguyen, 2019). In this way,

De Lissovoy (2019) explains that the educational implications relate less to "the inclusion of a specific content and more the irruption of an alternative and marginalized standpoint across the divide of the colonial world" (p. 427).

The World of Watchmen

As a project in "speculative world-making and historical reenactment," *Watchmen* weaves past, present, and future to "[re-familiarize] viewers...with a reality from which too many often turn away, while also immersing the audience in a world where reality can unfold otherwise" (Simek, 2020, p. 392-393). Broadly defined, speculative fiction is a "super category for all genres that deliberately depart from... 'consensus reality' of everyday experience" (Oziewicz, 2017, p. 2). Simek (2020) adds that speculative fiction emphasizes the "explicitly counterfactual" within alternative worlds, histories, and futures that differ from our own (p. 386). In calling attention to aspects of the world that markedly depart from our own pasts and presents, *Watchmen* invites us to dream new worlds (Imarisha, 2015) and imagine what might be possible.

As a character within this universe, Lady Trieu eventually becomes a foil to more-than-human protagonists, Angela Abar/Sister Night and Dr. Manhattan. In HBO's *Watchmen*, Tulsa's police force conceal their identities with costumes and masks following an attack on law-enforcement by a White supremacist organization. Angela Abar, a Black police detective, born in Vietnam and orphaned as a child when her parents are killed by a Vietnamese insurgent attack, is the central protagonist of the series. The audience later learns that her husband, Cal, is actually Dr. Manhattan who bound his powers and blocked his memories in order to lead a "normal" life with her. The explicit conflict between Angela, Dr. Manhattan, and Lady Trieu is clear by the end of the season—Lady Trieu aims to harness Dr. Manhattan's power for herself, killing him in the process. One of the tensions left unexplored, however, is "that Angela, who has inherited the trauma of a genocidal massacre, is married to a man who carried out destruction on a similar scale, and to a similar multigenerational effect, in Vietnam" (Rosenberg, 2019). Exploring the trajectory of Lady Trieu in HBO's *Watchmen* through the lens of refugeetude demonstrates how notions of "other" are both challenged and reinscribed within this world even as the series critically foregrounds familiar systemic problems from our own world: "White supremacy and the elusiveness of justice in the racist United States" (Simek, 2020, p. 388).

The interaction between speculations on possible pasts and futures and the challenges and contradictions that emerge demonstrate textures of a world that is different and not-so-different from our own. In the world of HBO's *Watchmen*, there would be no such thing as refugees who were resettled in the United States after the wars in Southeast Asia; in this reality, Vietnam becomes the fifty-first state of the union—glimpses of which we consume throughout the series. Even so, refugeeness emerges in the way that the Vietnam of *Watchmen* strangely echoes the Vietnam of our current reality; refugeeness emerges in Lady Trieu's own displacement from her family and her belief that, "Legacy isn't in land. It's in blood" (Lindelof et al., 2019). While not necessarily refugees in name, the depictions (and fate) of Lady Trieu and other Vietnamese people in the series teach us about the pervasiveness of the politics of belonging (Yuval-Davis, 2011) and hold pedagogical possibilities for disrupting the production of particular subjectivities as problems or "[crises] to be resolved" (Nguyen, 2019, p. 111).

The Case for Lady Trieu

As Lady Trieu's opening scene unfolds, she explains that she is not offering the Clarks money for their land, but legacy. The offer is simple: in exchange for their land, she will give them a baby that she created from the couple's genetic material obtained from a fertility clinic that Trieu Industries now owns. As Lady Trieu gives the Clarks ten seconds to decide, she tells them that she will find a loving home for the baby should they decline her offer. "He'll just never know where he came from," she says (Lindelof et al., 2019).

Near the end of the series, the audience learns more about Lady Trieu's legacy. In a flashback, we see Lady Trieu's mother, Bian, speak the words attributed to the Bà Triệu (Lady Trieu) of ancient Vietnamese history and folklore, "I want to ride the strong winds, crush the angry waves...reclaim the land, remove the yoke of slavery" (Cuse et al., 2019; Andaya, 2020), as she secretly self-inseminates Adrian Veidt's genetic material. Lady Trieu's mother is a Vietnamese refugee employed as a domestic worker for Veidt AKA the masked adventurer,

Ozymandias. Bian's actions and declarations are at once triumphant and subversive— "[acts] of liberation" (Simek, 2020, p. 395).

The character of Lady Trieu initially holds such promises of counternarratives that could open "a window into ignored or alternative realities" (Delgado & Stefancic, 2001, p. 39). Named after a legendary, Vietnamese woman warrior "celebrated for [her] struggles against foreign occupiers" (Duong & Sharif, 2020, p. 180), the Lady Trieu of *Watchmen* moves through the series with power, purpose, and potential to "reclaim the land" and fight for liberation. As a historical and mythological figure, Lady Trieu and other women in Vietnamese history, have often been constructed to achieve particular, often colonial, ends. Tran (2012) elucidates that the figure of the "Vietnamese woman" has been represented in three particular reified forms: "a sign of Confucian oppression, of Vietnamese uniqueness or of Southeast Asian cohesiveness" (p. 411). The Lady Trieu of *Watchmen* encompasses opportunities to retell and reinvent popularly held notions of Vietnamese womanhood and refugeeness—particularly within the context of United States imperialism and militarism.

Conceptual Frameworks

Refugeetude

Through the narrative of a Vietnamese woman, Nguyen (2019) introduces their conceptualization of refugeetude— "a continued state of being and a mode of relationality" that describes a recognition and "coming into consciousness of the forces that produce and structure 'refuge' and 'refugee'" (p. 110). Similar to conceptualizations within Critical Refugee Studies (Espiritu, 2014), refugeetude distances itself from legal frameworks and, instead, reframes refugees as actors within their experiences (Nguyen, 2019). Refugeetude critically reorients and redirects the conception of refugee as temporary or as solely a legal attribution, but instead as "an enduring creative force" (p. 110). Expanding notions of temporality, agency, and relationality, refugeetude makes visible interconnections between past, present, and future.

As a speculative work, *Watchmen* primes "the audience for questioning the dominant status quo" (Oziewicz, 2017, p. 11). Dominant frameworks conceive refugee and refugeeness as temporary, irregular, or a "disruption of political subjecthood" (Nguyen, 2019, p. 111); however, refugeeness and self are entwined. Refugeeness is a combination of social, political, and legal constructions (Malkki, 1995) and subjective experiences (Lacroix, 2004). Although the "ending" of the wars in Southeast Asia within HBO's *Watchmen* deviates from our own reality and Vietnam becomes the U.S.' fifty-first state, violence and war are entrenched aspects of the series' past and present. While Vietnamese refugees do not exist in the world of the series, in the same way, refugeeness emerges through the displacements experienced not only by Lady Trieu (and her mother before her), but also the series' protagonist, Angela Abar. Raised in Vietnam in a military family and later orphaned by a Vietnamese insurgent attack, Angela's relationship with displacement and colonialism is complex. While the series "only explores her relationship to Vietnamese culture in reference to [the] bakery she runs as a cover for her real work" (Rosenberg, 2019), glimpses of Angela's multifaceted connections to movement, generational memory, and trauma indicate several opportunities to engage with notions of refugeeness.

Refugeetude conceives refugeeness as "an experiential resource for developing significant and durable ways of being in and moving through the world" (Nguyen, 2019, p. 111). Engaging with the wars in Southeast Asia as a foundation for articulating refugeetude, analyses can be expanded to contemporary and speculative forms of mass displacement. Indeed, "examining and theorizing how refugeeness might engender modes of perceiving, critiquing, and resisting" (Nguyen, 2019, p. 111) the systems and structures that produce refugee subjectivities and lived experiences is particularly pressing within the context of "reinvigorated U.S. imperialism and globalized militarization" (Espiritu, 2014, p. 1). Given the ways that refugees have been criminalized (Nguyen, 2019) and produced as simultaneously in need and undesirable (Espiritu, 2014), understanding the concept of refugeetude and how refugeeness is not a temporary condition, but rather a "catalyst for thinking, feeling, and doing with others—for imagining justice" (Nguyen, 2019, p. 111) contributes to a nuanced reading of HBO's *Watchmen* broadly and the character of Lady Trieu, in particular. Refugeetude underscores "how refugee subjects gain awareness, create meaning, and imagine futures" (Nguyen, 2019, p. 111).

Feminist Refugee Epistemology

Feminist refugee scholars Espiritu and Duong (2018) introduce the term "feminist refugee epistemology" (FRE) as a way to "reconceptualize war-based displacement as being not only about social disorder and interruption but also about social reproduction and innovation" (p. 588). Situated within transnational feminist studies (Alexander & Mohanty, 1997), and Critical Refugee Studies (Espiritu, 2014), analyses through FRE "[draw] our awareness to routine, intimate and private sites where power is both reproduced and contested" (Shalhoub-Kevorkian, 2015, p. 2).

FRE provides a framework to examine Lady Trieu as an agent within the world of *Watchmen* as it not only recognizes the impact of refugeeness, but also uplifts resistance and resilience. As Critical Refugee Studies acknowledges and resists how refugees have been constructed within the western gaze and locate them "not in the violent legacy of decades of war and social upheaval, but within the bodies and minds of the [people] themselves" (Espiritu, 2006, p. 410), FRE engages the "intimate politics of the everyday" to center the ways refugees enact their hopes, politics, and dreams (Espiritu & Duong, 2018, p. 588). To that end, FRE "[asserts] the refugee as a knowing subject whose displaced condition teaches us... as well as one who produces knowledge" (Vang, 2018, p. 428). Specifically, FRE provides a way to engage deeply with the "unseen" and "private sphere as gendered space for creative loss and grief but also of creative, improvised, and experimental refuge-making practices" (Espiritu & Duong, 2018, p. 590). Thus, FRE supports an analysis of Lady Trieu's motivations, the way that she was produced within the series, and the actions that she takes throughout. By focusing on the range of Lady Trieu's actions, in addition to the moments in which she may have been instrumental to the plot, the nuances, details, and implications of Lady Trieu as a character, subject, and actor can emerge.

Integrating Frameworks and Implications for Pedagogy

Just as refugeetude provides language and a frame to understand "that lived experiences of refuge(e) constitute a form of subjectivity" and expands its boundaries to "include a range of times, places, and subjects" (Nguyen, 2019, p. 112), FRE engages the perspectives, desires, and needs "of the forcibly displaced as they create improvised, fluid... healing, and survival strategies" (Espiritu & Duong, 2018, p. 588).

Within and beyond the world of *Watchmen*, I believe that those who have been displaced may be considered "refugees"—whether or not nation-states recognize them as such. In this chapter, the purpose of applying the framework of refugeetude and approaching analyses through the lens of FRE is not to affix the label of "refugee" upon particular people, but to consider the way that refugeeness is taken up, exhibited, and experienced. In this way, we are able to enact pedagogies of displacement that build on decolonial frameworks through "a complex and difficult confrontation that cannot magically transcend the coordinates of coloniality" (De Lissovoy, 2019, p. 424). Lady Trieu is the focus of this piece, as opposed to other characters within the series who might also be read through these frameworks and lenses, because she is a central character within the series who is named after a legendary Vietnamese woman warrior and whose implications cannot be disassociated from the colonial histories and realities in which we, as the audience, are watching the series. The movement between the world of *Watchmen* and our current world is a part of such pedagogies of displacement that engage movement and emplacement. Brophy (2018) explains that such a "moving pedagogy" reveals how "experiential knowledge and localized subjectivity...change the interpretive and pedagogical frameworks we bring to engaging with stories...of migration and displacement." (p. 634).

My choice to engage both refugeetude and FRE as a combined lens is tied to my recognition that exploring the character arc and subjectivities of Lady Trieu necessarily requires an understanding of temporality and relationality not only as frameworks, but as practices. Refugeetude uplifts how refugee subjects impacted by forced displacement "come to understand, articulate, and resist their conditions" with the potential for "intergroup solidarities" (Nguyen, 2019, p. 112). FRE textures refugeetude as an analytical lens in the way that it supports a "[reimagination] of the interiority of refugee lives" and uplifts the "quotidian details of displacement and emplacement...to highlight these strategies as epistemological in nature" (Espiritu & Duong, 2018, p. 590). Both refugeetude and FRE allow for an engagement with themes of colonialism, imperialism, migration, and relationality that frames refugees as "producers of knowledge" (Espiritu & Duong,

2018, p. 590).

Learning from Legacies

Lady Trieu's introductory sequence on HBO's *Watchmen* poses the question: What does legacy mean? From this opening, the audience quickly understands that Lady Trieu defines legacy through lineage, through generational inheritance. As the truth about Lady Trieu's lineage, her role in creating the drug "Nostalgia," and her ultimate objectives come to light throughout the series, there is both a sense of movement and a desire for rootedness that underlie her overt and covert undertakings.

Lady Trieu's Legacy:
Land

Lady Trieu's conception of legacy and how it might be entangled with place emerges throughout her interactions with other characters in *Watchmen*. Shalhoub- Kevorkian (2009) reminds us that "space is…not only a material landscape but also a linguistic and symbolic one, replete with concepts of memory and historical legacies" (p. 154). Lady Trieu first meets the series' protagonist, Angela Abar (in her Sister Night persona), when Angela and FBI Agent Laurie Blake visit the trillion-aire's compound at the base of the in-progress Millennium Clock to investigate an occurrence that may be tied to one of Trieu's advanced devices. Bian, Lady Trieu's "daughter" greets Detective Night and Agent Blake and invites them for tea in the vivarium on her mother's directive. Upon entering the large domed structure, filled with foliage from Vietnam, Lady Trieu approaches the group:

> I'm sorry for the humidity. We have to get it just right for the plants. On her deathbed, my mother made me promise I would never leave Vietnam, so I found a loophole. Now, Vietnam never leaves me. (Lindelof et al., 2019)

This justification for the vivarium alludes to Lady Trieu's consciousness of not only what it may mean for a place to be home (and whether home must be a particular "place"), but also of a refugeetude that discerns the "space of in-between, an ontology of interstitiality" (Nguyen, 2019, p. 113) that refugees occupy. Whereas refugees may be constructed and understood in our reality by what they "lack" due to this ontological precarity, Lady Trieu creates a spectacular and vibrant refuge anew.

At the same time, Lady Trieu's immense wealth and resources in the present day are juxtaposed with life in the Vietnam of *Watchmen* after Dr. Manhattan "ended" the conflict. At the start of the seventh episode, the audience views an old newsreel that briefly follows the life of Jon Osterman and how he became Dr. Manhattan. As an "immigrant, son of a clockmaker," Osterman epitomizes a meritocratic, "American Dream" narrative when "from humble beginnings," he later became an "immortal god, impervious to the passage of time" and "forever [altered] the history of humankind by developing miraculous new wonders" (Osei-Kuffour et al., 2019). "And then, Vietnam," the old reel indicates.

Watchmen presents the dilemma of Dr. Manhattan's role in the wars in Southeast Asia by asking through the newsreel: Was he a "liberating hero who single-handedly ended the war and delivered his country its fifty-first state? Or was he a cold blue conqueror who decimated an entire way of life" (Osei-Kuffour et al., 2019)? As the audience engages with this alternative Vietnam and glimpses Angela's childhood in the new state:

> The streets of Saigon look somewhat similar to what they do in the real present: very colorful, sidewalks crowded with stools and low tables, and somewhat neglected. It seems that even in a hypothetical scenario in which the United States won the war with the assistance of a supernatural being, Saigonese quality of life is very similar to how it actually is had this not happened. (Do, 2019)

Interspersed with her grandfather's memories of the massacre in Tulsa's Greenwood District, the audience witnesses Angela's memories of her parents' death as the Vietnamese bomber yells, "Death to the invaders!" Placing Lady Trieu, *Watchmen*'s Vietnam, and Angela's past in conversation demonstrate that "refugee is not a transitory experience and that refuge...[remains] elusive" (Nguyen, 2019, p. 114). Applying FRE's notion of temporality as "fluid, dynamic, and multidimensional" and the "multiplicity and openness of the spatial" (Espiritu & Duong, 2018, p. 589), the complexities of identity, memory, and refugeetude emerge through interactions (and, later, connections) between Lady Trieu and Angela. While not "claiming that a refugeeness sticks to/with certain refugee bodies or communities," Lady Trieu's attachment to legacy implies, "a descendant of refugees, who has never been displaced, can come to inherit refugeeness through immersion in a social field, through stories, memories, and exchange" (Nguyen, 2019, p. 117).

Lesson from land. As aspects of Lady Trieu's refugeetude emerge through these vignettes and juxtapositions, the connection to Vietnam as a form of legacy showcases both an emplacement and entanglement with place and potential pedagogical frames for displacement and (re)settlement. Indeed, because of the echoes between our world and the world of *Watchmen* in regard to Vietnam, the movement between realities offers opportunities to add to Subedi's (2013) conception of pedagogies of displacement by asking the question: What places belong to us? What does it mean to belong to a place? Who decides?

Lady Trieu's Legacy:
Blood

Lady Trieu's lineage slowly unfolds during the series. While we learn relatively quickly that Lady Trieu's "daughter" is actually a cloned version of her mother, the audience does not learn the full scope of Lady Trieu's parentage until the last episode of the season. In a flashback, Lady Trieu travels to Karnak—Adrian Veidt's luxurious, Antarctic complex—to introduce herself to her father and to request financial support for her plan to save humanity. Before revealing her true identity, Lady Trieu captures Veidt's attention by giving him credit for saving the world by manufacturing a common threat in the form of a squid-like alien. Assured by Lady Trieu's flattery, the two have an easy conversation as she continues to praise his accomplishments.

"But it's a rerun," she says of his continued efforts. "You had a genius idea twenty years ago, but you're still doing the same thing. Just smaller. Great, you stopped the clock, but what happens if you let it start back up again" (Cuse et al., 2019)? Surprised, Veidt indicates that the world would be right back where it started before he had intervened. He believes that without a constant reminder of an other-worldly threat, the different nations of the world would once again be on the brink of nuclear war with each other.

"What if I could make every nuclear weapon in the world disappear?" Lady Trieu asks (Cuse et al., 2019). To do so, she reveals her plan of harnessing the abilities of Dr. Manhattan— "someone with no limitations" (Cuse et al., 2019). Revealing that she suspects Dr. Manhattan is not on Mars as he has led those on Earth to believe, Lady Trieu shares that she has launched a probe that will reach Europa (a moon of Jupiter) in five years' time to confirm his location. After Veidt scoffs at her attempts to locate Dr. Manhattan, he questions the purpose of such an endeavor.

Lady Trieu aims to verify Dr. Manhattan's location, she tells Veidt, so that she can "destroy him and take his power" (Cuse et al., 2019). "If I can take his power, I can fix the world. Disappear the nukes, end starvation, clean the air. All the things he should have done" (Cuse et al., 2019). She just needs someone to fund the creation of her already-designed quantum centrifuge capable of absorbing Dr. Manhattan's energy and transferring it to her. Lady Trieu briefly pauses to look at Veidt. "So, I was hoping you would stake me forty-two billion dollars" (Cuse et al., 2019). He should do so, she indicates, because she is his daughter. Of her mother, Lady Trieu shares:

> Her name was Bian. She was one of the Vietnamese refugees working here in '85. She shot herself up with some of your *legacy* and slipped out into the night. And you didn't even notice she was gone because she was just a cleaning woman.[2] (Cuse et al., 2019)

Veidt scorns her—indicating that he saw Lady Trieu's mother as a thief; thus, he sees Lady Trieu's intelligence as stolen. Referencing his own legacy, Veidt explains that while he inherited a vast amount of wealth from his parents, he had decided to give it all away because he wanted "to demonstrate that I could achieve anything, starting from nothing" (Cuse et al., 2019).

We see that refugeeness is "a substantial experience that can be the basis for the formation and development of a way of being in the world" (Nguyen, 2019, p. 117) through Lady Trieu's description of her mother, Veidt's response, and Lady Trieu's subsequent actions and focus on what exactly constitutes home and legacy. For example, Lady Trieu's ensuing personal endeavor to clone her mother so that she could be present during the culmination of her self-described "life's work" showcases the "intersection between private loss and public commemoration" (Espiritu & Duong, 2018, p. 593). Moreover, we know that Lady Trieu's veiled search for "home" results in a pragmatism that recognizes "there is ultimately no home in... the United States, especially one that views refugees as undesirable" (Nguyen, 2019, p. 123). This form of refugeetude does not mean that Lady Trieu is hopeless, however. Instead, Lady Trieu sets her sights on "saving humanity" and "fixing the world" (Cuse et al., 2019; Osei-Kuffour et al., 2019)

The interplay between how Lady Trieu conceives legacy and how Veidt speaks of inheritance reveals the chasm between their relationships with displacement. The raced, classed, and gendered overtones of their interaction provide opportunities to consider the form that Lady Trieu's refugeetude takes. Lady Trieu reframes Veidt's rejection of their shared blood as an opportunity to both enact her agency and disrupt Veidt's very notions of who is deemed as worthy. Nguyen (2019) indicates that while refugeetude can mean agency:

> It resonates more like a way of being (an ethos) that does not acquiesce to the entrenched global order structured by forms of racial, capital, and mobile inequality. An agential subject may be one actualization of refugeetude, but it is not the only or primary one. (p. 119)

While Lady Trieu most certainly is an agential subject in the series, before and after this particular interaction with Veidt, her consciousness leads to a range of expressions that includes the way she calls back to this conversation when she sees Veidt again many years later. As Veidt later finds himself stranded on Europa after taking Dr. Manhattan's place, he spells out "Save me, daughter," at the precise moment that Lady Trieu's space probe is set to capture images of the moon of Jupiter. While not produced by Lady Trieu, the way that she reads this "letter" from her father indicates that this private message is actually "discursive [and] performative" in a way that alludes to "the complexities of history and memory, displacement and emplacement" (Espiritu & Duong, 2018, p. 591). While she immediately rescues him, she has him frozen in a golden mold so that she can awaken him at the precise moment that she is ready to complete her "life's work." The audience recognizes at the end of the season that Veidt had been a golden statue in Lady Trieu's vivarium for the entirety of the series.

When Agent Blake sees the golden statue for the first time in Lady Trieu's inaugural episode, she asks, surprised: "Is that Adrian Veidt?" Lady Trieu responds, "Indeed it is. A truly great man. So much of my success grew from the seed of his inspiration"—a statement that takes on new meaning as the audience later realizes Lady Trieu and Veidt's connection (Lindelof et al., 2019). Agent Blake wonders why Lady Trieu chose to have Veidt rendered to reflect his old age. "Because he is old. In my culture, our elders are revered," Lady Trieu responds. Agent Blake says, "Well, yeah, but this is America, sweetheart" (Lindelof et al., 2019). The tension between Lady Trieu's words of reverence and what the audience knows to be the strained nature of her relationship with Veidt positions her action of freezing him as a trophy to be "indecent." Nguyen (2019) builds on Hannah Arendt's conception of indecency:

> Refugeetude is thus thinking, feeling, and acting that might be described as indecent within the prevailing social, cultural, and political milieu. Indecency is not necessarily oppositional, radical, or controversial but is more so surprising, unexpected, and revealing—what Arendt calls truth. (p. 123)

When the Millennium Clock is ready to be activated, Lady Trieu wakes Veidt so that he might see her accomplishment; Lady Trieu reveals to Veidt that she will soon destroy Dr. Manhattan and absorb his powers. She repeats the words that he shared with her the last time they spoke, "I brought you back so you could be here in person to watch me achieve anything having started from nothing" (Cuse et al., 2019). By echoing Veidt's sentiments back to him, Lady Trieu demonstrates her refugeetude; Nguyen (2019) explains, "It is, at the core, to see one's situation and identify sources of violence and injustice that have shaped one's (and also others') coming into being" (p. 119).

Lesson from blood. Lady Trieu's refugeetude emerges through her various interactions with Veidt in her attempt to be acknowledged as his daughter. The way that this exploration of legacy unfolds sees Lady Trieu stepping into her power—despite her father's blatant contempt. Even as Veidt rejects Lady Trieu, she continues to conceive legacy through blood and inheritance. The various movements that Lady Trieu experiences during her efforts to garner resources, build the centrifuge, absorb Dr. Manhattan's powers, and "save" the world (in addition to Veidt's literal movements from Antarctica, to Europa, and back to Earth again) do not shift her view of legacy. We must ask: Who are we connected to? What forms such relationships/attachments? Why? Is legacy our destiny?

Lady Trieu's Nostalgia

As the world prepares to witness the animation of the Millennium Clock—actually the quantum centrifuge that will destroy Dr. Manhattan—Lady Trieu gives a speech to all those at Trieu Industries, including a recovering Angela. After overdosing on an entire bottle of her grandfather's "Nostalgia" pills, Angela awakens in Trieu Industries, learning that Lady Trieu has been administering her recovery treatment. The trope of legacy and inheritance surfaces again as Angela learns about her grandfather, a survivor of the Tulsa race massacre, by actually becoming him through his memories and experiencing moments from his past in vivid detail. Understanding trauma emerges not by reaching a singular and static interpretation of it but comes from an examination of how "trauma unsettles us and forces us to rethink our notions of experience…" (Caruth, 1995, p. 4). A traumatic "event is not assimilated or experienced fully at the time, but only belatedly, in its repeated possession of the one who experiences it" (p. 4). Abraham and Torok (1994) explain that intergenerational trauma is a phenomenon that describes traumas that are passed unknowingly from one generation to the next. Now outlawed, the audience learns the drug Nostalgia was designed by Trieu Industries. Lady Trieu explains why she engineered Nostalgia in her invocation, which she now considers one of her greatest failures:

> I gave people the means to visit the past so they could learn from it, so they could evolve and transform and better themselves. Instead, they became fixated on their most painful memories, choosing to experience the worst moments of their lives, over and over again. And why? Because they were afraid. Afraid that once unburdened by the trauma of the past, they would have no excuse not to move gloriously into the future. (Cuse et al., 2019)

While the character of Lady Trieu seemingly rejects this impulse to dwell on painful memories, the drug that she designed gave the world an opportunity to:

Look for history outside the public realm of state-sanctioned commemorative discourses and memorials—and to engage other realms, such as feelings and emotion, in order to search for the quiet ways that...stories get (re)told. (Espiritu & Duong, 2018, p. 593).

In fact, the pharmaceutical Nostalgia and Angela's experience taking someone else's Nostalgia make painfully visible "how trauma can linger in bodies, families, and communities across spaces and generations" (Kwan, 2015, p. 7). Moreover, one of the side effects of Lady Trieu's detoxification treatment for Angela is the meshing of her grandfather's emotions via his memories and her own vividly re-experienced memories. Angela's recovery treatment includes being hooked to a tube that leads to an unknown location outside of the room. Lady Trieu's tutorial informs her that "foreign memories have invaded [her] brain"—a phenomenon that Trieu Pharmaceuticals calls a "recollective infestation" (Osei-Kuffour et al., 2019). The remedy, the tutorial indicates, is to exterminate the blight by connecting the patient to a natural host to flush the Nostalgia from the cortex. "This tube...it's connected to a natural host? My grandfather?" Angela asks with tears in her eyes (Osei-Kuffour et al., 2019). As Angela undergoes Lady Trieu's treatment, she consistently asks to see her grandfather, whom she assumes to be at the other end of her tube. Lady Trieu emphasizes that seeing her grandfather would not be a good idea because Angela is still in the process of parsing apart where she ends, and her grandfather begins.

Lady Trieu visits Angela to check on her throughout her recovery. Over a shared meal, the two women talk about how they found themselves in Oklahoma. Before the audience knows that Cal and Dr. Manhattan are one in the same, this conversation between Lady Trieu and Angela establishes that there may be more to Cal's story than we know. Even more so, Lady Trieu seemingly draws a connection between memory and the production of self, the connection between history and identity. Although "this does not mean that self-reinvention is not possible but that such acts are subject to the inevitable capriciousness and contingencies of history" (Nguyen, 2019, p. 122). Lady Trieu comments on Cal's apparent amnesia, "I can't imagine what it was like. No sense of who he was or who you were. His whole life up to that moment, gone" (Osei-Kuffour et al., 2019). Similarly, Lady Trieu indicates that Bian would not really be her mother, despite being a clone, if she did not have her mother's experiences or memories. For that reason, Lady Trieu reveals that she has been gradually slipping Bian her mother's memories through a Nostalgia IV drip. Lady Trieu's enactment of legacy through memories demonstrates a particular manifestation of refugeetude—a desire to maintain connections between generations. Moreover, Lady Trieu's refugeetude impacts the value that she places on memories and experiences as significant to the essence of a person.

Previous interactions between Lady Trieu's daughter/mother and Lady Trieu, in addition to scenes between Angela and the daughter-version of Bian, demonstrate how Bian literally "enters the structure of feeling—that which has not yet solidified but can be felt—of refugee" (Nguyen, 2019, p. 117). Seeking out Lady Trieu in the middle of the night after being awakened by a bad dream in an earlier episode, Bian shares, "I was in a village. Men came…and burned it. And then they made us walk. I was walking for so long. Mom, my feet still hurt." "Good," Lady Trieu replies. In the moment, the audience does not know the significance of this small interaction (Espiritu & Duong, 2018)—potentially focusing, instead, on Lady Trieu's subsequent conversation with Angela's grandfather (who is in the room while Bian seeks comfort from her mother).

While Bian as a daughter was experiencing particularly intense nightmares because Lady Trieu was reincorporating her memories as a mother, the metaphor for refugeetude is clear as Bian "[retains] traces—consciousness, knowledge, and feeling—of refugeeness, traces that are foundational to a present and future conception of self" (Nguyen, 2019, p. 117). Lady Trieu's consciousness emerges in her presentation of the philosophical dilemma of whether identity, memory, and history can ever be divorced when she says that Bian would not be her mother unless she had her mother's memories. The difficulty of "recovering the self" and "keeping identity" (Nguyen, 2019) is ongoing, although Bian eventually does realize that she is Lady Trieu's mother.

Lesson from memory. While Lady Trieu sees the drug Nostalgia as one of her greatest failures because of the way that people's most painful memories haunted them, Lady Trieu also views memories as integral to someone's essence—they elucidate who a person has been, who they are, and who they can be. Even as Lady Trieu conveys throughout the series that legacy is blood rather than land or other forms of inheritance, she also ensures that her "mother" is truly able to be there with her, not only in the flesh, but also in the mind. In this way, we might expand pedagogies of displacement by asking: How are we rooted? What do we build? What do we pass on? How?

Implications of Refugeetude for Pedagogical Thinking

In *Watchmen*, Lady Trieu's refugeetude is articulated through negotiations of legacy. Taking into account history, memory, trauma, and inheritance allows for pedagogical considerations of what exactly we might pass on and how. Lady Trieu's subjectivities as a Vietnamese refugee woman, her relationships with the other characters, and her eventual fate depict a character ultimately on the periphery. Even so, the connections that Lady Trieu has to other characters in the series shape and inform her actions throughout. Her journey demonstrates how her refugee subjectivity extends beyond past and present moments; however, her refugeetude "is not an unequivocal, categorical, or fully formed understanding" (Nguyen, 2019, p. 119). Her awareness emerges in different ways— "a... form of awareness, critique, and being that develops with an impetus to understand the threads that link past, present, and future forms of displacement" (Nguyen, 2019, p. 126).

Engaging with the refugeetude of Lady Trieu through the lens of FRE reminds us that integrating the "material, political, and creative dimensions of knowledge production" (Espiritu & Duong, 2018, p. 589) with an awareness of "everyday and out-of-sight struggles" (Espiritu & Duong, 2018, p. 587) can make visible the ways that those constructed as "problems" (Espiritu, 2014; Nguyen, 2019) come into being and make meaning through interactions, attachments, and relationality. Learning about the deep-rooted effects of the past and the interconnections that various characters had to one another allows for a recognition of both possibility and solidarity. Nguyen (2019) shares, "In refugeetude, is to be entangled in plurality and coexistence, to hold on to the many tensions that bind" (p. 126).

The Potential for Interdependence

By the time that Angela listens to Lady Trieu's invocation as the Millennium Clock's activation nears, she is more fully recovered and is able to distinguish her own memories from those of her grandfather. Convinced that her grandfather will be on the other end of the tube to which she is connected, Angela is determined to confront him. As she follows her tube down a hallway to a locked room, she discovers that she is actually attached to an elephant who is sprawled on its side. Simek (2020) explains:

> Personally reliving her own childhood traumas as well as her grandfather's life history, marked by multiple incidents of racial violence, has not "unburdened" her of the past, or dispelled the literal-metaphorical elephant in the room, which appears here at once as a life reduced instrumentally to human needs, as a symbol of Lady Trieu's power and ambition (her namesake's iconography often shows her riding an elephant), and also as a weight or distress borne but also perhaps relieved through relation. (p. 396-297)

This moment of shock and "indecency" of a human intravenously connected to a non-human, animal (known for its memory) signals a form of "critical juxtaposing" (Espiritu 2014, p. 21) that might "reveal the contours and contents of power," surfacing the possibilities of "forging a past together across time and space" (Espiritu & Duong, 2018, p. 595). While potentially disturbing, the scene shows that Angela is not able transcend her own familial legacies; a collective and interdependent approach to memory may lead to healing such generational wounds (Simek, 2020). As a symbol and as a result of Lady Trieu, the surprising connection between Angela and the elephant denotes the possibility of being able "to make crucial linkages between [refugees] and others who have undergone and are undergoing similar experiences" (Nguyen, 2019, p. 123-124).

Lady Trieu's ultimate desire to obtain Dr. Manhattan's powers constructs her as the actual villain in HBO's *Watchmen*, keeping her in a perpetual position of "other." Nguyen (2019) indicates that "most refugees in the world experience their condition as refugees indefinitely, sometimes for an entire lifetime" (p. 113-114). This lingering subjectivity emerges in *Watchmen* in the way that Lady Trieu is constructed as separate from the other characters even though her story arc was interwoven with several of them. Ultimately, she is "defeated" by her father. In this way, refugeeness is "psychic, affective, and embodied, enduring in time and space, adhering itself in various ways to the bodies, hearts, and minds of refugees, former refugees, and subsequent generations" (Nguyen, 2019, p. 114). Despite this ultimate positioning, Lady Trieu's wealth, intelligence, and power are assets earlier in the series. In fact, she develops collaborations with other characters and entities in *Watchmen*, such as Will Reeves (Angela's grandfather), precisely because of the resources that she is able to afford them. In Reeves' case, Lady Trieu is able to not only reconnect him with his granddaughter, but deliver the destruction of the Seventh Kavalry (AKA Cyclops)—the White supremacist organization that had terrorized Black communities and communities of color in Tulsa and beyond.

While Lady Trieu's final motivations of "saving humanity" by absorbing Dr. Manhattan's powers are constructed as "oddly generic" (Rosenberg, 2019), the actions that she takes, the literal innovations (Espiritu & Duong, 2018) that she develops, and the promises that she keeps along the way exhibit an awareness, and, indeed, resistance of dominant power structures. This "horizontal assimilation" that Lady Trieu illustrates through her final act before achieving her ultimate goal, shows:

> Other modalities of connection, affiliation, and commitment. Refugeetude could become shared intimacies between refugee subjects and cultivated affinities with others. In its most potent form, refugeetude is refugee subjects recognizing who they are, how they have come to be, and who they might become with others. (Nguyen, 2019, p. 124)

Lady Trieu indicates that she is fulfilling her promise to Will Reeves by giving him justice as she stands before Angela and the White supremacists who had also attempted to harness Dr. Manhattan's power. Before destroying the White supremacist organization, Lady Trieu reads from a paper given to her by Reeves that clearly denounces the harm caused by White supremacy. Though interrupted by one of the leaders in the organization before she is able to finish reading Reeves' words, she keeps her promise to him by destroying them. Lady Trieu's partnership with Reeves shows a form of "cross-group, interhistorical relationality" (Nguyen, 2019, p. 124) that offers possibilities for radical solidarities. The way that Lady Trieu's imperfect partnership with Reeves unfolds—given that she also collaborated with the Seventh Kavalry in order to double-cross them—aligns with how "tensions, antagonism, and conflict can and do arise...as different groups are pitted against one another" within refugeetude (Nguyen, 2019, p. 125). Understanding, however, that solidarity is a possibility, particularly within what Espiritu (2018) calls the "refugee settler condition," "initiates a more complicated understanding of how to be in refuge and how to be with others who may seem...disconnected and removed from one's experience" (Nguyen, 2019, p. 125). Similarly, Lady Trieu's layered actions at the end of *Watchmen* encapsulate how she "[pushed] against but also [bridged] multiple borders, boundaries, and barriers" (Espiritu & Duong, 2018, p. 589).

Embodying this "condition of possibility, [this] method of knowing and affecting the world" (Nguyen, 2019, p. 121), Lady Trieu attempts to become Dr. Manhattan. As a figure who experiences all of time simultaneously, Dr. Manhattan embodies the feminist conceptualization of temporality that connects power and time (Espiritu & Duong, 2018, p. 589). In this way, Dr. Manhattan's abilities mirror how "refugees inhabit a multilayered temporal consciousness" (Espiritu & Duong, 2018, p. 589) that emphasizes the concurrence of past, present, and future. Critiquing Dr. Manhattan, Lady Trieu tells Angela that he never answered any of the calls for help that he received through the Manhattan Booths. Similar to Lady Trieu's comment to Adrian Veidt that she would do all of the things with Dr. Manhattan's powers that "he should have done" (Cuse et al., 2019), such as ridding the world of nuclear weapons, Lady Trieu imagines the possibilities beyond their current situation. She believes that justice is possible.

The legacies of Lady Trieu in *Watchmen* center on what she has inherited from the past and how those inform the future that she hopes to see. Her lineage, in addition to individual and collective memories and traumas, ostensibly motivate her eventual desire to not only overcome, but to set aside past traumas to create a new world and "move gloriously into the future" (Cuse et al., 2019). While HBO's *Watchmen* frames her ending arc as an almost arrogant belief in the power of the individual, Lady Trieu's desire to ensure that her parents are present—through resurrection or through reanimation—illustrates a recognition of her rootedness and a desire to maintain the connections that she has to her legacies. Lady Trieu's arc and eventual fate illustrate her enduring position, the particular legacies that have been passed on to her:

Both refugee subjects and refugeetude come into being through contacts, attachments, and investments within everyday social and political interactions; they take form in encounters with power, that might prescribe and delimit, as well as in moments of clarity and communion, that might inspire and broaden. (Nguyen, 2019, p. 118)

Pedagogies of Displacement: Revisited

Although we cannot know when refugeeness may emerge, understanding refugeetude as we consider teaching, learning, sharing, and creating together recognizes that particular subjectivities are not temporally or spatially constrained, but are affective, embodied, and enduring. Throughout Lady Trieu's arc on *Watchmen*, pedagogies of displacement that recognize both movement and emplacement emerge—through Lady Trieu's negotiation of legacies with land, blood, and memories. Through these different movements in the series, the category of "refugee" is troubled and connections between Lady Trieu and others in *Watchmen* who have been displaced may be drawn to those displaced within our own reality. Moreover, engaging with Lady Trieu's refugeetude provides opportunities to ask questions that allow for deeper engagements with displacement. Understanding refugeetude is understanding "the possibility of some other desire, some other attachment, and some other way of relating can be felt, if not formalized or instituted" (Nguyen, 2019, p. 126). This understanding offers the pedagogical possibility of fluid framings of ongoing, complicated entanglements with power, space, time, and each other.

Notes

1. The epigraph is from Michelle Johnson, "Art Should Make You Uncomfortable: A Conversation with Vu Tran," World Literature Today, November 2018, www.worldliteraturetoday.org.
2. Emphasis added.

References

Abraham, N. & Torok, M. (1994). *The shell and the kernel: Renewals of psychoanalysis.* Chicago: University of Chicago Press.

Alexander, J.M. & Mohanty, C.T. (Eds.), (1997). *Feminist Genealogies, Colonial Legacies, Democratic Futures.* Routledge.

Andaya, B.W. (2020). Rethinking the historical place of 'warrior women' in Southeast Asia. In V.A. Lanzona & F. Rettig (Eds.), *Women warriors in Southeast Asia* (pp. 267-293). Routledge.

Brophy, S. (2018). Introduction: Fugitivity, Futurity, and a Moving Pedagogy. *Canadian Review of Comparative Literature, 45*(4), 629-635.

Caruth, C. (1995). Introduction: Trauma and experience. In C. Caruth (Ed.), *Trauma:Explorations in memory.* Johns Hopkins University Press.

Cuse, N., & Lindelof, D. (Writers), & Toye, F.E.O. (Director). (2019). See how they fly [Television series episode]. In D. Lindelof (Executive producer), *Watchmen.* United States: HBO.

De Lissovoy, N. (2019). *Decoloniality as inversion: decentering the west in emancipatory theory and pedagogy. Globalisation, Societies and Education, 17* (4), 419-431.

Delgado, R., & Stefancic, J. (2001). *Critical race theory: An introduction.* New York University Press.

Do, M.N. (2019, Dec 21). Watchmen breaks the promise of Lady Trieu's naming. *Reappropriate.* http://reappropriate.co/2019/12/watchmen-breaks-the-promise-of-lady-trieus-naming/

Duong, L., & Sharif, L. (2020). Displaced subjects: Revolution, film, and women in Việt Nam and Palestine. *Verge: Studies in Global Asias, 6*(1), 168-197.

Espiritu, E.L. (2018). Vexed Solidarities: Vietnamese Israelis and the Question of Palestine. *LIT: Literature Interpretation Theory, 29*(1), 8-28.

Espiritu, Y.L. (2014). *Body counts: The Vietnam War and militarized refuge(es).* Oakland, CA: University of California Press.

Espiritu, Y.L., & Duong, L. (2018). Feminist Refugee Epistemology: Reading Displacement in Vietnamese and Syrian Refugee Art. *Signs: Journal of Women in Culture and Society, 43*(3), 587-615.

Grande, S. (2004). *Red Pedagogy: Native American Social and Political Thought.* Rowman & Littlefield.

Imarisha, W. (2015). Introduction. In W. Imarisha & A.M. Brown (Eds.), *Octavia's brood: Science fiction stories from social justice movements.* AK Press.

Kwan, Y. Y. (2015). Encountering memory and trauma: Transgenerational transmission of trauma in Cambodian Americans (Unpublished doctoral dissertation). University of California, Santa Cruz, CA.

Lacroix, M. (2004). 'Canadian Refugee Policy and the Social Construction of the Refugee Claimant Subjectivity: Understanding Refugeeness. *Journal of Refugee Studies, 17*(2):147–166.

Lindelof, D. (Executive Producer). (2019, October 20-December 15). *Watchmen* [Television broadcast]. United States: Warner Bros. Television.

Lindelof, D. (Writer), & Kassle, N. (Director). (2019). It's summer and we're running out of ice [Television series episode]. In D. Lindelof (Executive producer), *Watchmen.* United States: HBO.

Lindelof, D., & Henry, C. (Writers), & Parekh, A. (Director). (2019). If you don't like my story, write your own [Television series episode]. In D. Lindelof (Executive producer), *Watchmen.* United States: HBO.

Malkki, L.H. (1995). Refugees and exile: From "refugee studies" to the national order of things. *Annual Review of Anthropology, 24*, 495-523.

Moore, A., & Gibbons, D. (2013). *Watchmen: The Deluxe Edition.* DC Comics.

Nguyen, V. (2019). Refugeetude: When does a refugee stop being a refugee? *Social Text, 37*(2), 109-131.

Osei-Kuffour, S., & Keichel, C. (Writers), & Semel, D. (Director). (2019). An almost religious awe [Television series episode]. In D. Lindelof (Executive producer), *Watchmen.* United States: HBO.

Oziewicz, M. (2017). Speculative Fiction. In *Oxford research encyclopedia of literature.* Retrieved from Oxford Research Encyclopedia database.

Rosenberg, A. (2019, Dec 16). If HBO makes a second season of 'Watchmen,' it should be about Vietnam. *Washington Post.* https://www.washingtonpost.com/opinions/2019/12/16/if-hbo-makes-second-season-watchmen-it-should-be-about-vietnam/

Santos, B.d.S. (2014). *Epistemologies of the South: Justice Against Epistemicide.* Routledge.

Shalhoub-Kevorkian, N. (2015). *Security Theology, Surveillance, and the Politics of Fear.* Cambridge: Cambridge University Press.

Simek, N. (2020). Speculative futures: Race in Watchmen's Worlds. *sympokē, 28*(1-2), 385-404.

Subedi, B. (2013). Photographic Images of Refugee Spatial Encounters: Pedagogy of Displacement. *Qualitative Research in Education, 2*(3), 277-301.

Tran, N.T. (2012). Woman as nation: Tradition and modernity narratives in Vietnamese histories. *Gender & History, 24*(2), 411-430.

Vang, M. (2018). The language of care: Hmong refugee activism and a feminist refugee epistemology. In L. Fujiwara & S. Roshanravan (Eds.), *Asian American Feminisms and Women of Color Politics,* eBook pp. 420–465.

University of Washington Press.

Yuval-Davis, N. (2011). *The politics of belonging: Intersectional contestations*. Sage Publications.

Epilogue

A Conversation with Jack Halberstam

by Jordan Corson

In place of a more traditional conclusion, we end with a "talking epilogue," a brief conversation between co-editor Jordan Corson and Jack Halberstam. Among other themes, Halberstam's work touches on posthumanism, pedagogy, and pop culture. In particular, in places like his 2011 book The Queer Art of Failure, *Halberstam uses dynamic forms of pop culture to assemble what he calls a "silly archive." Rather than aiming to include these texts in a broader order of things, Halberstam, much like the chapters in this volume, sees the potential of pop culture to provoke other worlds and alternative, subversive possibilities.*

Jordan Corson: As we start, I just want to say, kind of coincidentally, I actually just finished *Wild Things* this morning.

Jack Halberstam: Thank you so much for reading it. It was a very difficult book to write in the end, and I actually have a whole other book now made up of chapters that were originally in this book but required their own structure. So that's what's going to make up the other volume. I just couldn't figure out how to combine the very literary academic chapters with other essays on architecture, anarchitecture, and the aesthetics of collapse.

JC: Yes, I mean, I've seen so much from your talks and writing, particularly the piece with Tavia Nyong'o in that issue of South Atlantic Quarterly. It's such a beautiful book but I was also surprised to see that so much from these pieces—themes like anarchism, for instance— didn't appear as much as I thought they would in this.

JH: It was very clear that if you want to track a category like wildness, and you don't want to get stuck in a kind of neo-colonial formulation of the category and so, to detach wildness from colonial structures of thought required a deep dive into modernism. I thought that maybe I could get around that but really, the hard work of making wildness into a category with which we can think needed to be done separately from a project on anarchism. So, I'm trying to figure out this second book, and whether it actually is a second book, or if it's just a standalone thing that has nothing to do with this one. But that's what happens when you write about wildness, it sort of writes itself, and you follow along.

JC: Yeah, that's fantastic. I think, turning to this project, if I can just provide a little context. We're doing a special issue in a journal this fall. And then this is an edited book of disparate themes, but essentially converging around pop culture, posthumanism, and education. So, we have chapters on everything from hauntology in video games to mentorship in comics, even monstrousness of youth in a TV show. It's a really dynamic volume.

I'd like to start off with your recent work on the wild. I really like how it pushes the boundaries of thought rather than trying to shore up and unify those boundaries. And in doing so it moves explicitly against the order of things. Thinking about this, how does *the wild* appear in pop culture? How is it foreclosed, not as a place, but more, what is the wild terrain of pop culture? And what can be learned from this? Or what can be learned in this?

JH: In *Wild Things*, I do a deep dive into literary modernism, and into the way in which the wild is represented both in a colonial context and then in a kind of decolonial disorder of things in which the wild becomes a vector for the declassification of knowledge. In other words, wildness offers a way to undo some of the logics we have inherited from the end of the 19th century. Expert knowledges from that time sought to tidy up human behavior, and offer systematic ways of thinking about the body, and the self, and desire, and so on. I follow the disorder of things away from these tidy formulations (homo and hetero, normative and deviant) and accordingly arrive at a messy and complex model of human embodiment. The first part of the book does not have much to say about popular culture, which is unusual for me.

But towards the end of that book, I return to pop culture, in order to make an argument about how people mistake the household pet for a relationship to the wild when, in fact, pets represent quintessential forms of domestication. People do not want to hear this because they are convinced that the pet offers a channel to non-human being and that their relation to the pet is wholly benevolent. This is a kind of self-deception, where one tells oneself that one is being so kind and so engaged with nonhuman animal life, when in fact, all we're doing is incarcerating animals. My chapter on pets returns to earlier work of mine on animation and offers a reading of the slightly disappointing film *The Secret Life of Pets*. And, as one respondent to my work said, this chapter sort of goes in a very different direction. In all of my work on animation, I think I'm making an argument that no matter the sort of sponsoring corporate interest in the animated film, there's always a kind of surplus aesthetic value to an animated film that escapes the tidy moral narratives that the studio intends. And so whether it's the struggle against appropriation in *A Bug's Life* or the fight with the human fishermen in *Finding Nemo*, or the struggle against redundancy in *Robots* or the organic feminist revolution in *Chicken Run*, or whether it arrives in the form of the rebellion of pets against ownership and abandonment in *The Secret Life of Pets*, these films do traffic in unruly narratives of resistance. Whatever little homily the writers of some of these films may have intended to disperse through child audiences, the films exceed these cliched lessons and they offer, sometimes in the form of algorithms, structures (narrative and pixelated) for wild anarchic narratives of human rebellion as routed through animal forms.

Narratives about human rebellion inevitably open onto stories about animal rebellion as well. The point being that pop culture is never simply the expression of some corporate agent. There's always some kind of representational value that exceeds this marketing frame. When I was writing about Pixar, for example, people asked me repeatedly, "but you're writing about these multimillion-dollar films that are consumed by millions of people around the globe, and there are tie-ins and products associated with them. You can't claim something like anarchy as associated with them." But my point was that when a studio had to work out how to represent rebellion, say in *A Bug's Life*, they needed to work out how to represent many bugs at once—the studio had to figure out an algorithm for multitudes! Representing a multitude cannot happen by repeating the form of one bug or creature many times, a multitude is the massing of many different units in one place. I made the argument that the formulation of an anarchic rebellion is actually within the algorithm and therefore escapes the tidy narrative. For me, this too is a form of wildness that we could expand to other aspects of pop culture. Pop culture does not stay firmly within the marketing strategy that has been outlined for it. You could say that probably about any text, but we are most suspicious of popular culture texts. And so, I think it's important to say that.

JC: You've mostly addressed it in that answer, but there is this concern that we've had throughout this project that, even in our impulses to resist humanism, to push against capitalist modes of production, these pop culture things still sit within, they're dominantly produced within an enterprise caught up in these things. I know that especially your work *The Queer Art Of Failure* touches on this, but how do you respond to this tension on kind of a larger scale, rather than individual texts escaping the frames in which they're produced?

JH: In other words, Jordan, you're saying, obviously, there are going to be moments where pop culture texts break free from the enabling conditions of capitalism, but for the most part, they're embedded in the structures that they repeat and affirm. And, again, all of that is true. And maybe it's even a moment to, I don't know, revisit Adorno and Horkheimer's The Culture Industry and wonder, again, how easily manipulated we are, by cultural products, that mold us into ready subjects for consumerism. But there's a reason that I think people became suspicious of the overarching and totalizing narrative of The Culture Industry. There are vectors like pleasure and desire that do not simply fall in line with the mandate to produce or consume, but spin off in ways that have no productive value whatsoever. Like the way in which, for example, child audiences repeat-watch something, over and over again, which means that the same film that has been bought once might be watched, you know, several hundred times. It's not just about newness. There's something in the child's brain that is willing to suspend the desire for newness in order to keep seeing the flow of imagery. From such a viewing position, the child is not watching to see a plot unfold. They are instead fascinated by the strange flow of visual imagery. That kind of fetishistic looking is out of sync with humanist values or with capitalist logics. And I think for people who are thinking about education and pop culture, and who recognize that pop culture is an incredibly powerful tool for education, especially when we're in a very mixed classroom where people may not have anything in common at all in terms of the cultural texts that they are drawn to, pop culture offers an exceptionally powerful pedagogical terrain. And to the extent that universities remain attached only to the "great traditions" versions of Western culture, it will always be a deeply elitist kind of culture that can never quite take on the cultural spaces where most people live and breathe.

JC: I do worry about that, though, a little bit, because part of me wonders what forms of governance are opened up by making this more legible, by us wandering into the terrain of trying to explore and understand these forms of pop culture that move towards more anarchic forms of being? And what does that risk?

JH: What worries you?

JC: There's this ongoing question of the tension between new forms of visibility and what comes with that visibility or legibility is an immediate governance. And when we try to explore and interrogate films, comics, all of these different forms of pop culture, does that then bring them into the fold of governing logics? Does that kind of tame them in a way? I worry that it's making them part of the order of things, even in an attempt to push against that.

JH: Well, that's on us in a way. I don't disagree with you that a lot of what we do in academia, the analysis and interpretation of texts, can easily be about bringing things back into order, especially unruly texts that seem to operate according to a different logic. But that's on us. We have to find different ways to write about things, and I've tried to do that at times. And other times, I've completely failed to do that. We also have to think differently about archives, and we have to rethink what we mean by education. In *The Queer Art of Failure* I tried to make the argument, along the lines of what Rancière did in *The Ignorant Schoolmaster*, for a project of intellectual emancipation, where academics have to—and have, for the most part—stop turning up their nose at middlebrow artifacts, and have embraced the fact that in a classroom, any text will do. It could be *Rick and Morty*. It could be Japanese Anime. It could be the *Black Panther* film, it could be a comic book from the 1920s. Because every cultural artifact has a different thing to teach us about the intensely complex systems of representation, reality, governance, and escape that we all inhabit. And I don't think that we're ever going to get quite right what constitutes the reaffirmation of the order of things and what contributes to a disordering logic of being. There is no theory that will take us there. But there are ways of approaching *things* that allow those things to throw us out of whack, that shifts the conventional relation between subject and object and that puts subjectivity itself into question—Jane Bennett's work often makes this kind of case for the vibrant life of things. And there are other scholars who take up deeply unorthodox relations to archives, to daily life, to pleasure and to beauty. This is what

Saidiya Hartman does in her book *Wayward Lives*, which makes an argument for the pleasure and beauty that resides in a kind of ambulatory relationship to freedom as exercised by Black girls on the streets of New York and Philadelphia at the start of the twentieth century.

JC: Is there something maybe a little bit more sustainable within that? I love Hartman's work, and Rancière's, but so much of it is moments, the verification of equality. And then, as soon as that is verified, the police re-form. It changes something, but it's not held. Another thing I'm wondering is, how might pop culture contribute to maybe a more sustained provocation for a world otherwise? And is there something pedagogical within that possibility? Whether they be the term you use, "oppositional pedagogies," or just pedagogy writ large, or even any way that pop culture can contribute to more planned efforts towards a world otherwise?

JH: What if that's the wrong question, Jordan? What if saying, "this isn't sustainable, these little moments aren't sustainable, we can't base a kind of hope for a different world on ephemera," what if that's not true? What if ephemera offers a different form of provocation to use your word? This was part of an argument that José Muñoz used to make in relation to queer utopia and queer performance—that they were located within the ephemeral and that this was their strength rather than a liability. And that the ephemeral glimpses of queer creativity lead to a kind of ecstatic communion, a being together that sustained queer life at times of duress. The mistake, I think, would be to think about change as a sustained, directed trajectory, in which something measurable and quantifiable gets achieved over time. The ephemeral does surely give way to disruption and just as quickly, the policing mechanism returns. But that doesn't mean that that moment didn't happen. Robin Kelly in *Freedom Dreams* proposes that just because some political movements from the past didn't necessarily succeed in their goal to overthrow the order of things, it doesn't limit their value in relation to contemporary struggles. I really like this idea because political movements don't just succeed or fail; political orders are constantly shifting and changing. The problem is that in a neoliberal order of things, very often, the forms of resistance are quickly co-opted back into a management style. In fact, just today, I read a deeply disturbing article in New York Magazine about the use of anti-capitalist posturing on dating apps!! The journalist claims that young men and women looking for sex on Tinder or Hinge pepper their profiles with terms like "biracial communist" or who claim to be attracted to "the end of capitalism." So this season's hot moniker is anarcho-capitalism and one young man had a profile that read: "Together we could: make art, dismantle the system, and eat grapes at the park."[1] An, of course, there is nothing wrong with such a profile… unless everyone has a similar profile on a billion-dollar platform where sex and capitalism are entwined in and ever more complicated dance. So, yeah, popular culture can take the sting out of radical, the anti out of anti-capitalism and the revolution out of anarchy!

JC: But can we go back to how to use popular culture for pedagogical purposes?

JH: Pedagogical magic happens whenever a light comes on for anyone in the room, and that could be any room. We would be incredibly pedestrian if we just put pedagogy into a classroom, right? After all, often, teaching is at its worst when it announces itself as teaching. And learning is at its most transformative in the moments when people are not aware that it's happening. For example, as much as I am an absolute fan of pop culture and subculture, I also have written about, and am very invested in, abstract forms of representation. One of the reasons for that is because narrative and figuration are comfortable vectors for many people: a narrative that has a beginning, middle, and an end, a form of representation that shows the figure struggling through time and space and arriving somewhere. These are comforting because they confirm something about the arrangement of reality that we find ourselves in. But abstraction doesn't do that, it sort of shocks us out of our comfort zone. Those are pedagogical moments too, when you're confronted by a work of art that you cannot make any sense of or that you are strictly prevented from making sense of. For me, it's all about these very heterogeneous archives, rather than picking one or the other.

JC: You almost see it as kind of a forced encounter. But what comes out of that is never guaranteed; it opens a possibility. There's not something inscribed in pop-cultural texts that says: "you will learn *this*, you will get *this* out of it."

JH: Right. I use pop culture all the time in my teaching, and I'm sure you do, too. But, it is amazing how quickly something goes out of style. You might be poring over a scene from *The Sopranos* and your students have never heard of the show! And a student could be speaking about hyperpop without the teacher knowing anything about this musical form. Particularly in the moment that we live in, where at the level of platforms like TikTok, every minute a meme is made, every second a new craze is unfolding, a new viral text is circulating, we have to give up the urge to be absolutely up to date. Nobody can keep up any longer, if they ever did, with the flow of images and viral texts that pass across the multiple platforms that we engage. So, for that reason, we need a very, very big arsenal for teaching. We need many tools, we need many weapons, we need many forms of expression. Not one kind of textbook. So, there are no pure spaces. In many ways, you can see this in my wildness book where the book's organizing logic gives way at times to a kind of incoherence. But that incoherence can, in its own way, mount a defense to the market processes by which ideas are swallowed whole and turned into cash.

JC: That brings up a question, and I think that you've already hit on it here, particularly talking about TikTok. Who gets to do this kind of work? Or to use your terms, who gets to produce and/or grapple with low theory?

JH: Anyone and everyone. People are producing low theory every day. It's what makes it low theory as opposed to high theory. Some kid on TikTok who put something together in their bedroom that they know has a kind of viral potential, and it does, that person is a better low theorist than you or I who cannot figure out for the life of us what the algorithm might be for a viral bit. That's what people are doing on TikTok; it's bits. I saw someone do a riff on *Finding Nemo*. And I thought I could have done that. That *is* my riff. But I didn't do it on TikTok, I wrote a book. And I think this person even mentioned me in their riff on *Finding Nemo*. But would I have been able to turn it into something that 13,000 viewers were following? Not at all. And I thought that I actually did very well at giving talks on pop culture. But that's child's play compared to the audiences that people have on these platforms. If you go to a university, and you give a talk to 200 people, you're not making a dent in public conversations, but if you find a way to turn some of that talk into a 30 second bit that goes viral...well, it probably has been stripped of its meaning in some way, but it is doing something. Academics certainly have taken in Twitter in recent years and I am not sure that this is a good thing. Still, some academics are excellent in that medium. But I'm not convinced by the stuff that I read on social media, at any rate. I wouldn't call that low theory; maybe it's fast theory or something like it. It has a level of one-upmanship that I don't think is part of the principle of low theory. Low theory is really about theoretical ideas that circulate at a very different level in the culture at large and have a different kind of frequency. And it's not that it's a less complex form of theoretical practice; it's just that it has different goals, and it reaches different audiences, and it takes up different objects. It's not a high level of abstraction for thinking about epistemology and ontology. It might in fact, be exactly what you're doing in your volume, trying to make sense of a very vivid and diverse world of pop culture as it shifts and changes across platforms over time, and as it passes through different bodies in different spaces. That's low theory.

JC: And there seems to be, at least the way I'm reading it, something very collective about that, which I really see in places like Tik-Tok (I think the word you used was "circulating). I get completely lost and I feel way too old; for example, I just saw this TikTok where people are lip-synching about the *Trolls* movie, but then performing that scene in ways that build on each other's videos. There's something learned and gained through participating together.

JH: That's amazing. I actually think TikTok, Instagram, some of these places where people are not just writing quick takes on things, but they're actually trying to find new forms of expression and engagement... that stuff is super interesting to me. It's like hyperpop, the way in which many people think hyperpop was born on TikTok. It doesn't shy away from either the popular or noise for that matter, but is willing to find weird combinations of all of those things. Hyperpop has a huge presence in Trans and Queer culture. I'm super interested in that kind of material and I'm learning a lot from working with students who are writing about these new forms of cultural expression that emerge from new platforms and new forms of collectivity.

JC: I just want to ask a simple final question. What pop culture are you playing with now? What's a new thing in the silly archive or the wild archive?

JH: That's a good question. I haven't been dipping into my silly archive. Recently, I've been a bit serious. I'm really thinking about my anarchist archive. And I'm still thinking about the *Lego Movie*, to be honest with you, because I'm really, really interested in unbuilding and I have this big project about how we unmake worlds. I still think Lego is one of the best tools for particularly showing kids that they can make things, but they can also unmake them. That remains a really valuable lesson that I am myself trying to absorb and incorporate.

JC: I love that movie so much.

JH: It's ridiculous, but we do; it's so good. Legos never get old, that's the thing about them. It's always an amazing experience to build and unbuild in the way that it allows. For me, it's both the physical space of the Legos but also the sort of the constraints that can be imposed via Legos… The pleasure of the undoing, all of that is available. I'm still communing with that.

Notes

1. Emilia Petrarca, "Occupy the Dating App" in New York Magazine (June 21 – July 4, 2021): 18 – 20.

CPSIA information can be obtained
at www.ICGtesting.com
Printed in the USA
JSHW021718030622
26633JS00004B/85